Librarians, Literacy and the
Promotion of Gender Equity

Librarians, Literacy and the Promotion of Gender Equity

LESLEY S. J. FARMER

McFarland & Company, Inc., Publishers
Jefferson, North Carolina, and London

LIBRARY OF CONGRESS CATALOGUING-IN-PUBLICATION DATA

Farmer, Lesley S. J.
Librarians, literacy and the promotion of gender equity / Leslie S. J. Farmer.
p.   cm.
Includes bibliographical references and index.

ISBN 0-7864-2344-7 (softcover : 50# alkaline paper)

1. Information literacy — Study and teaching.
2. Information retrieval — Study and teaching.
3. Gender identity in education.
4. Library orientation for school children.
5. Media programs (Education).
6. School librarian participation in curriculum planning.
I. Title.
ZA3075.F37   2005   028.7'071—dc22   2005020999

British Library cataloguing data are available

Cover photograph: ©2005 Image 100

Manufactured in the United States of America

*McFarland & Company, Inc., Publishers
Box 611, Jefferson, North Carolina 28640
www.mcfarlandpub.com*

Contents

To Chris Farmer,
my technology collaborator

Introduction

Have you heard these comments?

"I can't get the boys to read anything besides gaming magazines."

"Girls just don't take computer classes."

"I'm worried about the messages that the media send; they seem to really mess up teens' self-esteem."

There's a problem, and both genders are suffering.

That problem has to do with the vast array of stimuli and information that surround today's youth. More than ever before, young people need to be able to decipher those messages, assess their validity and relevance, and decide how to act upon them. More reading material is being produced and disseminated than ever. Mass media now impact the world almost instantly. Visual images bombard the senses throughout our waking moments, and audio even affects us in our sleep. In the 21st century, digital information has come into its own and has transformed other formats. Digital photography and video, in particular, can be manipulated easily and repurposed for completely opposing agendas than originally intended.

To understand, analyze, and act upon all this information requires learning an increasingly complex set of skills and developing a broad knowledge base. Numeracy not only involves mathematical algorithms but broader issues of data representation. Reading print differs from reading electronic text. Visual literacy involves knowing universal principles as well as culturally imbedded connotations. Aural literacy requires making sense of nuanced soundscapes. Media literacy involves understanding commercial agendas. Technology literacy encompasses tool-based skills as well as critical thinking and ethical practice. Literacy in the 21st century is a multifaceted issue.

Nor is information value-neutral. Most conscious messages are contextualized, usually in societal terms, and young people react to them within that psychological framework. In some cases, the context becomes more important than the message itself-or gives a particular message more value. Moreover, when two messages or pieces of information conflict, either with a young person's existing mindset or with other factors, the context may determine how that individual will decide to act on the information.

A real example helps make this issue concrete. One message might be that inner beauty counts more than outward appearance, and a conflicting message may be that first impressions count — and that appearance should be the main concern. When teens look at how they personally interact and also see celebrity images, they are more likely to go along with the message that pushes appearance.

Many of these messages align with gender norms or expectations. For instance, girls experience information about birth control with a different mindset than boys. Even in early childhood, messages about bodily functions are experienced through a different lens, depending upon one's gender. As children develop, societal mores increasingly affect how they process and act on information. "Now that you're growing up, young lady, it's time to stop acting like a tomboy." "Real boys don't cry." "Don't worry about math; girls don't need to know that." "Why spend your time reading when you could be building your muscles; are you some kind of sissy?"

Is this a "good" thing or a "bad" thing? Ultimately, natural consequences will sift out that issue. However, when young people are not aware of the context of information, or when they blindly accept information, then they give up intellectual rights and may be prone to undue influence and manipulation by others who may be unscrupulous. Both girls and boys need to discern information about both genders and learn how to act upon it. Cutting themselves off from information because it has traditionally been linked to one gender diminishes both sexes, and limits one's self-actualization.

Where do librarians fit into this picture? Since a core set of functions in librarianship includes collecting, organizing, storing, and retrieving information efficiently, librarians need to address how format impacts these tasks. How can technology provide access to information worldwide? What equipment is needed to "read" a variety of non-print and electronic materials? What happens when storage media such as 5.25-inch diskettes and software programs such as WordStar are no longer supported; will that information become extinct?

Moreover, since the main reason that librarians do these processes is to support society in accessing and using information, librarians need to help users learn those skills. At this point, culling authentic and relevant information may be more difficult than simply finding information *per se.* Knowing what tools to use to analyze and organize information helps users become more efficient learners and employees. As information professionals, librarians have a responsibility to help others become self-sufficient learners.

This instruction and guidance is particularly important for young people as they develop physically, intellectually, emotionally, and psychologically. In the process, librarians need to be aware of gender issues — and help youth to discern them as well. Particularly as young people are developing their sexual identity, they need information that will support their inner search and self-realization. The more that librarians can help them in this endeavor, the greater the chances for gender equity and full participation in society.

Thus, this book focuses on librarians and their role in fostering gender equity for 21st century literacies. It emphasizes the development of professional knowledge and skills to better understand current issues related to the following literacies: reading, technology, information, numeracy, visual, aural, and media. Each chapter deals with some aspect of literacy, and how gender and technology affect it. Ideas for library involvement are given, and exercises to help explore related issues are provided in each case.

Chapter 1 focuses on gender's impact on how these literacies are learned, experienced, and used. Librarians need to provide resources and experiences that engage both genders, separately and together. Exercises help readers explore gender issues.

In order to optimize literacy competency, librarians need to design learning activities carefully. Chapter 2 details those steps, and takes into account gender and technology issues. The library has a unique role to play in providing gender-inclusive experiences. Exercises concretize teaching and learning techniques.

Chapter 3 explains the properties of technology, noting the associated literacies needed in order to take advantage of digital approaches. Technology has also generated strong gender-linked images and practices, which are explored. Teaching and learning should change significantly when technology is integrated meaningfully. This chapter looks at these different factors, and notes how libraries work in this environment to help students become technologically literate. Exercises help readers appreciate the impact of technology.

Reading remains the central literacy in the United States. Chapter 4 spells out the principles and key concepts of reading literacy, and covers current trends in teaching reading literacy. It also explains how technology affects reading. Gender-related issues on reading habits and skills are detailed, and ideas on instructional best practices are provided. The library can offer a variety of resources to help all students learn how to read and to enjoy that skill. Exercises offer insights on reading literacy issues.

Chapter 5 explains the principles, concepts, and current thinking about information literacy and research processes. Technology has become a cornerstone in information literacy. Gender influences how young people approach information literacy, so these differences will also be explored. Exercises explore information literacy ideas.

A separate chapter on numeracy highlights the challenges of numerical representation and analysis in terms of gender. Alternative methods for exciting both girls and boys about mathematical thinking are posed in Chapter 6, and exercises offer concrete ways to engage in numeracy.

Certainly as the United States becomes more pluralistic, society uses visuals to communicate and teach. Moreover, as technology has put a new "spin" on visual literacy, gender issues also arise. Chapter 7 explains the principles and concepts of visual literacy, and notes current trends in teaching these skills. Libraries need to embrace visuals, both in terms of resources as well as instruction. Exercises explore issues of visual literacy, particularly from a cultural perspective.

Sometimes overlooked but pervasive is aural literacy: identifying and making meaning of life's soundscapes. Educators still largely use oral language, and students live in a rich environment of music and other sounds. The role of aural literacy and accompanying resources is explored in Chapter 8. Supporting exercises take advantage of technology to further sound study.

Mass media impact today's young people both consciously and unconsciously, and certainly influence their concepts of gender. Chapter 9 explores the characteristics of media literacy and current best practices in relating to mass media messages. Ideas for library involvement in media literacy are offered. Exercises help readers become more aware of media literacy and its impact.

While these literacies may be parsed to determine their unique characteristics, in actuality they intersect to a large degree. Chapter 10 examines how gender and technology fit into this complex convergence. As an information center, the library offers an optimal learning environment to explore literacies holistically. Exercises provide ideas for next steps in gender equity relative to digital literacies.

An extensive bibliography and index complete the volume.

Are our young people up to the task of making sense of their complex surroundings and serving as contributing citizens? Yes, but it will take the full measure of society to help them. Our world is too interdependent and sophisticated for either gender to be relegated to second-class citizen status, and we have to take full advantage of each person's gifts and potential. As keepers of civilization's knowledge and as expert information processors, librarians play a unique role in helping young people become fully literate in the 21st century.

1

Gender and Learning

Getting boys to read? Getting girls interested in engineering? Gender impacts the way that individuals get, process, and share ideas. To help young people gain broad literacy competency, librarians and other educators need to be aware of how gender influences learning. This chapter details developmental and societal issues related to gender. Libraries need to provide resources and experiences that engage both genders, separately and together. Exercises about gender issues help readers explore issues.

How Boys and Girls Learn: The Role of Biology

Are boys and girls hard-wired differently? Does their chemistry differ? What role does society play in how girls and boys learn? These questions are still being debated. At conception the human embryo has the potential to become either sex; molecular chains of events lead to the disintegration of the less-favored sex organs within the first two months (Lehrman, 1997). While few traits or organs are entirely sex-linked, gendered expectations remain to an extent. The main issue is to ensure that variations are supported and valued.

The Role of the Brain

Hormones and chemistry certainly make a difference in learning. For example, testosterone, which is usually found in greater quantities in males, stimulates activity, risk-taking, and overt aggression. Interestingly, when girls have higher testosterone levels, they score higher on tests, but for similar levels, boys score higher on spatial tests but lower on verbal tests (Gurian and Henley, 2001). Such behaviors are valued in some sports and businesses. In other cases where following directions and sitting still are valued, such as during traditional schooling practices, testosterone would seem to be a handicap. Similarly, the chemicals serotonin and oxytocin are less present in males, which make them more impulsive and empathetic to others' emotions. In school, this can translate into more attention-seeking behaviors by boys; interestingly, when girls exhibit these behaviors, they are more apt to be reprimanded (American Association of University Women, 1992).

Each part of the brain is associated with unique functions. The basal ganglia, which controls physical movement sequencing, engages more quickly in males. Broca's area, the motor area for speech, is more active in females. Who walks and who talks? Male brain hemispheres have a thicker right brain where sequencing and abstract perception dominates; females usually have thicker left brains, which center on image and holistic thinking. Moreover, females' larger corpus callosum, which connects the two sides of the brain, enables them to coordinate the whole brain more easily than males (Sousa, 2001). The simple message for librarians is to engage different parts of the brain in order to address all students' strengths and needs.

Because of these biological variations, boys and girls may respond to stimuli differently. Females have better directional hearing, and males have greater spatial ability. Girls respond more to people than things, the reversal of boys' behavior (Moir, 1991). When a male is threatened, the lower half of the brain dominates, which results in "fight or flight." In contrast, the threatened female brain activates the upper part: the cerebrum thinking center. For this reason, girls may take fewer risks than boys, both physically and intellectually, so establishing a safe learning environment can help both genders to take positive action.

The process of learning changes the brain in a fortunate way. Beyond the obvious growth and pruning of neuron connections, specific parts of the brain grow denser with learning and practice, peaking at puberty. Emotion plays an important role in these changes because the chemicals associated with feelings—adrenalin, dopamine, serotonin—interact with those associated neurons. Thus, success in problem-solving can bring pleasure, which reinforces those neuron connections. Additionally, when more parts of the brain are engaged in learning, the chances that change will occur increase. The sensory cortex receives the information, the integrative cortex near the sensory cortex makes meaning of the information, the frontal integrative cortex creates ideas from the meaning, and the motor cortex acts on the ideas (Zull, 2004). Kolb (1984) earlier described this phenomenon in terms of experiential learning: experience, reflection, abstraction, and active testing. Girls tend to score higher as concrete experience learners, while boys favor abstract conceptualization, which is the dominant traditional mode of education in the United States (Philbin & Meier, 1995). Fortunately, Kolb asserted that the entire experiential cycle should be utilized. In concrete terms, students might experience taking water samples, for example; discover patterns about the samples while entering the data; develop a hypothesis to explain the data findings; and then test their hypothesis in another setting. To generalize, as girls and boys get actively involved in academics, they can use different parts of their brains and learn from each other, complementing their gender advantages and filling in their intellectual gaps.

Developmental Issues

Gender differences also align with physical development, even at the prenatal stage (e.g., the male's brain is larger and less flexible). In infancy, boys are less bothered by loud noises than girls, who prefer soft tones and singing; on the other hand, girls have better hearing and are able to distinguish emotional nuances. Boys are more active and more easily angered; girls are more easily saddened. As toddlers, boys have greater muscle and roam more. Girls develop better vocabulary and have better visual memory; they also multitask better than boys (Gurian and Henley, 2001). While some differences even out over time, having initial advantages in specific modalities of perception and processing can impact later learning.

In adolescence, development is significantly gender-linked. While biology continues to play a role in differentiation, by this point, the psychological and social factors take on much greater importance. Even the timing of the onset of puberty is viewed differently by boys and girls. Early male maturers tend to gain more power and popularity while females who mature at an earlier age tend to be self-conscious and uncomfortable with such physical changes. In particular, girls tend to lose their "voice," confidence and self-esteem in early adolescence as they try to relate to peers and their own morphing bodies. Appearance becomes more important to them, and societal messages often reinforce rigid expectations for females; not surprisingly, two-thirds of girls have a negative body image (Orenstein, 1994; Pipher, 1994). Interestingly, athletic girls have higher esteem than their non-athletic peers, but in co-ed sports those same female athletes lose their self-confidence (American Association of University Women, 1992). Thus, bodily changes can impact learning as girls vie for social acceptance more than academic prowess, and thus cut themselves out of challenging courses that appear to be male-dominated, such as engineering. In the process, girls do not learn those sets of skills as well as males (Knight, 1997). It should be noted that this phenomenon is culturally contextualized; where rites of passage empower both boys and girls, self-deprecation is observed less often. African American girls, for example, do not experience such a decline in self-esteem, but rather feel that they can play a more substantive role within their society as they mature. In fact, some librarians are uncomfortable with relatively loud Black girls. The down side, though, is that these same girls often lack academic self-confidence (American Association of University Women, 1992).

Other cognitive learning style preferences arise from these physical differences. For example, girls tend to approach problem-solving cautiously and reflectively while boys take greater risks and act more impulsively. Thus, librarians may need to allow students more time to think rather than pick on the first hand raised. Girls tend to be more field-dependent learners; that is, they contextualize meaning. This behavior favors collaborative learning. On the other hand, boys' ability to separate emotion from reason, and to be more field-independent, favors abstract reasoning and traditional teaching strategies. Girls also appreciate processes while boys favor product. Even girls' worldview often differs from boys': Time is considered fluid, measured in terms of relationships rather than in objective units; power is limitless rather than zero-sum; leadership is based on facilitation rather than power; individuals are more important than rules; and the world is to be lived with, not exploited (Miller, 1976).

The Social Side of Learning

As touched upon above, societal expectations carry as much weight as nature. Social development, which starts and continues with the family, grows to include neighbors and relatives, and then community and larger entities. By age five, gender expectations are evident. By puberty, peer influence overtakes familial ties, largely because youth need to determine their self-identify and their social place in the world. Generally, students with positive self-concepts and strong social skills succeed academically.

Beginning with prehistoric divisions of labor based on body build and functions (e.g., child-bearing), male and female roles have been articulated in an effort to establish a social order. When either sex displays the other sex's characteristics, the "natural order" can appear to be threatened, so societal expectations have often confined both genders' preferences—usually with male traits valued more than female. Over centuries, details about gender roles have been refined, some of which remain fairly global (e.g., warriors tend to be male and babysitters tend to be female) and others that depend on a specific culture or sub-group (e.g., healers or cooks). Over specific eras as well, social status has changed relative to gender; for instance, early agricultural societies were often matriarchal while industrial societies were often patriarchal. At least since the scientific revolution, rationalism and objectivity (preferred by males) have been valued more than intuitive, personal knowledge (preferred by females).

Within the last half century, societal expectations about females and males have been tested repeatedly; today's youth grow up in a different social climate than that of their parents or grandparents, by and large. Many businesses reflect "flatter" bureaucratic hierarchies, and deal with organizational well-being as much as the bottom line. The glass ceiling has become more permeable, and career options have increased for both males and females. Both sexes can self-realize their full potential to a greater extent.

During this same period, more attention has been paid to female ways of knowing, which are based on Gilligan (1982) and Belenky (1986). Belenky noted that women: (1) keep silent about their knowledge; (2) listen to others' voices, known as received knowledge; (3) listen to their inner voice, known as subjective knowledge; (4) look for separate and connected knowledge, known as procedural knowledge; and (5) integrate different points of view contextually, known as constructed knowledge.

As a result of these different dynamics, gendered roles and expectations are not easily explained or designated in many parts of the United States. So even while traditional roles and social messages sound loud and clear, nuances and contradictions pose alternative options, which provide more options for both genders—but more difficult decision-making.

Learning in School: Boys vs. Girls

Do boys and girls experience school in the same way? Yes and no. In general, girls work harder, are more motivated, earn better grades and are more satisfied with school than boys. Boys are less comfortable with rules and authority than girls, and are more apt to think that their teacher does not like them (Black, 1995). Wherein lies the issue?

Gender differences in school behavior start from the first year. In examining how children interact in playground games, Pellegrini, et al., (2002) found that boys play a greater variety of games, especially chase and ball games, and that girls play more verbal games. Facility in playing games is an accurate predictor of boys' social competence, and both genders' adjustment to first grade. Boys tend to express their emotions through actions while girls use words, which also reflects boys' interest in things and girls' interest in people and relationships.

How do these differences impact learning in primary school? Girls develop earlier than boys, so their bodies can process stimuli meaningfully at a younger age. It takes boys longer to learn, yet they have shorter attention spans and need more teacher time than girls. Gender-linked subject matter, related to kinds of reasoning, already surfaces by third grade. Boys demonstrate better general math skills and three-dimensional reasoning, and girls excel in verbal and reading abilities. Learning disabilities start early too as boys are more likely to be hyperactive and need reading remediation. Moreover, more boys are held back in grades than girls.

Puberty accentuates other gender-linked learning issues. For instance, boys achieve academically after puberty while girls start to drop out of some advanced science courses. Girls' IQ scores drop off during middle school, although they rise again in high school. Boys tend to pursue power while girls pursue a comfortable environment. Boys' social acceptance is usually based on physical strength and athleticism, while girls' acceptance is typically based on beauty and peer relationships. Additionally, boys' social hierarchies tend to be stable while girls' are fluid. Girls are more likely to be depressed, but boys are more likely to successfully commit suicide. Still, teens look for experiences that create intense feelings (Park, 2004). Because learning is largely a social process, the emotional lives of adolescents need to be acknowledged and leveraged to bring out the best in each gender — and to build up their less-utilized traits. Indeed, a New Boys Movement has focused on the plight of adolescent boys, noting how society has constrained boys' psychological options (e.g., boys don't cry, boys should hide their feelings) (Smith & Wilhelm, 2002). Thus, collaborative skills take on more nuanced meaning in adolescence. Additionally, personal coping skills need to be explicitly taught in order to help students overcome personal frustrations so they can focus on academic endeavors.

As part of this psychological picture, the issue of motivation needs to weigh in. If students have no motivation to learn, if they ignore learning opportunities, they will not be successful academically. Motivation first requires attention, which may be self-initiated or "caught" by the librarian. Martin (2002) found that boys exhibit significantly less cognitive engagement and less concentration than girls. On the other hand, boys are less stressed and fearful than girls about learning, and may demonstrate a more playful attitude about learning, which can motivate them and help them achieve (Scherer, 2002).

Still, to hold students' attention and engage them in learning calls for a faceted sense of motivation. Each event and each situation shapes motivation, students are not simply motivated or unmotivated. Thus, a specific subject or even concept can affect the level of motivation (e.g., Scherer, 2002, noted that history is rated low as an engaging subject, and computer-enhanced learning is rated high), and the student's personal status or response to a situation (e.g., family stress, or a disruptive classroom) also impacts motivation. Pintrich and Linnenbrink (2002) posit four components of motivation: self-efficacy, attribute theory, locus of motivation, and achievement goal theory. Girls tend to underestimate their self-efficacy. Moreover, girls tend to blame themselves for their failures while boys tend to blame others; in contrast, successful girls think they are lucky while boys who achieve pat themselves on their back (American Association of University Women, 1992). Girls' intrinsic motivation is more likely to be based on interpersonal factors than that of boys, which complements achievement goal theory, in which boys are more performance oriented while girls are mastery oriented. Boys also actively seek a "zone of flow," where total attention is paid to the activity at hand to the exclusion of any other matter (Csikszentmihaly, 1998). Unfortunately, this flow more often occurs outside school. Being aware of students' self-perceptions and interests, both within school and outside, can help librarians look for ways to provide intriguing learning activities that foster intellectual risk-taking in a safe environment.

Overall, today's girls and boys reflect a wide range of interests and learning styles. Individual differences overrule sex-linked traits. Perhaps because the United States has become more pluralistic, lifestyles have become less stable, and social messages have diversified, young people's personal experiences are more varied. However, social expectations can shape students' self-perceptions. On one hand, television and other forms of instantaneous communication have helped spread common cultural experiences such as those presented on *The Simpsons* and *American Idol.* On the other hand, stereotypical images and expectations are communicated daily in the mass media and in daily life. Particularly when students are stressed or uncertain about themselves, they are more likely to regress to stereotypical behavior. In brief, young people are trying to find their identities within society, which bounce between the dynamics of personal uniqueness and social acceptance, both of which involve sexual issues.

The Impact of Technology on Learning

Learning with technology may be considered from two different standpoints: attitudes toward technology and use of technology to do tasks. The former includes the factors of affinity, confidence, lack of anxiety, and perceived usefulness (Gressard & Loyd, 1986). When Ames (2003) examined learning styles and computer attitudes, she did not see any significant gender difference in computer attitude, but she found that abstract sequential learners, who tend to be male, like to interact with computers more than abstract random learners, who tend to be female. Ames recommended that students be introduced to computer use early so their brains can be change more easily.

Another way to approach technology and learning is in terms of the resources and tools that are available to students. Technology provides more access to resources, particularly in terms of global information, and it motivates students because of its novelty and multimedia choices.

It should be noted that gender expectations relative to technology have changed over the years. To what extent do today's students — the NextGens or Millennials — differ from prior generations? A more salient question might be: how does the world differ? A key factor is technology. The proverbial Digital Divide is largely a generational issue now, between youth and their elders; if young people want to get their hands on a computer, they can find a way. As Abram and Luther (2004) contend, today's youth were "born with the chip." This same phenomenon impacts learning since teens, in particular, find themselves as technical experts to their parents and teachers; the days of hierarchical transmission of sanctioned knowledge may soon become extinct. Intuitively, this new generation learns experientially, and favors higher-level thinking over facts and rote learning.

As evidenced by their active use of instant messaging (IMing) and a variety of electronics, both sexes can now multitask, holding multiple conversations simultaneously. Both sexes consider collaboration as a natural value. Both genders like to express themselves and take advantage of the many technology tools: IMing, blogs (web logs), zines (online alternative magazines), and video. To this extent, then, technology has the potential to help both boys and girls learn. Indeed, the cutting edge technology user may well be the 14-year-old Japanese girl. Both sexes have "what William Gibson calls a techno-cultural suppleness—a willingness to grab something new and use it for their own ends" (Mann, 2001, 101).

These changes impact education, if for no other reason than students expect to use technology in school. Thus, the greatest challenge may be training older faculty to incorporate technology authentically into learning activities—and to learn in concert with their students.

Feminism and Learning

Today's girls believe that they can be anything, although they might not think they *want* to be anything or have the ability to be anything. At this point, their biggest barrier might be adults who hold more traditional views.

In the 21st century, feminist critical theory and women's studies hold their own in academia. While not as high-profile as they were in the last two decades, their perspectives have been mainstreamed and diversified. The second generation of feminists did not "suffer" for their economic and social gains to the same extent as their mothers. Feminism experienced a third, more nuanced and particularized wave that explored differences among women and fostered women's studies; male-bashing practically vanished, although wage discrepancies and promotional glass ceilings still exist in some occupations. A fourth wave of feminism has now begun, which seems to be striving for more inclusivity.

In terms of learning, students are starting to be exposed to feminist points of view in their research. Although most of this writing is geared to academic audiences, the underlying ideas of populist points of view, contextual reality, and issues of social justice permeate high school curricula. They help students question the status quo and gather more data in order to develop a fuller understanding.

On the other hand, more writings about male issues have emerged. As boys fall behind, particularly in reading, more attention has been paid to raising sons. Such treatment has focused on interventions rather than a world view of education or social status, which makes sense since male-oriented scholarship has dominated education for centuries.

While differences between females and males are significant, in total more variation exists within each sex. Additionally, as boys and girls mature and grow older, they have even more in common. Other factors—individual, cultural, and situational—largely shape who we are. What seems clear is that gendered education has to be exposed, and strategies to acknowledge such practices and offer gender-equitable learning activities need to be implemented, supported by librarians' and other educators' own gender awareness and knowledge. Ultimately, though, students have the most need to see how gender impacts their own self-perception and learning; by embracing their own gender and understanding their counterparts' approach, *all* students can learn more effectively.

Gender and Learning Exercises

Note: Activities marked with an * are appropriate for elementary grades or include accommodations for younger students; unless otherwise noted, all the activities may be done by middle and high school students.

LIKE MOTHER, LIKE DAUGHTER*

Pair mothers and daughters, fathers and sons (at the least, same gender adult relative/guardian and child). Have them compare:

1. The role of reading literacy when growing up, and in terms of parenting
2. The role of information literacy when growing up, and in terms of parenting
3. The role of technology literacy when growing up, and in terms of parenting
4. The role of visual literacy when growing up, and in terms of parenting
5. The role of media literacy when growing up, and in terms of parenting
6. Career exploration and expectations when growing up
7. Family expectations about gender when growing up
8. School expectations about gender when growing up
9. Social expectations and peer pressure about gender when growing up
10. Parent vs. child expectations about gender.

Visual and media literacy may need to be defined and distinguished for this exercise.

WHO AM I?*

This series of questions looks at students' self-perceptions, linking them to issues of literacy and expectations.

1. Ask students to respond to each of the following questions spontaneously.
   • Who am I? (*Write ten different answers.*)
   • Who do I want to be in ten years? (*Write ten different answers.*)
   • Who will I be in ten years? (*Write ten different answers.*)

(Optionally, request that they rank order their answers, most important first.)

2. In same-sex pairs, ask them to compare their answers in terms of self-perceptions, expectations, and values.

3. Assign quartets comprised of a girl pair and boy pair. Again, ask the quartets to compare their answers in terms of self-perceptions, expectations, and values. In the process, they should create a visual aid or chart to show their conclusions.

4. Each quartet will report their findings.

5. Lead a class discussion on the process (e.g., who took leadership at each step) as well as the products.

IT TAKES A VILLAGE SOCIOGRAM*

The extended family includes those relatives, friends, and other significant people who support and guide a person.

Ask students to:

1. Draw a circle in the middle of a page, and write her/his name inside it.

2. Draw other circles in the space around the central one, labeling each with the name of a significant extended family member.

3. Draw a line from each outside circle to the central one, and label each line with a word or phrase describing that person's influence on the student's life.

4. Compare personal family circles with those of their fellow students.

Older students can create more sophisticated sociograms, where the size of the circle can indicate the relative degree of influence, coloring in of the circle can indicate negative influence, and distance between circles can indicate closeness of the relationship. The thickness of lines between circles can indicate amount of communication, and arrows can indicate the communication's direction.

TALKING IT OUT

Usually, persons understand one another when their backgrounds, experiences, or values are similar. Ask students to:

1. List three people with whom they can talk easily, and indicate why communication with them is easy.

2. List three people with whom they have difficulty talking, and explain why communication with them is hard.

3. Review their lists, and discover any patterns.

4. Discuss how they can use new knowledge to improve their literacy skills.

THE POWER OF WORDS

Most words bear connotations or link to values. Likewise, whether accurate or not, genders often have specific words associated with them. This exercise examines what words might be gender-linked.

1. Ask students to read the set of words below.

2. Ask them to put a plus sign in front of five words that most closely reflect themselves, and a minus sign in front of five that least reflect themselves.

3. Ask students to underline five words that most closely reflect their own gender, and draw a line in the middle of five that least reflect themselves.

4. Ask students to circle five words that most closely reflect the opposite gender, and draw a diagonal through five that least reflect themselves.

5. Ask boy-girl pairs to compare their results.

6. Lead a class discussion on the results, and the social implications. How might words impact literacy?

Aggressive	Egotistic	Modest	Sloppy
Friendly	Energetic	Neat	Sly
Air-headed	Enthusiastic	Nosy	Smart
Arrogant	Generous	Optimistic	Snobbish
Assertive	Goofy	Out-going	Strong
Flirty	Gossipy	Pessimistic	Submissive
Bossy	Helpful	Pushy	Successful
Classy	Humble	Rebellious	Talkative
Clever	Independent	Reflective	Teasing
Complaining	Jealous	Sarcastic	Thorough
Critical	Kind	Secretive	Touchy
Cute	Lazy	Serious	Trusting
Dependable	Loud	Showy	Truthful
Detailed	Methodical	Shy	Understanding
Diplomatic	Mellow	Silly	Weak

Alternatively, attach a label, using one or more of the above words, to each person's back. Suggest that groups of students (6–8 members) interact with each other based on the label. See if the students wearing labels can self-identify their labels. To process the experience, ask students:

1. How did it feel to not know the label?
2. How did you treat the person differently?
3. How did you interpret other people's attitude towards you?
4. Did gender factor into the interaction?
5. Do you think you subconsciously wear a label that you can't see for yourself?

MY ROOM, MYSELF*

Ask students to photograph or draw their bedrooms, including objects that have personal meaning for them. Request that they state why those objects are significant. Discuss what gendered connotations emerge in the process, such as the types and names of favorite toys. This activity is probably best done in same-sex pairs to help students feel comfortable talking about their possessions. The class can then divide by gender to see if patterns emerge. Then the two sexes can compare their findings without compromising privacy issues.

DER, DIE, AND DAS

In some languages, nouns are gendered. French and Spanish, among others, have male and female nouns. German has three: male, female, and neuter (der Wolf, die Maus, das Boot; interestingly, a girl is das Fraulein.) English does not have gendered nouns. Some metaphors and similes also have gender connotations. Do these practices correlate with cultural attitudes about gender?

Ask students to identify an object in the room that somehow represents or symbolizes a personal value for them, and ask them to explain why. It is a good idea to model this exercise; for instance: "I chose this thick book because I value ideas, like the book, and think I have lots of ideas similar to those in the book. I also chose a thick book because it looks serious, and others will think I look serious."

In processing this exercise, ask students to reveal what they learned about each other. What gender issues, if any, emerged? Were any objects chosen that could have gender-linked connotations?

THE EMOTIONAL SIDE*

Request that students describe their emotional state by completing this grid.

Emotion Emotion	Source of Followed	What Action Could I Have Acted?	How Else
happiness			
sadness			
pride			
shame			
anger			
fear			
surprise			
frustration			

Ask students:

1. Do you discern possible gender patterns or stereotypes from this grid?
2. Do you think your behaviors reflect personal- or gender-based decisions?

Students may want to submit these tables anonymously. The teacher/librarian can share some of the behaviors with the class, asking students to determine which gender they believe was involved. Older students might compare how they behave now with how they remembered behaving five years earlier.

PUBLIC AND PRIVATE MASKS

How people behave in public may differ from their behavior in private. What they say may differ from what they think. Sometimes gender factors into these discrepancies. Both private and public behavior and attitude can be influenced by others. Thus, when dealing with literacies and learning, a student may hold one value but demonstrate another value in public: s/he may want to learn how to read but, swayed by peers who do not see the need for reading, does not show interest in reading when in school. How do these public and private masks impact learning?

Have students complete this chart (examples are given here).

I Know	*I Don't Know*	
Others Know I don't eat meat.	I play tennis. If I'd be a lousy liar.	Whether I'm a good listener.
Others Don't Know I have perfect pitch.	I'm afraid of being alone. How well I'd do in physics.	Whether I have dyslexia.

Same-gender pairs can then compare charts, and compare findings with an opposite-gender pair. What gender patterns emerge? How might public and private values impact learning?

Another factor that can impact learning is that people have different opinions about what should be public and what should be private. Sometimes these public-private "fences" are gender-linked.

Ask students to decide which of the following topics ought to be public knowledge, and which should remain private:

1. Names of family members
2. Ages of family members
3. Where the family lives
4. Family income
5. Family divorce
6. Family substance abuse
7. Neighborhood location
8. Personal religious affiliation
9. Personal health history
10. Feelings about one's own body image
11. Personal work habits
12. Personal leisure habits
13. Personal eating habits
14. Personal achievements

15. Personal obstacles
16. Academic areas of success
17. Academic areas of frustration
18. Personal goals in life

What patterns emerge? Are any results gender-linked?

To expand the exercise, students can draw a target with a series of concentric circles, and label it as follows. Place the number of each item above in the circle that represents the most communication comfort. Process as done above.

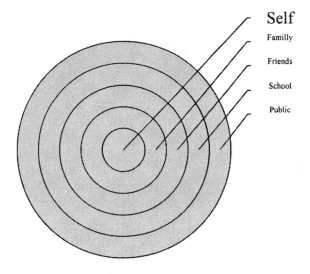

CONDITIONS FOR LEARNING

Ask students to self-assess their learning preferences along each continuum below. Then, request that they draw a line connecting their points. Next, ask them to compare their learning "profiles" to reveal possible gender patterns. For easier comparison, duplicate the continuums on transparencies so charts can be overlaid.

Alone	Large Group
Compete	Collaborate
Silence	Noisy Environment
Low Light	Bright Light
Informal Seating	Formal Seating
Morning	Night
At Leisure Pace	At Rush Pace
Text Information	Image Information
Task-Oriented	Performance-Oriented
Read Broadly	Read Deeply
Lots Of Small Tasks	A Few Big Tasks
Memorize	Create
Structure	Open-Ended
Small Details	Big Picture
Facts	Ideas

Concrete	Abstract
Practical	Ideal
Passive	Active
Watch	Do
Ponder	Experience
Think	Feel
Process	Product
Sequential	Random
One Right Way	Many Ways

DEALING WITH SEXUAL STEREOTYPES

Societal or cultural expectations can be gender-linked, sometimes impacting students' goal-setting and academic effort. This exercise makes those stereotypes explicit, and helps students to think about their reactions to them — and to consider possible actions.

The following sex-role stereotypes adapted from Project Born Free (Pederson & Hernandez 1997) have been reversed for the sake of this activity (the parenthetical wording is the actual one). Ask students to react to them as written. Afterwards, tell them the actual truism, and see how they react. It could well be that students will reject the stereotypes, which reinforces the actual truism.

1. The same product is evaluated more highly if it is attributed to a female (male) than a male (female). *Can you think of a case where a teacher graded a paper differently when the person's name was known than when the paper was anonymously graded?*

2. Males (females) who are competent and achieve are viewed as deviant from male norms and thus anxious, whereas males (females) who see themselves as lacking these traits may suffer low self-esteem. *Would you rather be deviant and anxious, or have low self-esteem?*

3. When a group of males and females are asked to predict how well they will perform on a specified task, males (females) state lower expectations for their performance then females (males). *Think of a task you do better than your peers; think of a task your peers do better than you. Would you answer differently if you could state your skill privately?*

4. Males (females) have a harder time deciding on a career that aligns with their self-concept than females (males). *Do you have an idea of what you want to do as a career? Is your idea based on others' opinions or your own?*

5. Learning about adult roles tends to be family-based for boys (girls) and job-based for girls (boys). *What adult roles have you practiced?*

6. Males (females) achieve less than females (males) in professional jobs, politics, and sports according to traditional measures of success. *In what situations are you more successful than your counterparts? When are you less successful?*

7. Males (females) tend to attribute their success to luck — and their failures

to lack of ability. *When unsuccessful doing a computer task, what do you think is the problem?*

Works Cited

Abram, Stephen, and Luther, Judy (2004, May 1). "Born with the chip." *Library Journal, 129,* 8, 34–37.
American Association of University Women (1992). *Shortchanging girls, shortchanging America.* Washington, DC: American Association of University Women.
Ames, Pat (2003). "The role of learning style in university students' computer attitudes: Implications relative to the effectiveness of computer-focused and computer-facilitated instruction." (Doctoral dissertation, The Claremont Graduate University, 2003). *ProQuest Dissertations and Theses* (AAT 3093249).
Belenky, M. F.; McVicker Clinchy, B.; Rule Golberger, N.; Mattuck Tarule, J. (1986). *Women's ways of knowing: The development of self, voice, and mind.* New York: Basic Books.
Black, Gordon (1995, Fall). *CSMpact for education: Do boys and girls experience education differently?* Rochester, NY: Harris Interactive.
Csikszentmihaly, Mihaly (1998). *Finding flow: The psychology of engagement with everyday life.* New York: Basic Books.
Gilligan, Carol (1982). *In a different voice.* Cambridge, MA: Harvard University Press.
Gressard, C., and Loyd, B. (1986). "Validation studies of a new computer attitude scale." *Association for Educational Data Systems Journal,* 18(4), 295–301.
Gurian, Michael, and Henley, Patricia (2001). *Boys and girls learn differently! A guide for teachers and parents.* San Francisco: Jossey-Bass.
Higgins, D., and Bryce, J. (1999). *Flow, enjoyment and positive experiences in computer gaming: Preliminary research, theoretical background, results and future research.* Unpublished [online], University of Manchester, Manchester, United Kingdom. Retrieved February 3, 2005, from http://www.playingfields.co.uk/content/gamingreport.htm.
Knight, Heather (1997, May 7). "Study finds few signs of an academic gender gap." *Los Angeles Times,* A1, 33.
Kolb, D. (1984). *Experiential learning.* Englewood Cliffs, N.J.: Prentice Hall.
Lehrman, Sally (1997, May). Woman. *Stanford Today, 25,* 3, 47–51.
Mann, Charles (2001, August). "Why 14-year-old Japanese girls rule the world." *Yahoo! Internet Life,* 99–103.
Martin, Andrew (2002). *Improving the educational outcomes of boys.* Canberra, Australia: Department of Education. Retrieved February 3, 2005, from www.decs.act.gov.au/publicat/pdf/Ed_Outcomes_Boys.pdf
Martin, Robert (2004, Winter). "A nation of learners." *Threshold,* 32.
Miller, Jean Baker (1976). *Toward a new psychology of women.* Boston: Beacon Press.
Moir, Anne, and Jessel, David (1991). *Brain sex.* New York: Dell.
Orenstein, Peggy (1994). *School-girls.* New York: Doubleday.
Park, Alice (2004, May 10). "What makes teens tick?" *Time, 163,* 19, 56–65.
Pedersen, P., and Hernandez, D. (1997). *Decisional dialogues in a cultural context: Structured exercises.* Thousand Oaks, CA: Sage.
Pellegrini, A. L.; Kato, K.; Blatchford, P.; and Baines, E. (2002), Winter). "A short-term longitudinal study of children's playground games across the first year of school: Implications for social competence and adjustment to school." *America Educational Research Journal,* 39, 4, 991–105.
Philbin, Marge, and Meier, Elizabeth (1995, April). "A survey of gender and learning styles." *Sex Roles: A Journal of Research.*
Pintrich, P., and Linnenbrink, E. (2002). "Motivation as an enabler for academic success." *School Psychology Review,* 31 (3), 313–327.

Pipher, Mary (1994). *Reviving Ophelia: Saving the selves of adolescent girls.* New York: Putnam.

Scherer, Marge (2002, Sept.). "Do students care about learning?" *Educational Leadership, 60,* 1, 12–17.

Smith, M., and Wilhelm, J. (2002). *Reading don't fix no Chevys: Literacy in the lives of young men.* Portsmouth, NH: Heinemann.

Sousa, David (2001). *How the brain learns.* 2d ed. Thousand Oaks, CA: Corwin Press.

Venezky, Richard (Ed.). (1990). *Toward defining literacy.* Newark, DE: International Reading Association.

Zull, James (2004, Sept.). "The art of changing the brain." *Educational Leadership, 62,* 1, 68–72.

2

Teaching and Learning

Education strives to prepare students to become happy and productive citizens. In a traditional world, that education generally consists of passing existing knowledge to the next generation, preserving the *status quo*. Today's students, however, need to be prepared for a world that has not yet been created. Thus, students need to learn skills and processes that will enable them to learn throughout their lives as well as collaborate and perform in unexpected situations. For example, a study entitled "Digital Transformation: A Framework for ICT Literacy," published by Educational Testing Service (2004) identifies 21st century literacy skills as the ability to:

1. Collect and/or retrieve information
2. Organize and manage information
3. Interpret and present information
4. Evaluate the quality, relevance, and usefulness of information
5. Generate accurate information through the use of existing resources.

In order to optimize literacy competency, librarians and other educators need to design learning activities carefully. This chapter details those steps, and takes into account gender and technology issues. The library has a unique role to play in providing gender-inclusive experiences.

The World of School

The world of school serves as a social microcosm, a conglomeration of sometimes conflicting cultures and expectations. While each site manifests a kind of school spirit, that psychological bind may be very loose — or stiflingly tight. In the latter case, students may have a hard time expressing their individuality or satisfactorily finding their own identity; instead, they may be forced into externally determined "packages." Within those parameters, students may confront predetermined concepts of gender that do not mesh with their self-concepts. Usually it is the student who suffers, although society as a whole will not reach its full potential when psychological aspects of individuals are cut off from humanity.

Growing Up in School

Librarians hopefully realize that children bring their gendered experiences the first day they enter the school doorway. Their first teachers, parents, have already provided countless messages about gender — through the toys and children's clothing they buy, the kind of parent-child interaction they have, and the behaviors they model for their children. Moreover, older children impact younger siblings; they model socially acceptable behavior including expected school behavior. Once children walk into the school building, they pick up social norms, particularly in the cross-grade environments of the playground and eating area. Not surprisingly, the single-sex bathroom often serves as an initiation into gendered behavior as boys compare their projectile abilities and girls compare their self-images. Thus, adults need to be sensitive to gender messages and to model positive gender behaviors and attitudes. Gender should not be ignored, particularly since one of the major tasks of growing up is determining one's own gender role; but both sexes need to be respected, and subtle variations in how gender is manifested should be applauded.

The Learning Community

The process of maturation, in all its variety, affirms the notion of lifelong learning. In the business world, a recent paradigm is the Learning Community. Underlying this model is the belief that all employees have tacit knowledge, which should be shared in order to benefit the entire company. Certainly schools should model a learning community where teachers are considered expert learners, but everyone can contribute to the body of knowledge and together they can improve the school. In this scenario, outsiders or neophytes are mentored and gathered into the fold, and their individual perspectives are taken into consideration. Such involvement of new members includes not only new teachers but also parents and students.

It should also be noted that, while learning goals ought to be identified and pursued, the community also needs to realize that goal setting and attainment is a never-ending cycle of inquiry. As new students, parents and school personnel enter the school each year, new needs and opportunities will emerge. Thus, a dynamic structure of initiation and socialization will exist alongside a perpetual inflow of new ideas and challenges.

Furthermore, in such learning communities, different ways of knowing and learning are respected and valued. Thus, sex-linked traits can be embraced and integrated for the greater good. School personnel need to be aware of the decision-makers and those rising in power, paying attention to gendered patterns. Who leads committees? Who serves as secretary? At the student level, are student-body leaders representative of the total student population relative to sex, ethnicity, and economic status? What gender patterns exist in terms of course enrollment; do boys predominate in advanced science courses, and do girls predominate in advanced language arts? Do both boys and girls cheerlead? Students need to see both sexes in leadership and supporting roles, and they need to learn and practice theses roles themselves in order to prepare for their contributions as citizens and employees.

The different attributes of the school culture as a learning community may be detailed as follows:

1. *Mission:* What is the school's purpose, and how will it strive to accomplish its goal?

2. *Culture:* What are the school's norms and expectations? Where are its tacit and explicit values and beliefs?

3. *Curriculum:* What is the scope and sequence? How is curriculum developed and improved? What skills, knowledge and dispositions are taught? What is the hidden curriculum?

4. *Staff:* What quantity and quality of classroom teachers and supporting professionals exist? How much authority and responsibility are they given? What voice do they have in governance issues? What is the professional relationship among staff? What is the relationship between school personnel and students, parents, and the community at large?

5. *Instruction:* What methods of instruction are used and valued? How are instructional decisions made? How does instruction meet student needs and interests? What attempts are made to provide cross-curricular and differentiated instruction? How are courses scheduled to carry out the school's mission?

6. *Materials resources:* What are the quantity and quality of textbooks and other classroom resources? What is the library collection? How is technology incorporated? What kind of access exists to worldwide resources? What supplies are available to the school community?

7. *Facilities:* How does the space support the school's mission? How are facilities maintained?

8. *Assessment:* What is being assessed and valued? Who is being assessed, and who assesses? What assessment instruments are used, and who decides what to use? Who interprets the assessment data, and acts on the findings? What is the impact of assessment?

This chart identifies representative practices of exclusionary and gender/diversity-affirming communities (Farmer, 1996).

Exclusionary	*Gender/Diversity-Affirming*
No mission or clear purpose	Strong mission statement supported by all stakeholders
Rigid, outdated norms	Open, positive and evolving norms based on community-wide consensus
Arbitrary, unarticulated curriculum	Cohesive, comprehensive scope and sequence with opportunities for cross-curricular options
Poorly trained staff with low morale	Highly prepared, motivated staff; good student-faculty ratio
Lecture and rote memorization	Wide variety of instructional modes to fit content and needs
Worn, outdated texts; no library or non-print resources	Ample and current textbooks and library collection; fully integrated technology
Cramped, inadequate classrooms; no labs	Well-maintained and spacious facilities supporting school mission
No assessment or accountability	Broad-based criteria and evaluation method to ensure fair accountability and effective improvement plans

The range of practices reflects, among other factors, gender-sensitive approaches. It should be noted that as school communities move from exclusionary to inclusive structures, those who are apt to lose power may fight to maintain their balance of power. Especially as women have traditionally experienced lower status, they may find it hard to assert their rights, even in today's society. Fortunately, as business practices have started to acknowledge the need for collaboration and effective leadership, education has also been more receptive to non-traditional governance structures and practices. Some of the factors that facilitate change include a shared articulated vision, broad-based consistent communication, an open and inclusive climate, thorough training, and supportive administrative management. Nevertheless, change can be difficult and create self-conscious reactions. Conflicting values need to be discussed, so that support for change is forthcoming. Positive change needs to be not only recognized, but also integrated and institutionalized so that a new equilibrium exists that absorbs a gender-equitable school culture.

Parents are part of this learning community. If parents are totally absent from the immediate educational picture, that scenario reflects an attitude about education. Too often school personnel have projected a superior stance relative to their contribution to student achievement, loudly asserting their pedagogical expertise. However, parents have the advantage of spending the first, formative years with their children, guiding their growth from an intimate perspective. Therefore, those educators, including librarians, who approach parents as deficient because of the latter's possible lack of formal education risk negating important and subtle contributions to student learning.

Women are more likely to be susceptible to this kind of attitude because they pick up on relational cues and because they may play a traditional role in their own families where the male serves as the public figure. Acknowledging such realities, school staff need to provide a welcoming, non-threatening atmosphere to parents. They could find out where mothers tend to socialize, such as local churches, and partner with those cultural institutions as a means of leveraging educational efforts. Hopefully, female school personnel reflect a variety of role models so mothers can identify with them, and feel comfortable talking and working with them in support of their children's success.

Generational Issues

As the retirement age for teachers has risen, it is possible that four generations of school staff may be working together. This range of age and experience can lead to philosophical clashes in terms of gender and education. For instance, traditionalists born before 1945 tend to like the status quo and want to build a legacy; they are used to hierarchical educational systems. Their mothers may have worked during World War II, but most were brought up to see the importance of homebound moms. The boomers, born after the war, are typically the power figures in education, but still believe in ideals and teamwork. Their own education ranged from Skinnerian behaviorialism to open classrooms, from a heavy emphasis on science to proper use of language and reading. They experienced the second wave of feminism of the 1960s and 1970s, and may have the scars to prove that their professional advancement took a toll. Younger boomers, born between 1956 and 1964, have been labeled the Me generation because they didn't have to deal with Vietnam or bra-burning women's liberation but feel that they deserve the benefits of the work of their parents and older siblings; still, they have delayed commitments and now may be experiencing mid-life crises (Sheehy, 1995). Generation Xers, who were born between 1965 and 1980, feel a real need to balance work and family; practical at heart, they are busy building their repertoire of skills so they can handle downturns in the economy. This generation experienced the third wave of feminism, which focused on different ways of knowing and gender studies; in contrast, their education reflected lessons learned from *A Nation at Risk* (1983), sometimes reverting to essentialism and sometimes reaching for critical theory and cultural literacy. When these generations mix, their expectations and needs may conflict, so the push for a more inclusive and gender-equitable school culture can help to assuage complications along the way. Along the way, the negotiations involved in finding a mutual ground of understanding and cooperation provide a positive model for students.

Standards

How do we know when students are well-prepared? First, the term "well-prepared" needs to be defined. Next, standards of achievement need to be identified, and authentic indicators of performance need to be determined. Assessment instruments need to be able to measure the degree to which students meet those standards, and all assessors must be able to guarantee consistent ratings.

As the school community examines the notion of preparation, its members typically think about future employment, citizenship, and the personal lives of their students. Certainly the U.S. Department of Labor's SCANS report (2001) emphasized the world of work. Increasingly, schools have been creating magnet academies to foster specialized expertise, from hotel management to the performing arts. As a result, standards may be couched in terms of employer-friendly language, such as "problem solving" or "effective communication skills." On the positive side, such standards, *if applied equitably to all,* assume that every student has the capacity to successfully enter the work field. On the negative side, homemaking may be under-valued, which may marginalize females, who continue to be more likely to stay at home than males. Another danger, particularly when a curriculum has a narrow focus for youngsters, is that students might not experience a full range of academic and co-curricular possibilities and thus limit their horizons. Finally, students may associate school only with work, and not realize the inherent joy of learning.

As school personnel and parents make academic choices for elementary children in particular, adult expectations may supersede the child's own interests. In patriarchal family structures, girls bear the brunt of this one-sided decision-making, although both sexes suffer because gender stereotypes may be reinforced and promulgated from generation to generation. In the process, the traditional notion of a well-rounded education may be lost, which not only limits students' self-potential, but also makes those students less capable of making wise political and personal decisions. Thus, schools at all levels need to ensure that standards reflect the whole child and that all students take a variety of courses in order to enable them to choose from a wide variety of futures.

Assessment of Student Performance

How students demonstrate the way they meet those standards bears close scrutiny. Do they have a variety of ways to show competency? To what extent can they choose how to perform? Do expectations differ between sexes? What is truly being measured: knowledge or presentation? For instance, when teachers grade literacy portfolios, students with more organized and tidier portfolios often tend to get higher marks than students with sloppy products. As teenage girls tend to place more importance on appearance, their grades may be artificially inflated because their writing *looks* good.

Similarly, students who think globally rather than sequentially (more likely girls), or who experience difficulty with the physical process of writing (more likely boys), might solve a mathematical problem mentally without writing down the steps and have points subtracted for their work, even though they know the under-lying mathematical principles. In the above cases, alternative ways to demonstrate mathematical processing include drawing diagrams, orally tracing the mental steps, or walking through the problem using a graphing calculator.

The assessment process also needs to take under consideration *who* is doing the assessment. It may be difficult for some librarians to acknowledge their gen-der biases as they grade, and make appropriate modifications accordingly. More-over, students should have opportunities to learn and practice assessment skills in order to self-assess their work and review their peers' efforts. This kind of shared decision-making may be threatening for some teachers—of either sex—because it implies sharing power. However, if schools are serious about preparing students to be lifelong learners and successful citizens, then evaluation and decision-mak-ing processes need to be part of the curriculum as well. Girls and boys may well differ in their criteria for judging and in their conclusions, but such differences should be brought to light and analyzed in order to determine the basis for such perspectives and then utilized to teach alternative ways of approaching decision-making. For example, girls tend to under-rate their academic competency, and boys tend to over-rate themselves. Girls consider school more important than boys, and their performance a matter of higher stakes (Newkirk, 2002).

Curriculum

What are schools teaching students? In the final analysis, a curriculum pro-vides the content that students need to understand and apply to become contribut-ing members of society. As standards become pervasive are considered the lynchpin of education, the curriculum is reviewed to ensure that the standards can be met through the course delivery and accompanying learning performances. It sounds simple enough, but the actual picture is more complex.

Chartock (2000, 65) lists six approaches to curriculum:

1. Teacher-centered (traditional)
2. Student-centered (humanistic)
3. Subject-centered (academic domains)
4. Broad fields (interdisciplinary)
5. Technology-based (behavioral)
6. Society-based (meeting social needs)

According to Wright (2000), contemporary schools tend to offer a combination of traditional, subject-centered but socially aware curricula. Tension between "teaching to the test" and constructivist inquiry-based learning activities dominates educational discussion.

Posner (1992) asserts that three levels of curriculum exist: the official (what is listed on the books), the operational (what is actually taught), and the hidden. The case for co-curricular considerations may also be made since the presence — or absence — of clubs and activities impacts students' learning. This is particularly true if curriculum is thought to include social and emotional learning experiences, hidden agendas that transfer underlying cultural values that may result in gendered teaching and learning.

The process of developing, approving, and delivering the curricula reflects the social norms of the school community. Thus, attention should be paid to decision-makers who make things happen: school board, superintendents, principals, other administrators, senior staff, and parents. In large schools, several spheres of influence may exist, such as department heads. Do these decision-makers have legitimate power or informal power? Did they get their power based on expertise or on whom they knew (referent power)? How willing are they to share their power? Despite the sexual revolution, males tend to serve in leadership roles, particularly in high schools. What are their attitudes about gender equity?

How, then, does gender play out in curriculum? Are students tracked into college preparatory vs. vocational programs, and are those tracks gender-linked? Does a wide range of courses enable students to explore career possibilities based on their interests, such as fashion or construction? Does enrollment in advanced classes, whether English or the sciences, reflect the relative proportion of boys and girls? Are both sexes encouraged to take pre-engineering or home economics classes? Are all sports equitably supported? Is content itself gender-conscious, addressing social issues affecting both boys and girls (i.e., sexual identity, health and fitness, career choices)?

Particularly as today's society demonstrates that social equality still does not exist between males and females, it becomes imperative that K-12 education prepare both genders to optimize the societal "playing field." For instance, boys are better at retrieving information, but girls understand narrative and expository text better than boys (Smith & Wilhelm, 2002). Teachers tend to intervene to solve girls' problems; boys are left to solve their own problems. Similarly, girls think themselves less able to solve problems, and are less likely than boys to argue with their teachers when they think they are right (American Association of University Women, 1992). On the other hand, girls tend to behave better than boys, and constitute a smaller percentage of students tagged "learning disabled." Indeed, a New Boys Movement has focused on the plight of adolescent boys, noting how society has constrained boys' psychological options (e.g., boys don't cry, boys should hide their feelings, etc.) (Smith & Wilhelm, 2002). At the least, the school community needs to affirm students' curricular strengths, provide a broad-based curriculum to accommodate differences in background knowledge and interest, and help students improve in those curricular areas where they are less well developed.

Choosing Resources

What resources do students have access to, and what resources do they actually use? Textbooks remain the principle learning resource, so teachers need to examine them carefully to ensure equity.

1. Do authors and other experts represent the population?
2. What perspectives are reflected? Is information given contextually?
3. How are pronouns and titles used?
4. What is the relative degree of coverage of male- and female-oriented examples? What status does each gender exhibit?
5. Do pictures represent both sexes, and do they show a variety of roles and settings?
6. Can students self-identify with respected figures in the texts?
7. Are different formats of information represented: textual, graphical, illustrative? Do CDs or websites accompany the text?

When students are involved in examining textbooks from a gendered perspective, they can realize for themselves the need for other resources to provide a more well-rounded perspective on content. Other supplementary textual material may focus on one perspective, such as women's diaries or Civil War soldier life, but the available collection of resources should provide a spectrum of viewpoints across the curriculum so all students can experience many different ideas. These resources need to also reflect different learning styles, in a variety of formats.

While resources are considered mainly in terms of content information, they should also include production tools: ways to manipulate and produce information. Thus, manipulatives can help kinesthetic learners explore mathematical principles. Productivity application software, such as authoring programs and computer-aided design, provide content-neutral, open-ended structures for structuring learning. Cameras and video equipment enable students to gather information *in situ*, and then edit it in order to justify a stance or demonstrate knowledge. Even simple drawing tools offer a way to understand and express ideas. Some of these tools are best used individually, such as reflective journaling; others lend themselves to collaboration, such as videotaping. By providing a variety of manipulation tools, each aligned with the intended learning outcome, educators (including librarians) can acknowledge the learning differences and commonalities of all their students.

Impact of Technology

Since 80 percent of future jobs involve technology, it is essential that technology become part of students' learning experience. Additionally, the characteristics of technology can engage students and help them focus their attention on the task at hand. The combination of text, sound, and image that technology facilitates enables students with different learning styles to interact with the same content. Technology's digital features allow students to manipulate and repurpose information according to their needs and interests. Furthermore, technology enhances the lines between school and home — and the world — through Internet access and telecommunications.

The 2005 National Educational Technology Plan developed by the U. S. Department of Education clearly realizes the importance of technology in teaching and learning, both because of the nature of today's digital world and the need for data-driven decision-making and accountability. The plan's six major action steps include:

1. Strengthening educational leadership
2. Considering innovative budgeting approaches
3. Improving teacher preparation
4. Supporting e-learning and virtual schools
5. Encouraging broadband access
6. Increasing digital content
7. Integrating data systems

Librarians who incorporate technology into the curriculum need to look at how to implement new strategies to meet existing standards, assess learning and student products of learning, and communicate student learning. It should be noted that technology is not the best approach for some kinds of learning. Here are some guidelines.

Use technology to:

1. Increase access to information
2. Provide repeated training
3. Combine, re-organize, and repurpose information
4. Facilitate asynchronous collaborative learning.

Avoid technology when:

1. Appropriate technology is not available
2. Immediate personal contact is important
3. Other means are more cost-effective.

For technology to be effectively used in teaching and learning, the following elements need to be in place:

1. Vision: in terms of learners, research-based practice, community commitment, and communication
2. Practice: in terms of site culture, research-based practice, alignment of elements, relevance of education, range of use
3. Proficiency: of teacher skills in productivity, planning, implementation, and assessment, and ethics
4. Equity: in terms of system-wide socio-economics, gender, race, special needs
5. Access: of resources, connectivity, support, facilities, learning opportunities, and administration
6. Systematic thinking about standards, culture, community, proficiency, development, accountability, and funding (North Central Regional Educational Laboratory, 2004).

Especially as schools consider alternative instructional delivery systems such as distance learning, Web-based courseware, and m-learning using mobile telephones (Clyde, 2004), the entire school community has to guarantee that school personnel as well as students are comfortable with technology and can use it independently.

Instructional Design

The central factor for student achievement relies on the design and implementation of a series of meaningful learning activities within a positive learning environment, whether within the school setting or outside it. These activities need to align outcomes, strategies, resources, and assessments—and consider the varying needs of learner subgroups and individuals, including the issue of gender. In the field of human resource development, current instructional design focuses on students. Wiggins and McTighe's (2001) model of understanding by design starts with the desired student outcome, and works backward to develop a curriculum that will enable the learner to perform successfully; the Association for Supervision and Curriculum Development provides online templates and a forum for exchanging units following Wiggins and McTighe's model (http://www.ubdexchange.org). Another popular model uses the acronym ADDIE to facilitate following the steps.

1. *Analyze* needs: check learner current level of knowledge and learning style preferences using check sheets, observation, questionnaires

2. *Design* instruction: identify outcomes, resources, and strategies such as lectures, displays, videos, panels, online experts, demonstration, role-playing, simulations, videotaping

3. *Develop*/produce/locate resources and learning environment

4. *Implement* the plan, including monitoring of processes

5. *Evaluate*: collect data and analyze it in order to improve the design, using tests, check sheets, interviews, observation, peer evaluation (Dick & Carey, 1996).

Instructional design is best considered as a process, hopefully one that involves collaboration between librarians and classroom teachers. Indeed, instructional design should also include student input since all parties need to know what is going on and share ownership in the learning. A sample scenario focusing on gender issues concretizes this notion.

Ms. T, a science teacher, notices how gender is affecting student perception of course content and learner behavior: girls take fewer risks, boys are condescending toward girls. Ms. T also realizes that the chemistry textbook has more male than female roles. In the library, Mr. L the librarian sees that boys use the computers more than girls. He also notices that the two genders approach research processes and handle frustration differently, to the detriment of the girls. The two educators decide to address gender issues as a means to change student behavior.

As the content matter specialist, Ms. T analyzes what students already know, and what they need to know, prerequisite skills, so all students can start in reasonably equitable playing field. Ms. T looks at possible gender-sensitive chemistry content, and makes sure that both sexes can relate to the topic. Are gender stereotypes reinforced, such as male researchers or female lab writers, in texts or in classroom behavior? Are these gender differences acknowledged?

As the expert in resources and information literacy, Mr. L identifies those competencies and prerequisites linked with the content area gender issue. For instance, if the information skill entails locating and comparing textual material, do students know how to use magazine indexes; if not, the learning activity may need to be modified. Mr. L. also needs to be sensitive to possible gender inequities relative to information skills; for instance, boys may be more comfortable using computers for Internet searching because they have had more experience and take more intellectual risks with remote online databases. In this scenario, an additional session might be provided to get all students up to speed in computer use.

The instructional design needs to consider:

1. *Time frame*: Both content and information skills require time to assimilate, with extra time needed to address technology prerequisites.

2. *Resources*: Ms. T and Mr. L should examine available resources that fit both outcomes—textual material that shows a variety of gender roles.

3. *Grouping*: Ms. T knows how students interact, and Mr. L can suggest student groupings that best facilitate research and content analysis, such as same-sex researching and jigsawed mixed-sex paired content analysis.

4. *Instruction*: Ms. T and Mr. L have to negotiate who will teach each process, and how students will get help or clarification in view of their learning needs and preferences.

As an overarching concern, Ms. T and Mr. L need to assess the process and outcome of their instructional design. How will students' perceptions and behaviors change; how will such learning be measured? In addition, how well does the instructional design facilitate learning, and how well was collaborative planning achieved?

The Social Side of Instruction

It has been said that teachers teach students—not subjects. The underlying message is that without students, no teaching occurs. Regardless of a librarian's expertise, if positive interactions do not occur, the library program will suffer—as will the students. Thus, for students to learn, librarians need to provide opportunities for youth to be actively engaged, participate in groups, interact frequently with their librarians, get timely and specific feedback, and see connections in real world contexts (Roschelle, 2004). Generally, teachers interact more with boys than girls, although that interaction involves more negative attention. Thus, educators need to find more equitable ways to interact with their students (Jones & Dindia, 2004). Students' education should also involve their families. In short, socialization is a vital part of education, and need to address issues of diversity, including gender.

Before thinking about student socialization, librarians must examine their own social style. Introverts and extroverts may interact with students differently, intuitive thinkers may behave differently than individuals who prefer reacting to concrete external realities. Even the comfort zone of physical space between two individuals differs by culture and personality. Some people prefer interacting with others of the same sex while others would rather work with the opposite sex. Some librarians like whole-class discussions while others prefer coaching individuals. Whatever the social style of the adult, self-awareness can help explain reasons for initial adult-student interaction. Even though the two parties may have different ways of reacting to one another, it is frankly the responsibility of adults to identify reasons for a possible disconnect and figure out ways to overcome first miscommunications. In the process, these adults can use this opportunity to help students learn different ways to interact socially.

One obvious aspect of socialization is communication. Respectful and inclusive language should be expected at all times. Verbal put-downs reverberate in some school halls, with the latest derogatory slang being almost unconsciously spoken throughout the day. "That's so gay," for instance, is a typical phrase used to imply that someone is stupid. Students who are gay/lesbian/bisexual/transgender know that the meaning is demeaning, and they feel upset or hostile when such language is used. In fact, constant use of homophobic language can constitute verbal sexual harassment. To make matters worse, *adults* also use words as an insult, such as coaches calling boys "ladies" to imply that they are weak or "sissy." In this case, stereotypes about female behavior are reinforced. Such name-calling only hurts and confuses students, particularly as they try to discover their own self-identity.

While this socialization process continues throughout life, as noted before, a major developmental turning point in social education occurs when students enter puberty. For girls, in particular, their self-esteem often declines in response to societal messages (often from mass media) about age-appropriate behavior and expectations. For both boys and girls to weather these pressures, they need to have a firm psychological foundation early in their education. They need to analytically critique those social messages to confront the underlying assumptions and agendas. They need to learn coping strategies to withstand those pressures, and behave according to their developing inner moral compass. In short, educators play a central role in this socialization process, and can provide a safe environment for social risk-taking and analysis.

One aspect of the social side of teaching focuses on expectations. Educators tend to treat students differently based on their expectation of their pupils' capabilities. When lowered expectations are based on prejudice — regarding sex, ethnicity, or social status — the results can be especially damaging because they force false labels upon groups of individuals. Some of the manifestations of such differentiated expectations include:

1. Waiting less time for students to answer
2. Giving less credence to students' ideas
3. Giving less informative feedback and inappropriate reinforcement (e.g., rewarding wrong answers)
4. Interacting less both verbally and non-verbally
5. Placing students farther back in the room
6. Demanding less
7. Emphasizing lower thinking skills and impoverishing the curriculum (Nichols & Good, 2004).

As a result, those students cannot assess themselves as accurately and have fewer tools to improve their performance. They have less autonomy, less choice, and fewer opportunities to learn.

Expectations also impact the notion of competition and cooperation. Traditional education in the United States has tended to focus on individual competition. Student achievement is measured relative to another's performance. This approach assumes a zero-sum solution where someone wins and another loses. With the advent of standards-based education, the emphasis has shifted, to some extent, to "meeting the bar" of excellence. In this way, students compete with a set level of competence. In this alternative scenario, everyone could theoretically "win" or be successful. Where individual progress is measured, students compete against themselves, in effect. The trouble with competition is that it fosters gender differentiation because boys tend to be more aggressive, which is reinforced in a competitive environment, and girls are reinforced to be quiet. In addition, girls are more likely to look at context and collection rather than give the right answer, which is more symptomatic of competitive activity.

Students' "social capital" can also affect teacher-student interaction, even though it may be unconscious. Family background, neighborhood status, community ties, social status among students all constitute social capital factors. With girls' sensitivity to relationships, it might be assumed that they would have more social capital, but boys who are more aggressive may "work" their social capital to gain power more effectively than girls. Since students with high social capital tend to achieve more academically, librarians need to be aware of these influences, and work to nurture those students in particular who need more social assets—across gender lines (Beaulieu, et al., 2001).

An alternative educational socialization skill is collaboration, which tends to favor girls' approaches to learning. Complex tasks that require a variety of skill sets offer authentic learning experiences that also draw on students' social competency and help them to work autonomously. The interdependence inherent in collaborative work also helps students respect each other's abilities and learn how to negotiate. Toward this end, students should have opportunities to work together in single- and mixed-sex groups. Even though students experience teamwork from the earliest grades, learning how social interaction can optimize production needs to be taught explicitly. Beyond the general idea of active listening and distributed leadership, other social skills need to be monitored by the group: setting standards, calling persons by name, maintaining eye contact, sharing feelings, responding to ideas, checking for agreement, and easing tension (Dishon & O'Leary, 1994). Students also need training in performing various roles within groups:

1. Coordinator/facilitator: makes sure everyone participates
2. Recorder: documents the group's work
3. Reporter: shares the group's work with the rest of the class
4. Reader: reads the task and clarifying group opinions
5. Materials handler: gathers and keeps track of needed resources

6. Checker: makes sure all group members know the correct answers
7. Assessor: makes sure cooperative skills are used
8. Timekeeping: keeps the group on task (Farmer, 1999)

During the actual practice of collaborating, librarians need to make sure that both boys and girls have a chance to learn and practice these roles. For instance, the librarian can assign roles, taking into consideration students' sex. If all the recorders are girls one time, then the next time all can be boys. When students share computers, librarians can monitor keyboard and mouse use to ensure equitable use. Regardless of the activity, group practice should be observed; when inequitable behaviors occur, interventions can be made in a timely manner. Classes should also debrief after an activity to check their progress in social skills, and discuss ways to improve their behaviors as needed.

One solution to the competitive-collaborative conundrum is to foster collaboration within groups and encourage competition, against a standard, between groups. In that manner, both approaches to group dynamics can be usefully employed to address the learning preferences of both sexes.

Socialization in learning must transcend the classroom and school site to include the community, both physical and virtual. Service learning, which enables students to test their understanding and assumptions of academic concepts in real-world settings, offers a way for young people to contribute to their community and bring their life experience into the classroom to refine their subject matter learning. This approach to teaching and learning can resonate with both genders. Girls, who tend to favor relational experience, can recognize service learning as a practical way to contextualize abstract notions. Boys, who tend to favor kinesthetic learning, can appreciate the problem-solving aspects of service learning as they seek ways to improve their livelihoods. Service learning also helps each gender experience other points of view and increase its repertoire of learning tools, creating grater empowerment. In short, service learning helps students make a difference in their lives.

Good Librarian Teaching Practices That Promote Literacy

Gurian and Henley (2001) surveyed successful teachers about developmentally appropriate educational measures that can facilitate equitable learning. Here are some of those tips that are applicable to librarians:

Kindergarten:
1. Foster experiential learning through hands-on learning environments (e.g., manipulatives, puzzles, games).

  2. Help children use digital cameras to capture positive behavior and learning.

  3. Provide a rich variety of print materials; create daily reading rituals.

  4. Bring in positive male role models.

  5. Channel children's energy positively; help girls express their energy through leadership roles.

  6. Let children express their feelings; use a feeling board to identify and express moods.

Elementary grades:

  1. Encourage hands-on learning and touching of objects.

  2. Encourage kinesthetic learning, including whole-body movement and engagement.

  3. Provide opportunities for a variety of positive learning experiences that use competitive, cooperative, and individual effort.

  4. Provide many, varied writing experiences.

  5. Encourage storytelling.

  6. Provide single-sex and mixed-sex groupings.

  7. Be sensitive to children who do not act in stereotypical gendered ways, and accept their differences.

Middle school:

  1. Express high expectations both academically and socially.

  2. Provide positive rite-of-passage experiences.

  3. Provide both single- and mixed-sex groupings.

  4. Facilitate one-on-one mentoring using community role models.

  5. Teach social and tension coping skills.

  6. Ensure equitable computer access and training.

  7. Balance sedentary and active learning experiences.

High school:

  1. Incorporate service learning.

  2. Help each sex understand the other sex.

  3. Help students learn and practice communication and negotiation skills.

  4. Encourage and facilitate intellectual risk-taking.

  5. Facilitate one-on-one mentors, and introduce adult role models reflecting a wide variety of interests and skills (e.g., male nurses, women engineers, single fathers, women sky-divers).

Many gender-equitable teaching practices cross developmental stages and curricular lines. The following list for librarians and other educators reflects a consensus of studies and teacher preparation processes.

  1. Get to know the students personally, and build on their personal literacies.

  2. Build a sense of mutual respect and trust.

3. Create a safe learning environment, and use student work to promote ownership of that environment.

4. Give the purpose and rationale for everything taught.

5. Help students get "in the zone"; provide students with a sense of control and competence, offer appropriate challenge, give clear goals and feedback, and focus on the immediate experience (Smith & Wilhelm, 2002).

6. Encourage hands-on and social learning.

7. Provide opportunities for in-depth learning and understanding.

8. Focus on meaningful tasks and authentic assessment.

9. Give students frequent, timely, specific, corrective feedback — including praise.

10. Facilitate creative, unique self-expression.

11. Teach responsively.

12. Ask engaging, critical questions; use an inquiry approach to learning.

13. Give students a voice; use small group discussion frequently (do male-only, female-only, male then female then male comments) (Crew, 1997).

14. Think contextually.

15. Practice sensitivity to cultural identities.

16. Practice sensitivity to differences in values at school and at home.

In addition, as educators of the school's largest classroom, librarians can offer unique teaching and learning experiences:

1. A variety of learning areas: to read, research, produce

2. Differentiated grouping arrangements: individual carrels, small group tables, study rooms, classroom presentation areas

3. A strong collection of — and access to — high-quality, appropriate educational resources in a variety of formats

4. Optimum environment for constructivist enquiry.

Works Cited

American Association of University Women. (1992). *Shortchanging, girls, shortchanging America.* Washington, DC: American Association of University Women.

Beaulieu, Lionel, et al. (2001). "For whom does the school bell toll? Multi-contextual presence of social capital and student educational achievement." *Journal of Socio-Economics, 30,* 2, 121–127.

Chartock, R. (2000). *Educational foundations: An anthology.* Upper Saddle River, NJ: Merrill.

Clyde, L.A. (2004, Oct.). "M-learning." *Teacher Librarian 32* (1), 45–46.

Crew, Hilary (1997, Summer). "Feminist scholarship and theories of adolescent development: Implications for young adult services in libraries." *Journal of Youth Services in Libraries, 10,* 4, 405–417.

Csikszentmihaly, Mihaly (1998). *Finding flow: The psychology of engagement with everyday life.* New York: Basic Books.

Dick, W., and Carey, L. (1996). *The systematic design of instruction* (4th ed.). New York: Harper Collins.

Dishon, Dee, and O'Leary, Pat (1994). *Guidebook of cooperative learning: A technique for creating more effective schools.* Holmes Beach, FL: Learning Publications.

Farmer, Lesley (1999). *Cooperative learning activities in the library media center.* Westport, CT: Libraries Unlimited.

_____ (1995). *Informing young women: Gender equity through literacy skills.* Jefferson, NC: McFarland.

Gurian, Michael, and Henley, Patricia (2001). *Boys and girls learn differently! A guide for teachers and parents.* San Francisco: Jossey-Bass.

Jones, S., and Dindia, K. (2004, Winter). "A meta-analytic perspective on sex equity in the classroom." *Review of Educational Research, 74,* 4, 443–471.

Kolb, D. (1983). *Experiential learning.* Englewood Cliffs, NJ. Prentice Hall.

Newkirk, T. (2002). *Misreading masculinity: Boys, literacy, and popular culture.* Portsmouth, NH: Heinemann.

Nichols, Sharon, and Good, Thomas (2004). *America's teenagers — Myths and realities.* Mahwah, NJ: Lawrence Erlbaum.

North Central Regional Educational Laboratory (2004). *EnGauge.* Portland, OR: North Central Regional Educational Laboratory.

Posner, G. (1992). *Analyzing the curriculum.* New York: McGraw-Hill.

Roschelle, Jeremy, et al. (2004, Fall). "Changing how and what children learn in school with computer-based technologies." *The Future of Children.*

Sadowski, Michael (Ed.) (2003). *Adolescents at school: Perspectives on youth, identity, and education.* Cambridge, MA: Harvard Education Press.

Sheehy, Gail (1995). *New passages.* New York: Random House.

Smith, M., and Wilhelm, J. (2002). *Reading don't fix no Chevys: Literacy in the lives of young men.* Portsmouth, NH: Heinemann.

U.S. Department of Education (1983). *A Nation at Risk:* The Imperative for Educational Reform. A report to the Nation and the Secretary of Education by the National Commission on Excellence in Education.

_____ (2005). *National Educational Technology Plan.* Washington, DC: U. S. Department of Education. Retrieved February 3, 2005, from http://www.nationaledtechplan.org.

U.S. Department of Labor (2001). *Secretary's Commission on Achieving Necessary Skills.* Washington, D.C.: Government Printing Office.

Wiggins, Grant, and McTighe, Jay (2001). *Understanding by design.* Englewood Cliffs, NJ: Prentice Hall.

Wright, H. (2000). "Nailing jell-o to the wall." *Educational Researcher, 29,* 5, 4–13.

3

Technology Literacy

Technology is not the wave of the future, it is today's norm. At this point, almost two-thirds of jobs incorporate some type of technology skills, and 80 percent of the fastest growing careers involve technology (Online content, 2000). Today's K-12 students have grown up with technology to such an extent that the last major digital divide is probably an issue of generations rather than socio-economics. Education reflects this reality in that teachers are often less knowledgeable about technology than their students. Such a situation may be uncomfortable to some educators who think that they, rather than their students, should be the experts; but if the paradigm is a learning society, then anyone can teach anyone. This change has gender consequences. If the school community — at any age — cannot connect with technology including the Internet, it will have a hard time learning and applying technological skills. While the issue of physical access is important, intellectual access is a necessity for comprehending and using technology-embedded ideas.

As a center of information, libraries play a unique role in providing both physical and intellectual access to technology so that students can use it meaningfully. This chapter looks at these different factors, and notes how libraries work in this environment to help students become technologically literate. Exercises help the school community appreciate the impact of technology.

Definitions of Technology Literacy

The International Society for Technology in Education (ISTE, 2000) has developed technology literacy standards that apply to primary students as well as to experienced teachers. Their six areas of competency include:

1. Basic operations and concepts
2. Social, ethical, and human issues
3. Technology productivity tools
4. Technology communication tools

5. Technology research tools
6. Technology problem-solving and decision-making tools

The International Technology Education Association (2000) has also developed technology literacy standards for students, but these focus more on learning *about and for* technology rather than *using* technology as an intellectual tool. Their foci include:

1. The nature of technology
2. Technology and society
3. Design (specifically, engineering design for problem-solving)
4. Abilities for a technological world (creating technological products)
5. The designed world (i.e., agriculture, energy, medicine, transportation, manufacturing construction, communication)

In other areas of the world, technology literacy is frequently reconfigured as Information and Communications Technology or as Information and Technology Literacy, which recognizes the overlapping concepts. The ISTE standards, while rather tool-based, offer the most delineated and most easily applicable set that can be expected for K-12 students in the U.S. Thus, they serve as the framework for this book's discussion of technology literacy.

Developmental Issues of Technology Literacy

According to Pink (2005), logical left-brain thinking dominated the Information Age. He contends that the more holistic right brain will rule the Conceptual or Knowledge Age. The left brain is useful for basic computer skills such as following directions, inputting information into electronic formats, and coding. The right brain enables one to find patterns in data and communicate meaning. Because of the variety of content and formats accessible through technology, educators can find resources that match students' various learning styles. In short, children engage their entire brains when using technology, depending on *how* they use it.

The question is not if children *should* use technology; today's students are technology natives (Kaiser Family Foundation, 1999). As far back as 1994 it was determined that the average age that children started using computers was between 18 and 24 months (Casey, 1997). By the time children reach the age of seven, their learning style is pretty much set, so even kindergartners ought to have learning experiences using technology in order to feel more self-confident about using digital skills. Since individuals with abstract sequential learning style preferences, which style is more often exhibited by males, tend to like computers more than individuals with other learning style preferences, early success with computers can take advantage of the brain's early malleability (Ames, 2003).

The issue is, again, *how* children use technology, particularly in early grades. The Northwest Regional Educational Lab (Van Scoter & Ellis, 2001) offers useful guidelines for technology use in light of child development factors. For example, to meet children's social and emotional development needs, one computer should be used by two students in a learning structure that ensures that both students have hands-on experience and opportunities to talk about their efforts. The American Association for the Advancement of Science (1999) found that more peer teaching and helping occurs when students use computers. In terms of language development, students should play with reading-rich digital resources and be encouraged to talk about their processes while using technology in order to develop more complex speech and reading fluency. To address motor development, word processing — if done using smaller keyboards—can actually be easier for some children than physically forming letters. Of course, computer use should be brief for little ones in order to prevent obesity and vision problems. Usually a combination of on-computer and off-computer activity within a learning activity yields the best academic and social results (The American Association for the Advancement of Science, 1999).

Gender Issues and Technology Literacy

While many factors account for differences in how students use technology, such as socio-economics and personality, on the whole, girls and boys have exhibited distinctive behaviors relative to technology.

Girls	Boys
Technology is a medium for connecting to others.	Technology is a source of power.
Technology is used to express.	Technology can be commanded.
Girls are concerned about nature relative to technology.	Boys want to conquer nature through technology.
Technology is a social activity.	Technology is a machine (yeah!).
Technology facilitates two-way communication.	Technology facilitates one-way communication.
Technology is a way to converse.	Technology is a way to the world.
Technology can lead to careers???	Technology is a career!
Technology is a means.	Technology is an end and a means.
Technology use improves with accuracy and reflection.	Technology use improves with risk-taking.

(Brunner and Bennett, 1997)

This picture has changed to some degree, though not systematically, as girls have had increasing access at home and more opportunities to use technology. Still, knowing the socially constructed issues underlying attitudes towards technology helps the school community address possible gender inequities.

Do girls get an even break in terms of technology literacy? Yes and no. The field is large enough for girls to have equitable access to a variety of software and telecommunications so that they can find their own voice within these parameters. Moreover, they are self-confident enough to reject applications that do not interest them. For example, boys tend to like action and competitive games; girls prefer software that promotes affiliation and complex characters. Girls also like technology's communicative elements, which they can contextualize across the curriculum and in their personal lives (Agosto, 2004). What girls seem to reject most often is their perception of the *culture* of technology: male-dominated and mechanical. On the other hand, girls often do not realize the long-term implication if they prematurely cut off options.

Even gaming experience can motivate students to learn computer programming; boys are thus more likely to pursue a computer science career (Agosto, 2004). Sadly, adults are part of that limiting option as they advise girls not to take advanced courses or model their own reluctant relationship with technology (American Association of University Women, 2000). It should be noted that girls should not be pushed into high tech careers heedlessly; the most important thing is to provide options from which students can choose knowledgeably.

The "break" point in terms of girls' involvement with technology has been puberty; up to that point, girls usually perform as well as boys relative to technology. According to the 2000 report of the American Association of University Women, if girls do not use computers by sixth grade, they are likely never to pursue science or technology. Therefore, if schools delay incorporation of technology until middle school, technology literacy may be too late for some girls. Since parents are more likely to purchase computers for boys than for girls, education's role in technology access is critical (Hackbarth, 2001). As girls enter adolescence, societal messages about appropriate behavior and peer pressure increasingly impact their self-image and overt behavior. Even in an online environment, boys are more apt to ask questions and communicate more; girls tend to use vaguer speech (McGrath, 2004). The "hard" sciences, including technology, become transformed into masculine endeavors; girls who show continued interest in these areas are perceived as tomboys and geeks, seldom as popular "with it" young women.

The school community needs to proactively support girls' engagement in technology by leveraging teenage girls' values of relationships, collaboration, social concerns, creativity, communication, and growing independence. Here are some ways to encourage girls' interest in technology, many of which can be done in school library settings:

1. Model and talk about effective use of technology for academic and personal applications (women, in especial, need to do this).

2. Invite girls on a personal level or in small social groups to take technology courses.

3. Design learning activities that incorporate technology and pose questions/situations that reflect girls' interests.

4. Emphasize collaborative technology projects, particularly utilizing presentation tools, web pages, digital imaging, and videotaping.

5. Hold girls-only technology training.

6. Establish a girls-only tech club.

7. Enlist college technology majors to be mentors for girls.

8. Train and employ girls as computer lab aides.

9. Enlist girls' help in developing web sites, particularly in terms of layout.

10. Invite girls to create electronic publications.

On the positive side, a significant number of young women in their twenties work in technology fields or use technology for other professional careers. They are creating technology products that attract females, building on feminine interests and values, and inventing fun, supportive web sites that demonstrate female tech power. They are also mentoring their younger "sisters."

Technology Literacy Resources

When librarians think about technology literacy resources for students, they have to consider both hardware and software — because one does not work well without the other — and they have to decide what kind of access is needed. In fact, the very first consideration is one of scope: the library, the school site, and the district. The library hardware must be compatible with other systems at the site so the school community can work easily from any location on campus. While some sites mandate one operating system platform, most cannot guarantee such constraints, so the library usually has to provide MacOS and WIN options. The library may also circulate computers, whether laptops, mobile carts, or even long-term desktop systems for students and teachers. Since the school needs Internet connectivity and the infrastructure for intranets, library-based computer systems should be linked to such networks, with broadband capabilities. Additionally, the library should have a web portal so the school community can access library digital resources such as catalogs and databases, as well as library publications, from home.

In the same manner, software decisions involve hardware availability. A decision about the library's scope of influence must be made here too. Will the librarian purchase and maintain the school's entire collection, develop digital collections that include subject-specific software programs for circulation or networking, suggest software titles for other teachers, or confine software decisions to library-only items? In some cases, the school may buy a site license for productivity program suites and other content-neutral software, such as Inspiration. Classroom teachers often do not realize that the librarian has the skills to select software and CD-DVD titles for specific academic areas; collaborating with them for learning activities can be one way to bring up that possibility. Librarians can also suggest software-reviewing web sites such as http://www.educational-software-directory. net/reviews.html, http://www.clrn.org, and http://www.evalutech.sreb.org. In general, open-ended and content-neutral software are preferable to address all kinds of student learning styles, and provide a more generic approach to technology literacy. Thus, basic reference titles, productivity tools, and exploratory software offer technology learning opportunities for the entire school community.

That same principle applies to web sites. However, because so many high-quality educational resources exist, making choices can be difficult. Libraries can "play it safe" by listing good educational metasites such as Internet Public Library (http://www.ipl.org), Library Index to Information (http://www.lii.org), Galileo (http://www.galileo.usg.edu), and Infomine scholarly Internet resource collections (http://infomine.ucr.edu). For younger students, directories such as KidsClick and Yahooligans provide access to pre-selected educational sites. Several public libraries have sites, targeted to teens, that can help with technology literacy: Tucson-Pima, Arizona (http://www.lib.ci.tucson.az.us/teenzone); King County, Washington (http://www.kcls.org/teens); and Pittsburgh (http://www.clpgh.org/teens/index. html).

Still, students and teachers alike appreciate subject-specific webliographies, which is a good practice even in terms of becoming technologically literate because these lists use technology as a means to access meaningful information. Still, focusing on technology literacy, lists can include:

1. Tutorials for learning tech skills: http://www.Learnthenet.com, http:// www.powerup.org, http://www.youthlearn.org/techno/hardware.asp
2. Technology project sites: ThinkQuest (http://www.thinkquest.org), Center for Digital Storytelling (http://www.storycenter.org), Girls for a Change (http:// www.girlsforachange.org)
3. Technology career sites: http://www.itsworking.org/home.html, http:// www.discoverIT.org.

Interestingly, few "just for boys" web sites exist, mainly because their technology interests are well taken care of in general directories. Realizing the need to proactively support girls' interests in technology, commercial and non-profit groups are creating more techie sites for girls, particularly teenagers—although girls do not necessarily want a site that is restricted to girls only (Hamilton, 2000). Rather, girls prefer clean-looking, lively interactive sites that speak to their personal needs. Girls Go Tech (http://www.girlsgotech.org/), developed by the Girl Scouts, helps girls have fun with technology and explore tech careers. Mentor Girls (http://www.mentorgirls.org/resources/category_11.html) links to more than 80 web sites, many of which provide tech career information. Girl Power (http://www.girlpower.gov), developed by the U.S. Department of Health and Human Services, includes teen-centric and career exploration activities. The University of Maryland, Baltimore County (http://research.umbc.edu/~korenman/wmst/links_girls.html) has an excellent, though unexciting, web site for girls and adults on technology-related issues.

Technology Literacy Instruction

The most important instructional question is: What are the ends and means of technology competence? How the school community answers this question reflects its attitude about technology. If tools are the emphasis, then girls, in particular, will devalue technology. If the focus is on real-life problem-solving and contributing to society, then girls will feel more connected to technological processes—and boys will still be engaged.

Because most students have used technology since they were preschoolers, they tend to think that they are proficient. Students tend to think that they are proficient Internet users even if they really are not (Fallows, 2005). Here are some other behaviors that fly in the face of assumptions. Lower socio-economic students spend more time with most types of media than their richer peers but are less likely to use computers, media use is highest just before the teenage years, young people prefer computers to television, and parents spend little time supervising their children's use of technology (Kaiser Family Foundation, 1999). Some adults fall into the same trap of assumptions, thinking that all students come fully equipped with some kind of technology chip inborn in their genes. Both girls and boys can feel uncomfortable about technology or consider it unnecessary for their own self-actualization. Furthermore, students—and some educators—fail to realize that technical skill often does not reflect knowledge about technologically related ethical issues.

All students need to perform basic mechanical skills in using technology (i.e., use of input and output devices, file management, word processing, emailing and Internet use), rather like the first rote steps in reading. Usually the best way to teach these skills is to demonstrate the basic steps and features using a data projector, provide reference directions with accompanying diagrams, and give students opportunities for hands-on practice and structured exploration. Most of these skills can be taught offline to minimize inappropriate use or potential computer crashes; even simple use of the Internet can be simulated with "captured" screens. Frequent, short follow-up sessions work more effectively than infrequent, long periods to help students remember how to perform a task and internalize it so it becomes automatic (such as touch typing). A good practice is to teach a tool as a prerequisite skill that leads to deep understanding; that is, using technology tools as a means to interpret, analyze and manipulate data and information and then generate new information to share.

The ability to choose the most appropriate technology tool for a specific task is, in itself, a key competency. Thus, by linking the tool to the task, librarians help students develop efficient technology strategies. For example, graphic organizers help organize thoughts, spreadsheets help analyze data and generate visual data patterns, databases help sort information, videotape captures processes instantly, authoring tools meld several formats for more powerful presentations.

Tight structures are appropriate for tool-based learning, but for more authentic tasks, students should have choices within given parameters or goals; for instance, they could pick different topics to investigate, use different technology tools to access and analyze information, incorporate different media to present their findings, and decide to work alone or in pairs. One effective learning approach is that of WebQuests, which uses pre-selected web sites to accomplish an authentic task. This framework especially appeals to girls because it usually involves collaborative work and uses an open-ended approach to problem-solving. In some cases where students may feel overwhelmed, librarians can break the learning task down into small enough steps that can help the student achieve success and feel self-confident. Just-in-time assistance can provide quick, focused instruction that has added value because it meets a specific, explicit need. Online digital reference service also provides a teaching opportunity as librarians help students locate and access information using technology; particularly since online inquirers choose not to ask for help face-to-face when in the library, this venue offers a new option for learning (Wilson, 2000).

In terms of gender, several issues impact technology learning. Even by the time children enter kindergarten, a range of experiences and abilities is evident. Students need to learn how to respect one another's level of expertise and provide support, if requested. Since girls tend to be less experienced in some aspects of technology features, librarians might consider sponsoring a girls-only tech club or provide extra training sessions for students who need additional help. School should serve as a safe place to explore and take intellectual risks, especially for girls. On the other end of the spectrum, boys may want to challenge legalities and security, so librarians should lead class discussions about intellectual property and system-wide maintenance to optimize performance. To develop self-sufficiency, particularly for girls, librarians can show students where to get assistance: help screens,

FAQ pages, web tutorials, manuals, and online email help. In some cases, students may have had negative experiences with technology or fail to see the reason for its use, so librarians need to remind students of the big technology picture: finding and using all kinds of information to improve and entertain one's self.

Some good web sites that help teach technology literacy follow. Literacy and Technology (http://oswego.org/staff/cchamber;literacy/indexlcfm) provides project-based resources that incorporate technology literacy. Tech4Learning (http://www.tech4learning.com) includes tech lessons and other resources, including help for learning multimedia skills. Regional Technology Education Centers (http://www.mcrel.org/lesson-plans/index.asp and http://www.ncrtec.org/tl/lp/) have tested lesson plans that incorporate technology meaningfully. Filamentality (http://www.kn.pacbell.com/wired/fil/) offers hotlists and web-based lessons as well as a means to create and have hosted one's own online learning "package." Learning objects (e.g., http://www.merlot.org and http://www.marco-polo.org), which can be accessed by topic or tool, provide peer-reviewed individual simulations and other technology-based activities that can be incorporated into lessons and units. Technology in the Early Childhood Curriculum (http://coekate.murraystate.edu/kate/2003/may/techec/default.htm) includes research-based practices and resources for adults and young children. Learn the Net (http://www.Learnthenet.com/English) offers low- and high-tech tutorials in English, Spanish, French, German, and Italian.

Best Technology Literacy Practices for Libraries

In school settings, it makes sense for librarians to collaborate with classroom teachers to facilitate technology literacy since the library often has the most digital resources. Indeed, technology offers a natural "hook" for teachers who might not otherwise use the library with their classes. Of course, librarians must demonstrate technology savvy and good coaching skills so they can truly serve as instructional partners in technology-enhanced learning activities. The fact that the majority of school librarians are female enables girls to see positive role models in action; too often the major barrier to technology engagement is the negative message sent by women who have experienced negative technology situations.

Librarians can also train their own student aides technological skills. Girls should be encouraged to explore tech activities, including software installation and troubleshooting. Students can write tech contracts with the librarian, stipulating which competencies they want to work on and on which they can then help others. This approach appeals to both sexes since it fosters safe risk-taking, empowers students, and facilitates social responsibility. A wide variety of technology-related jobs can be performed by library aides: creating desktop publishing flyers and guide sheets, reviewing web sites, writing online book testimonials, installing software, cleaning hardware, demonstrating and coaching others in using computer programs, photographing and videotaping library orientation and instruction, and developing multimedia presentations about technology skills.

Librarians can take proactive stances in technology skills training independently as well. Library web portals are becoming a mainstay service, offering access to digital resources, areas for students to discuss books and favorite non-print materials, and instructional aids such as Webliographies and research guides. Increasingly, librarians are creating web-based tutorials and WebQuests on technology skills such as evaluating web sites and using digital databases (e.g., http://www.samnet.net/ludlowhs/lmc/fr_orient_WQ.htm and http://www.wayne.k12.in.us/bdmedia/index.htm). They can establish 24/7 reference service as easily as posting their school email address on the library web portal, although consortium-based reference service provides more robust and timely service. Librarians also sponsor computer clubs, videotaping services, video yearbook crews, and web designer groups as a way to combine the social aspects of technology and useful skills (Dobosenski, 2001).

Facilitating youth technological literacy has been a growing activity in education and industry. Focused efforts to support girls reflects another national trend. These programs often include field trips, career women speakers, and college student mentors. Some initiatives enable girls to use technology as a way to improve the community. Libraries, especially public library systems, have also provided opportunities to enhance technology competency, often in collaboration with other agencies.

Gen GIT (http://www.genyes.org) incorporates library research projects into their program. Several public libraries offer after-school technology programs where students learn various tech tools and then work with community members to develop technology products such as web sites. One of the most successful approaches is teen-created technology-based products. YouthAccess.org, a series of programs developed by Libraries for the Future, targets 10- to 18-year-olds outside school hours. Ejournalism builds on community issues to teach teens media literacy and research skills. MyHero (http://myhero.com) is a zine used as a vehicle to research all types of heroes. Imagination Place focuses on encouraging girls to develop science and engineering skills. The public libraries that conduct these programs typically work with community resources, and provide a welcoming place for teens (Farmer, 2005). In school settings, such library-related initiatives are usually tied to after-school homework centers, jointly sponsored by youth agencies.

Clearly, school libraries can offer a myriad of positive learning opportunities for students. By collaborating within the school — and within the community — school librarians can showcase the advantages of libraries: welcoming, neutral spaces with developmentally appropriate and engaging technology resources and services that foster technology competence.

Technology Literacy Exercises

Note: Activities marked with an * are appropriate for elementary grades or include accommodations for younger students; unless otherwise noted, all the activities may be done by middle and high school students.

I AM A ROBOT*

By following the flow of information, students get a clearer idea of the influence of technology. Elementary students can reenact how information is created and disseminated through role-play: acting out each step in the cycle. Older students can draw information cycle flowcharts. Students can also look at distribution of sexes along the cycle.

TECHNOLOGY IN YOUR FUTURE

Some students, particularly girls, may not realize the extent to which technology has permeated employment. Students can interview employees to find out how technology is used, what technology skills are needed, and what academic preparation should be included in order to be eligible for jobs. Students should note male-female representation in different jobs, and trace the preparation needed.

FACT AND FICTION IN TECHNOLOGY

Technology trends are often reflected in science fiction. Ask students to brainstorm technology-related features that might appear in science fiction works; the lists should include quantity and quality of male and female characters, attitudes towards technology, use of technology, function of technology, access to technology. Students can analyze writing in same-sex pairs, and then compare findings with the opposite sex.

HACKING

Computer hacking continues to negatively impact education and industry. Ask students to research the life of hackers, brainstorming factors to consider: educational background, access to technology, technology expertise, reasons for hacking, skills needed to hack, age of initiation into hacking, gender balance, social context, length of hacker practice, consequences of hacking, advantages and disadvantages of hacking, ethical and legal issues. Students can focus on different aspects of hacking or research different hackers, and then compare results.

TECHNOLOGY FUNCTIONS

Sometimes the use of technology makes tasks easier or helps us perform them faster; in other cases, using manual tools is more effective. Ask students to make four lists: functions that computers do more efficiently or effectively than humans, functions that computers do less efficiently or effectively than humans, functions that a computer might do more efficiently or effectively than humans in the future, and functions a computer will never do more efficiently or effectively than humans. Ask students to note if gender traits apply to these functions.

DESIGN THE PERFECT COMPUTER

What are the possible functions that computers can perform? In same-sex pairs, ask students to design the perfect computer. They should determine the specific features of the computer, and note what functions can be featured. Students should also determine which features are now available, which are being developed now, which are feasible in the near future, and which are unlikely to exist. Do gender patterns emerge in terms of desirable features?

COMPUTER ETHICS

Students' moral development lags behind their competency in using technology tools. The situation is analogous to having the ability to build a bomb but not the wisdom to know when *not* to use it. First, ask students to brainstorm technological issues that might involve ethics: security, privacy, intellectual property, intellectual freedom, filtering. Next, create small groups to locate codes, policies, and procedures relative to these issues. To contextualize the issue, ask them to create a scenario in which the ethical issue might arise, and then recommend appropriate policies and actions to support their stance. See if gender trends emerge in terms of scenarios or actions.

SEARCHING, SEARCHING

No one search engine is perfect; different ones work better for locating different kinds of information. In groups of four or six members, ask students to identify a topic to research. Request that mixed-sex pairs use the same search engine to research the same topic, and then compare their process and results. Next, ask the other pairs to compare their results using different search engines. As a class, compare the process and product for different topics to see what patterns might emerge.

HISTORICAL TECHNOLOGICAL COMPETENCY

Technology literacy has changed as technology itself has changed. For instance, at one time it was thought that technologically literate students needed to know how to program a computer. In small groups, ask students to research the technology competencies expected of K-12, higher education, and professionals over the years (starting as early at WWII). Note if gender expectations are part of these competencies.

REALITY IS IN THE HAND OF THE BEHOLDER

Image editing allows one to change visual images significantly so that it becomes increasingly difficult to authenticate sources. Start by taking the students through Kathy Schrock's site on Web evaluation (http://kathyschrock.net/abce-val/), feature by feature. Next, instruct them to read this site about image manipulation: http://www.snopes.com/rumors/cnn.htm. Then ask students to search for images that have been distorted, finding how images were changed and for what reason. See if any gender trends, in terms of authorship or message, emerge.

Works Cited

Agosto, Denise (2004, Jan.). "Gender, educational technologies, and the school library." *School Libraries Worldwide, 10,* 1, 39–51.

American Association for the Advancement of Science (1999). *Dialogue on early childhood science, mathematics, and technology education.* Washington, DC: American Association for the Advancement of Science.

American Association of University Women (2000). *Tech-savvy: Educating girls in the new computer age.* Washington, DC: American Association of University Women.

Ames, Pat (2003). "The role of learning style in university students' computer attitudes: Implications relative to the effectiveness of computer-focused and computer-facilitated instruction." (Doctoral dissertation, The Claremont Graduate University, 2003). *ProQuest Dissertations and Theses* (AAT 3093249).

Brunner, Cornelia, and Bennett, Dorothy (1997, Nov.). "Technology perceptions by gender." *NASSP Bulletin, 81,* 46–51.

Casey, Jean (1997). *Early literacy: The empowerment of technology.* Englewood, CO: Libraries Unlimited.

Dobosenski, Laura (2001, Sept.). "Girls and computer technology: Building skills and improving attitudes through a girls' computer club." *Library Talk, 14,* 4, 12–16.

Fallows, Deborah (2005). "Search engine users." Washington, DC: Pew Internet and American Life Project. Retrieved February 3, 2005, from http://www.pewinternet.org/pdfs/PIP_Searchengine_users.pdf

Farmer, Lesley (2005). *Digital inclusion, teens, and your library.* Westport, CT: Libraries Unlimited.

Furger, R. (2004, Sept. 3). "Success stories for learning in the digital age." *Edutopia.*

Hackbarth, S. (2001, April). "Changes in primary students' computer literacy as a function of classroom use and gender." *TechTrends, 45,* 4, 19–27.

Hamilton, Anita (2000, Aug. 21). "Meet the new surfer girls." *Time,* 156, 8, 67.

International Society for Technology in Education (2000). *Technology standards for students.* Eugene, OR: International Society for Technology in Education.

International Technology Education Association (2000). *Standards for technological literacy.* Reston, VA: International Technology Education Association.

"Kids and media at the new millennium." (1999). Menlo Park, CA: Kaiser Family Foundation. http://www.kff.org/entmedia/1535-index.cfm.

McGrath, Diane (2004, March). "Closing the gender gap." *Learning & Leading with Technology, 31,* 6, 28–31.

Online content for low-income and underserved Americans (2000). Santa Monica, CA: The Children's Partnership. http://www.childrenspartnership.org.

Pink, Daniel (2005, Feb.). "Revenge of the right brain." *Wired,* 70–72.

Van Scoter, Judy, and Ellis, Debbie (2001). *Technology in early childhood: Finding the balance.* Portland, OR: Northwest Regional Education Laboratory.

Wilson, M. (Summer, 2000). "Evolution or entropy? Changing reference/user culture and the future of reference librarians." *Reference & User Services Quarterly.* 39: 387–390.

4

Reading Literacy

Reading remains the central literacy in the United States. In the 2001 No Child Left Behind Act, reading plays a major role, and elementary school students in particular often spend hours daily on reading activities. Yet a 2004 study by the National Endowment for the Arts asserts that adults are reading less; only a third of males read literature regularly. Perhaps more alarming is that the reading decline by 18- to 24-year-olds comprises 55 percent of the total decline of the adult population. Other studies paint a different picture, such as the Pew Internet and American Life Project, which researched people's reading of Internet documents and came up with 70 million a day. What is happening?

This chapter spells out the principles and key concepts of reading literacy, and notes current trends in teaching reading literacy. It also explains how technology impacts reading. Gender-related issues on reading habits and skills are detailed, and ideas on instructional best practices are provided. The library can offer a variety of resources to help all students learn how to read *and* enjoy that skill. Exercises offer insights on reading literacy issues.

The Importance of Reading and Writing

One of the special characteristics of humanity is its ability to use language. Furthermore, the capacity to preserve language on recordings has enabled humans to progress much more quickly than if they had to depend solely on oral communication. The oral tradition, to be sure, has helped social and psychological development as people, for centuries, have shared local mores through storytelling. In addition, reading and writing have led to intellectual control and abstract thought. (Donalson, 1978).

Nevertheless, throughout most of history, only the elite were allowed to read and write. The invention of the printing press, with its potential for low-cost broad dissemination of information, threatened both church and state. Even in 19th century industrial society, broad-based education was frowned upon because it was feared that the masses would no longer be docile and would revolt. In 19th century

Britain, the elite thought boys wasted too much time reading and ought to be working. Interestingly, those in power actually co-opted the populace by establishing free public schools so children could study literature rather than polemics, thereby structuring their time and guaranteeing the *status quo* (Willinsky, 1990). In short, reading lays a foundation for democracies so that those who cannot read may now find it difficult to participate in governing themselves.

The definition of literacy itself has changed over the years. In the Middle Ages, it referred to the ability to read Latin. Writing was not required to be literate since the scarcity of writing surfaces and the skill to use ink and quill precluded most people from attaining writing literacy. At one point, a literate person just had to read a familiar text, such as the Bible. Later, literacy required that a person be able to decipher an unknown text. Highly literate individuals were identified by their ability to read and understand sophisticated texts. Typically, functional literacy today refers to procedural knowledge, being able to read and write, in order to function in society (Blake & Blake, 2002). As icons replace text on computer screens and text may refer to visual artifacts as well as print, reading literacy is in danger of becoming an amorphous concept. Therefore, in this volume, reading literacy shall be confined to orthographic literacy: the ability to derive meaning from orthographic (i.e., writing system) text, produce meaningful text, and self-regulate this process (Knuth & Jones, 1991).

Nowadays, reading (i.e., orthographic) literacy is considered essential for everyone. The ability to comprehend and act upon textual information is imperative to vocational and personal success by many societies. The National Literacy Act of 1991 stated that by the year 2000, every adult in the U.S. would be literate and able to compete in the work force. UNESCO declared 2003 to 2012 as the Decade of Literacy, asserting that literacy was a major global challenge, particularly for females. The first benchmark was not met; the second goal points out the fact that reading and writing competency require ongoing diligence by all of society. In the final analysis, schools must make every effort to help students see the value of reading in their own lives and then help them read confidently and independently.

The Reading Process

While the brain is built for language, children are not born readers. The process of learning to read involves a sophisticated series of steps that use several parts of the brain. The back half of the brain identifies pattern; the occipital lobe serves as the primary visual cortex. The frontal lobe strategizes and coordinates physical behavior. The limbic system responds from experience over time. The reading process involves linguistic, logical-mathematical, and spatial intelligence. Because the oral and written language parts of the brain are located close to each other, educators should stimulate both areas when helping students read — by introducing pictorial cues, rhymes, and repetition of words (Teele, 2004).

In order to read, children need to understand phonemes of spoken language (auditory processing), realize that phonemes can be represented by print (orthographic visual processing), and have phonemic awareness: that a few phonemes can be arranged to make many different words (concept formation abilities). As the brain processes the same configuration of letters repeatedly, it begins to store them as a single bit of information or a word. By chunking these letters, the brain can overcome limited processing space, enabling it to decode automatically and concentrate on comprehending ideas, as well as incorporating syntactic and semantic understanding (Sousa, 2005).

Developmentally, reading readiness begins before birth as the fetus feels sounds that are both chaotic and rhythmic. By the age of one, children can see and touch pictures, and even turn pages with help. By age two, they can fill in the words of familiar stories and "read" to their toys. By the age of age three they can link text and pictures, and recite whole books. At that point, they are ready to follow text, retell stories, and move to letter recognition (Reach Out and Read National Center, 2005). On the other hand, if children have no reading material at home and have not experienced the world of print in libraries or bookstores, if their parents do not share reading experience or help them build their vocabulary, those children are likely to be unprepared to read when they enter school. Sadly, letter recognition in kindergarten is a strong predictor of reading ability in tenth grade (Everhart, 2004).

Because language and thought are socially constructed, reading literacy is influenced by societal values and norms. What are the beliefs and habits of reading exhibited by a child's family and peers? What is the importance ascribed to a specific reading activity? What are competing activities or options? Who controls the choice of text: the state department of education, a teacher, a librarian, a parent, the child him/herself? What are the psychological and physical states of the reader? Can the reader identify with the subject matter or genre? (Pearson & Taylor, 2002). Some of these questions are situation-based but others reflect enduring beliefs. Just as sex development is socially constructed to a significant degree, so is reading development.

Proficient Readers

In order to determine effective reading promotion activities and remedial interventions, the characteristics of proficient readers need to be identified. Five main issues focus on learning how to read: decoding, reading skills, relating reading and language, factors interfering with reading, and the specific acquisition of reading competence (Resnick & Weaver, 1979). Basically, one decodes a word and links it with prior experience, such as hearing the word in a meaningful context; at that point, one comprehends the word. Beginning readers focus on decoding, and more experienced readers focus on comprehension. Over time, proficient readers develop a repertoire of reading strategies so they can self-monitor their experiences, and they store their information in organized knowledge structures. Reading also involves reading for intent, predicting the text, analyzing and contextualizing it, and either accepting or rejecting it (Knuth & Jones, 1991; Block, Gambrell, & Pressley, 2002). Predictors of reading success include: vocabulary size, ability to use expressive language, recognizing alphabet and naming letters, and knowing the purpose of books. Other specific practices of fluent readers include the ability to:

1. Vary reading strategy to match the type of text and reading objective
2. Value literature
3. Think about the author
4. Complete literacy tasks in spite of failure or ambiguity
5. Seek help or information
6. Summarize and synthesize
7. Process after reading
8. Share reading experiences (Colvin & Schlosser, 1997; Pearson & Taylor, 2002).

Several factors can account for reading problems: the reader him/herself, the text, and the environment or context. Physical and developmental issues often underlie reading difficulties. Some students have auditory weaknesses so they have a difficult time distinguishing between phonemes and sound-symbol relationships, or may have an attention deficit that makes it hard for them to settle down and listen. Vision limitations or mental processing of visual stimuli can impact reading development. Some students have difficulty mentally visualizing written concepts. Reading difficulty can be attributed to genetics, neural problems, or lack of early stimulation, among other reasons. Likewise, the child's cognitive skills and prior educational experiences can delay reading development. Psychologically, the child's attitudes and motivation impact the degree to which s/he engages with the text.

The text itself also influences reading development. Is the subject matter and writing style developmentally appropriate? Can the child identify with the topic or point of view? How readable is the text in terms of vocabulary, sentence structure, and length? What textual features provide reading structure or cues, such as pictures, captions, graphs, headings, summaries, tables of contents, or glossaries?

As mentioned before, the context also influences reading development. What reading materials can the child access and choose? What is the purpose for reading?

What reading activities are provided? What instructional support is available? Does the child have opportunities for social interaction linked with reading? (Pearson & Taylor, 2002).

Struggling readers need to learn the same reading skills as their proficient peers, but require more instructional time, more precisely sequenced learning activities, and immediate feedback. Early intervention is important (National Institute of Child Health and Human Development, 2000). Surprisingly, for basic reading skills, meaningful text is not as important as explicit direct instruction; in effect, students are learning how to use basic reading *tools*. Whether the hammer is being used to make a bookcase or a house is not the issue: it's knowing with which end to pound.

A Word About Writing

Increasingly, writing and reading have become intertwined. Writing is, in effect, the process of generating reading text. As education focuses more on students as producers rather than passive consumers, the act of student writing has gained attention. Even in preschool, youngsters often dictate captions or stories about pictures they make; in the process, they are dual coding their thoughts, which strengthens their learning. This activity also demonstrates the value of writing, so that students become more motivated to learn how to write skillfully for themselves.

As students get older, that link between writing and practical applications needs to continue. Completing job applications, creating resumés, and writing cover letters are tasks that resonate for both genders. Writing one's feelings can serve as a safe, private outlet for frustration, particularly for boys who do not want to share their feelings—although broadcast blogging (i.e., web logging) has attracted many teens who want to air their perspectives.

Writing development mirrors reading development in terms of phonics, vocabulary, language structure, and construction of meaning. English-Language Arts Content Standards for California Public Schools (1997) lists six types of writing that should be covered in public education: summary, narrative, response to literature, persuasive, expository, and business letter. Summaries help students pick out main ideas in texts. Narratives help students comprehend and apply story features. Response to literature can employ both cognitive and affective domains. Persuasive writing helps students apply skills in logical justification. Expository writing recognizes the importance of factual text. Business letters link writing to careers. Boys tend to be more comfortable writing about factual information, eschewing lyrical personal writing. The text to be consulted in the writing process can also impact writing efforts; if students do not have related prior knowledge or do not value the assignment, their writing will reflect that lack of experience or interest.

Students are more apt to learn writing skills if they value the process and have a good reason to do it. Librarians can collaborate with classroom teachers in asking students to write original stories in book form, sharing their writing through author parties, and adding their works to the library's collection for others to read. The library can also archive student publications such as school newspapers and literacy magazines. Librarians can work with classroom teachers to develop career exploration units that combine research, reading and writing activities that can be leveraged into paying jobs and worthwhile careers. Students can also write for the library: flyers and announcements about upcoming events, book and web site reviews, and directions for using library resources such as online databases.

Gender and Reading

The research is clear: girls like to read more than boys, and they value reading more than boys do. Girls read a greater variety of materials, and they read more often. Girls outperform boys in literacy, particularly in narrative and persuasive writing, and the discrepancy grows as youngsters get older. The Educational Testing Service found that the gap in writing between eighth grade boys and girls was six times the gender gap in mathematics (Smith & Wilhelm, 2002). However, boys improve their performance when they read for information or have to act based upon the reading. It appears, though, that education seems to set different values for different forms of reading / writing literacy, and those preferred by boys tend to get the short end of the stick (Sullivan, 2004).

Some of these gendered reading literacy differences have physiological roots. For instance, boys tend to use only half their brains at a time, unlike girls whose neural connections cross brain hemispheres; so boys need extra physical stimulation to gear up their brains. Girls develop their verbal skills earlier than boys, which impacts the listening prerequisite of reading. Boys are also more likely to be diagnosed with learning disabilities that impact reading skills. Boys who are kinesthetic learners may also have more difficulty sitting down for extended periods of time in order to read (Ligamari & Goodwin, 2004). (It should be noted that little boys who move around during story hours may well be responding to the story's rhythm; sometimes librarians stifle the very action that shows engagement.)

Social values and norms also reflect gendered reading habits. Boys are less likely to read for pleasure, and not consider reading to be manly (Newkirk, 2002). Nor do boys like books that are chosen for them rather than by them. The fact that English teachers are most apt to be female than male does not help the situation. In fact, Martino (1998) posits that if P.E. coaches taught reading, boys would improve their skills. Martino also notes that girls' superior reading ability does not seem to translate into better jobs, which may actually reinforce boys' apparent dismissal of reading. On the other hand, fathers tend to pay more attention to their sons than their daughters, and have a more playful approach to literacy; therefore, librarians should consider targeting fathers when providing parent workshops on family reading (Herb & Willoughby-Herb, 1994). Jon Scieszka's Guys Read web site (http://www.guysread.com) provides a good starting point for male reading bonding.

Smith & Wilhelm (2002) synthesized decades of research on gender-linked reading practices. Here are some of their major findings. Boys tend to read less, value reading less, and underrate their reading ability. They prefer to read for utilitarian reasons than for leisure. Boys tend to choose informational texts, escapism and humor, science fiction and fantasy, graphic novels / comic books periodicals, and electronic texts; overall, they prefer to read something that is "real" and connects to their "now." Girls read more fiction and poetry. In addition, girls read stories about both genders (sometimes foregoing their own feminism to identify with a male protagonist) while boys generally do not like reading about girls. On a more psychological level, as boys develop their sense of masculinity, they tend to reject feminine traits; thus, if girls are associated with books and reading, then boys may generalize that behavior and avoid reading "to play safe" among their peers. In general, boys tend to be more critical of reading material than girls. Girls also like to talk about reading while boys prefer to physically act out or respond to reading. Girls are more likely to look for underlying significance and implications while boys tend to stick to literal and material interpretations. More surprisingly, girls examine relationships in stories while boys ignore them — to the extent that they will actually omit female characters when retelling a story. Interestingly, too, boys tend not to write about emotions, and as girls get older they self-censor and control their emotions; in both cases, young people tend to constrain themselves, perhaps more than they need to (Goldberg & Roswell, 2002).

Several strategies can address these issues: choice of texts, instructional practices, incorporation of technology, and contexts for reading enjoyment.

Choices of Texts for Boys and Girls

Back in the middle ages, no literature was written specifically for youth. Early reading material consisted of Latin grammars and religious texts. Not until Newbery in 1744, with his book *A Little Pretty Pocket-Book,* did book publishers aim to both instruct and delight children. Periodicals for young people date back to the late 19th century. Young adult literature, *per se*, is a 20th century concept. Now in the 21st century, reading materials for youth come in several formats, including web pages and e-books (Dresang, 1998).

Youngsters read a wide variety of texts in their daily lives: street signs, cereal boxes, directions, television captions, schedules, sports statistics, games, baseball cards, hip-hop lyrics. Fortunately, the underrated comic book has been transformed into the trendy graphic novel so students can enjoy reading dual-coded material that is "acceptable" by society. Indeed, the artificial borders between school reading and real world reading should be eliminated so that youngsters can see the relevance of lifelong reading habits.

Because boys tend to read about boys, and girls will read about either sex, adults may be tempted to suggest books that evoke traditional male roles, such as Matt Christopher and Tom Clancy, to gain boys' interests. Yet if those authors constitute the whole of boys' reading, then boys will feel that they have fewer gender role options and may perpetuate stereotyping. Furthermore, as boys mature, their reading interests coincide more often with girls' interests. Just as the human body needs a variety of foods in order to grow healthy, so does the human mind need textual variety. Therefore, schools should encourage students to transcend the *status quo* and improve their future surroundings. Since one of the charges of schooling is socialization, educators can model good reading habits and leverage students' need for belonging by encouraging them to suggest good reading materials to their peers.

Another part of the problem of choosing reading material is that some genres are less valued in formal educational settings. Narrative literature, for instance, is encouraged to the detriment of non-linear text such as periodicals and technical manuals. The latter usually require different reading strategies, and both genders need to know how to navigate both approaches. Reading online incorporates additional skills such as hyperlinking and scrolling.

Boys, in particular, prefer historical documents to textbooks. They like reading "the real thing," and appreciate different perspectives (e.g., a Black soldier's diary in comparison to a white general's directives). Both genders like storied texts, and reading material that evokes feelings, especially humor (even if boys hide some emotions or miss some of the subtle nuances). Boys also like reading that stimulates visual thinking — as well as texts that include visual elements. The use of these non-fiction materials can give both sexes a variety of ways to represent themselves, relate to others, and negotiate with cultural knowledge (Alloway, 2002).

Older elementary schoolers especially like series for their predictability and "comfort level." Students also like to have several opportunities to engage with the same characters or settings, and will even reread the same text if they enjoy it deeply. Those students who like to collect things, again usually boys, will sometimes competitively read "everything" by the same author.

Still, Brozo (2002) suggests that boys read books that have positive male archetypes. He lists the following examples: pilgrim (e.g., Soto's *Pacific Crossing*), patriarch (e.g., Lynch's *Shadow Boxer*), king (e.g., Winston Churchill), warrior (e.g., Nelson Mandela), magician (e.g., Weaver's *Striking Out*), Wildman (e.g., Hobbs'

Far North), healer (e.g., Bakkan's *The Fields and the Hills*), prophet (e.g., Spinelli's *Maniac Magee*), trickster (e.g., Dahl's *James and the Giant Peach*), lover (e.g., Carter's *Talking Peace*). For girls, books that recount the heroine's journey should also be considered. Murdock (1990) traces the quest as follows: separation from the Feminine, identification with males, undergoing trials, finding a boon of success, sensing spiritual aridity, descent to the goddess and reconnection with the Feminine, healing the mother/daughter slip, healing the wounded male, integrating the Masculine and the Feminine. Some of the ways that students can examine these archetypes is through concept maps, hero quest simulations, mock resumés, mock interviews, letters to these archetypes, mass media connections with contemporary heroes, virtual trips, and emails to experts. The use of heroes in literature also helps boys and girls learn empathy and develop moral philosophies.

Regardless of the reading material choice, educators need to realize that their favorite reading material might not coincide with children's preferences. A quick reminder about preferences in movies and music should make that point obvious. Still, students are apt to read what a likeable teacher suggests—and assert that they "never read trashy YA novels but only touch National Book Awards"—sometimes out of a need for approval. Thus, adults need to be careful not to discount certain authors or genres, just in case the student favors those selections for the moment. A more fruitful approach is to engage students in meaningful conversation about their reading experiences in order to draw out deeper thinking or delight in the process. Librarians can also sponsor student peer reviews and Xtreme Reader clubs—both face-to-face and online—to reinforce student-based reading recommendations. In the final analysis, all students should have the power to choose the reading material that appeals to them. In the process, they can become experts in their reading "field," which empowerment reinforces their reading habit and facilitates academic achievement in general (Alloway, 2002). Another way to look at text choice is: Which practice helps students become better readers—reading one novel a month or reading the newspaper daily; reading a variety of series or reading one award winner, reading lots of leisure books but not the book assigned in class, or reading *just* the assigned book? The answers to these questions reveal much about personal philosophies of reading (Smith & Wilhelm, 2002).

Reading Instruction: The Librarian's Perspective

Reading literacy requires explicit instruction. Having in mind specific desired student reading outcomes helps educators focus their efforts to optimize results. In addition, thinking about the overall reading process at the same time enables educators to take advantage of spontaneous learning moments. While librarians are not reading teachers, *per se*, they can support reading instruction significantly.

Beginning Reading Strategies

At the beginning, students need to decode text; librarians can label resources throughout the library, and use picture books as a way to show how images can provide clues about the meaning of words. They can help students improve their listening skills by reading aloud, particularly rhyming stories and poems, and asking students to echo the sounds (Wolfe & Nevills, 2004). They can also share alphabet books, and help students do activities with letters. To help students gain lexical knowledge, librarians can demonstrate the use of dictionaries, and can point out phrases as they read from oversized books. Showing students the spine labels for books also helps students understand and apply alphabetic principles. To facilitate semantic and syntactic knowledge, librarians can use predictable books such as *Brown Bear, Brown Bear, What Do You See* and fairy tales to show linguistic patterns. To build vocabulary, librarians can introduce books with specialized vocabulary, particularly with non-fiction titles. Because picture books often include vocabulary that is beyond beginning readers' decoding ability, librarians can read those stories aloud and explain the new words. Jokes and word play can also help students understand words that have different meanings depending on the context. Librarians can also provide reading drill and talking storybook software programs and include beginning reading web sites on library web portals.

Before, During, and After Text-Based Instruction

Literature plays an integral part of reading literacy. However, merely reading a book aloud will not foster reading comprehension to any degree. Rather, reading instruction begins before physically accessing, continues actively when engaged in the text, and follows after the book is closed.

Before. When instructing, librarians should "frontload" the experience by giving students a good reason to read the text, providing context or background information to help them understand the text, and book-talking the text to get their attention and engage them emotionally. Students are more apt to be engaged in reading a story if they connect emotionally with the character, a task that is harder for boys. Librarians should draw upon students' prior knowledge so they can connect more easily with the text, and ask predicting questions that will build reader suspense about the text. Librarians should also explain unfamiliar vocabulary so students do not get mentally "stuck" and forget the flow of the text. Advance organizers (e.g., concept maps, concept wheels, storyboard, T-charts, K/W/L charts, Venn diagrams, word webs, timelines) can help students see the underlying schema or main ideas of the text, guiding their mental focus (Teele, 2004).

During. What is the author trying to say? That is the main comprehension task. Librarians can point out reading cues: headlines, pictures and captions, frequency of words, glossaries, paragraph structure. They can also help students develop mental images of the story. How does the author communicate his/her ideas? Librarians can help students see how the text structure, writing style, and accompanying images impact comprehension. To help students understand the reading process, librarians can read a text aloud and use reflective talk to share their own thinking process. "Hmm, I wonder why the author used this example?" "In conclusion — this must mean that the author is going to summarize his main points." "I never thought of houses from the dog's perspective before!" These phrases demonstrate to students how the reader can question the text and relate it to personal experience.

After. This stage constitutes the "so what" of the reading experience. When the reader comes upon new ideas, s/he can choose to ignore, disagree, or agree with the text. By defining the purpose of the reading ahead of time, librarians can optimize the likelihood that students will incorporate that new information. Follow-up activities facilitate that process. Students can act out the story, draw pictures about the story, summarize or retell the story orally or in writing, predict what might happen after the end of the story, link it to other stories, generalize from the story, or consider how it fits into the rest of their school or home life (UCLA, 2004).

Progression and Differentiation in Reading

Reading experiences should also be structured to build one upon the other sequentially so students can see their progress; students should be encouraged to keep track of their reading. While the above actions feature the librarian as an active instructor, these processes can be implemented in small cooperative groups for older students. As students progress in school, they can take increasing control of their learning so that the librarian basically structures the environment in which learning occurs. Different groupings can be arranged according to the reading task at hand (e.g., homogenous grouping to teach advanced reading skills, heterogeneous groups to discuss cultural implications, same-sex groups to share personal experiences). In these groups, the librarian can pay attention to how students structure their thinking and writing, and provide timely feedback to aid in the reading process (Frater, 1997). Boys, in particular, prefer to read *efferent* material that gives instant information such as repairing a car or getting a joke; *esthetic* reading, which emphasizes the pleasurable *experience* of the reading process, is not as interesting for boys, although it is highly valued in schools (Smith & Wilhelm, 2002). Afterwards, librarians can display exemplary student work (Noble & Bradford, 2000).

Domain-Specific Reading

By high school, students can approach reading as a domain-specific process. That is, how a historian reads a document differs from how a scientist reads a document. Thus, every high school teacher is a reading teacher, although most subject specialists are uncomfortable with that philosophy. It is true that, regardless of academic discipline, students need to be able to understand how to read textual information: by reviewing, looking at the table of contents and index, skimming the headings, examining the tables and charts, and reflecting on guiding questions. Students should also question the text, consider the context of the information, and experiment with the ideas presented. Normally, students do not need to think about the perspective advocated in a textbook because review committees have looked at gender and ethnic issues to minimize prejudicial information. Still, students should reflect on ideas that challenge their present knowledge and consider the relevance and accuracy of the information given as well as facts that are omitted.

Individual academic domains do look at information from different perspectives, which should be the focus of reading competencies. Each domain, for instance, has its own specific vocabulary. In addition, each focuses on different reading approaches such as experimentation or argumentation. Here are a couple of examples: (1) History: How do primary and secondary sources contrast in terms of information and perspective? How do different types of text impact understanding (e.g., diary, other primary documents, literature reviews)?; (2) Science: What are the main concepts and the supporting details? How are ideas organized? It should be noted that students tend to feel competent in specific domains, and do not always transfer their learning to other subject areas or generalize their learning. Thus, the more that the entire school community members look at each other's practices, the more they can build on them and develop interdependent learning activities. To prevent academic "siloing," librarians are in a unique position to link one type of reading with another. For instance, if students are reading *Out of the Dust,* make sure they examine the Library of Congress American Memory collection (http://memory.loc.gov/) for primary sources on the Depression, including Dorothy Lange's photographs. Students could also read biographies of the times, such as that of President Franklin Delano Roosevelt, and commentaries of young people in the Depression, as described in Stanley's *Children of the Dust Bowl: The True Story of the School at Weedpatch Camp.*

Librarians can also emphasize the experience of reading as an important activity in itself. Students can begin to see how reading provides a escape from other life stresses, involves solving problems (e.g., mysteries), and offers a stable and predictable mental setting. Teachers and librarians can remind students that an initial reading might focus on decoding, but that a repeated reading can focus on comprehension — and a third reading can focus on the sheer pleasure of the story.

Social Practices That Foster Reading

Reading competency requires personal responsibility and emotional engage-ment as well as intellectual attention. Most students know this fact intuitively, for if given no control in their reading experiences, some students will find a sense of control by choosing to ignore reading in school. For that reason, educators need to value personal literacies, such as diaries and comic book reading, and encour-age students to share their out-of-school experiences. Students need choices in what they read and how they respond to and act on their reading, at least in terms of supplementary activities. On an individual basis, librarians can provide stu-dents with novel and challenging reading in areas where students want to improve — or where teachers feel students can be successful (Smith & Wilhelm, 2002).

For both genders, reading should acknowledge and foster social aspects: through reading and literature circles, tutoring and reading to others, poetry slams, book testimonials (e.g., oral reports, book reviews, public service announcements), singing, building on home literacies, sharing reading and writing strategies, post-ing "golden quotes." Educators can provide ample opportunities for students to work together to build on texts:

1. Decorate a room to reflect the reading matter's environment (e.g., Roaring Twenties, Okie Great Depression, medieval town, Renaissance London)
2. Produce a newspaper of the times
3. Develop a web page or multimedia presentation on an author
4. Present a simulation where each character is interviewed
5. Create a photo album of the times and locale of the story
6. Create opportunities for competition relative to reading, such as:
   • Battle of the books
   • Trivia fact relay
   • Number-of-pages-read competition
   • Literature question of the day
   • Read-aloud marathons

When students are engaged in oral literacy activities, teachers and librarians need to make sure that the activity is meaningful and that the audience pays atten-tion to the speaker. For many students, dramatic readings and performances can be very engaging, providing a way for them to identify with the characters and sit-uations; in fact, for some readers who struggle because they have a hard time visu-alizing the text, dramatization helps them comprehend the text. However, some students are uncomfortable center stage, so adults and classmates need to be sen-sitive to those feelings. There are ways to ameliorate the situation: Establish group norms for mutual respect and acceptance, help students feel free to take intellectual risks in class, permitting students to videotape their presentations at home, ask students to carry out behind-the-scenes responsibilities, allow "duo" presentations (this works best using an interview or newscaster format). Students can enjoy males' renditions and storytelling sessions; this approach may encourage the intimidated to try presentations at a future date. This approach can be broadened to include out-of-class experiences such as community reading buddies, family book clubs, and father-son discussion groups.

The Role of Technology in Reading and Writing

The digital age has impacted the world of reading. Youth can access reading materials from around the world, which not only validates the importance of written material, but provides real world information. The nature of text changes via sound, video complement text and images. Also, documents have changed from two-dimensional to three-dimensional artifacts as readers can explore in non-linear fashion and link to other documents. Even the process of reading changes online as readers scroll down a screen or click from screen to screen; readers can also change the size of text, change fonts, and modify the background color in digital documents. Indeed, the differences that arise from reading online require that students develop new schemas to handle the process, which can actually improve their reading schemas for print-based reading (Dresang, 1998). Technology features also help students with special needs: computer software can read files out loud, and online translators (e.g., http://www.babelfish.com) can help English language learners access information. Digital libraries (e.g., http:// www.icdlbooks.org) provide access to world literature, and enable students to hear and see the text simultaneously. Adding glamour to reading, online streaming video programs feature Screen Actors Guild members reading children's books aloud) (http://www.bookpals.net/storyline/welcome).

These new reading features can help students become better readers—or can cause reading difficulties. The presence of technology can entice and motivate students—and can make print texts even less attractive. Technology helps some students, especially boys, focus better; however, the high stimulus level can shorten students' attention level. Hypertext enables students to explore information to the degree wanted or needed — or become confused and disoriented as they follow one link after another. The incorporation of non-textual elements in web pages can provide dual coding assistance — or can distract readers. Changing fonts and backgrounds can help students read text more easily — or can result in students spending more time tweaking a text's appearance than reading. Technology offers more options; both adults and students need to know enough about those tools to use them effectively in support of reading.

Technology also augments the reading experience by providing contextual information. Students can contact authors via email and videoconferencing. They can virtually visit places around the world, and so can create mental images that help in understanding text. For years, educators have been using slides, film, and video to provide background information about specific reading materials, and have incorporated recordings and audiotapes to bring text alive through sound. Now the options are myriad.

For educators, technology provides wider access to lesson plans, bibliographies, and other teaching/learning aids, such as graphic organizers and online writing assistance (e.g., http://www.graphic.org and http://owl.english.purdue.edu). Besides drill practice software, which can help students with beginning reading skills (e.g., http://fonikzcom), more sophisticated software and web sites aid children in speed reading and vocabulary building (e.g., http://www.starfall.com and http://www.vocabulary.com). The advantages of such software include increased interactivity, focused effort, timely and specific feedback, and logical sequencing of skills. Increasingly, software is being used to diagnose students' reading, even to the point of identifying processing difficulties, and then offering individualized instruction to improve student skills. Sousa (2005) recommends the three following research-based products: Earobics Literacy Launch (http://www.earobic.com), Fast ForWord Reading Language Program (http://www.scientificlearning.com), and Lindamood Phonetic Sequencing Program (http://www.lindamoodbell.com). Computers also come equipped these days with read-aloud programs so that students with visual impairments or reading problems can listen to (and see) scanned text. Prescriptive reading programs, such as Accelerated Reader and Reading Counts, help students determine a comfortable reading level and suggest books accordingly. While these programs are controversial because of their testing style and external motivational approach, they do reinforce reading habits and give students self-confidence and reading choice.

In terms of writing, word processing helps students feel more comfortable about editing and rewriting because they do not have to recopy their entire papers by hand and can concentrate on expressive writing instead. Students can also peer review their writing using tracking-changes features of word processing programs; portable digital assistants (PDAs) can also facilitate file-sharing as students beam their work to one another. Spell check, grammar check, and thesaurus features help scaffold writing, particularly for students with learning disabilities. Web sites also offer writing advice (e.g., http://webster.commnet.edu/grammar). In addressing the needs of students with special needs, writing prompt and predicting software programs, such as Write Aloud, aid more challenged students. On the other end of the scale, classes can participate in online community-based reading and writing projects such as epals and image exchanges (e.g., http://www.monsterexchange.org) (Leu & Kinzer, 2003; Wollman-Bonilla, 2003), online reading buddies, blogs, youth writing (e.g., http://education.indiana.edu/cas/adol/teen.html), journalism (e.g., http://www.digitaljournalist.org), digital storytelling (e.g., http://www.ThePotter-Projecti.com and http:// www.storycenter.org), and even simple images (e.g., kids.ot.com:80/) and animated film-making (e.g., http://www.digitalfilms.com).

As detailed in the chapter on technology literacy, the incorporation of technology raises gender issues. Male reluctant and lower-achieving readers may respond more positively to reading in a technologically rich learning environment. Kinesthetic learners, again often boys, like the key and mouse action that keeps their fingers busy and their senses focused. The melding of visual, sound, and textual features captures their attention. Boys like the control they feel with computers, and are willing to take the time and intellectual risks to master the machine and the reading involved. For that reason, interactive reading and writing software can work with this population. On the other hand, educators need to make sure that girls feel included in this technology world. For them, open-ended productivity software and opportunities for online communication are more attractive. Both genders need to learn how to read and write digitally since their futures are likely to involve such skills.

In short, technology offers a variety of communication channels and a variety of tools to aid and augment reading processes. Of course, incorporation of technology requires training and preparation for adults, more than for students. Librarians and other educators need to feel comfortable using technology tools — or comfortable having students teach them. Making sure that the resources, both software and hardware, are available and in good working order can be a time-consuming process; both technical support and clear rules about technology use are imperative. Even locating appropriate web sites and software requires careful evaluation, which the librarian can provide.

The nature of instruction changes with the incorporation of technology; the learning environment tends to foster more inquiry-based learning and collaborative work. Additional time may need to be built into the lesson in order to train students in the technical skills required to accomplish the learning task. The learning curve for such efforts can be steep; fortunately, the first time is the hardest; over time, tool use becomes more automatic, just as the reading process becomes automatic, and a repertoire of good reading materials can be amassed and shared with colleagues.

The Role of Libraries

In an age of constant testing and strict alignment to specific content standards, libraries play a vital role in promoting reading through an effective program consisting of a strong reading collection and varied, individualized services in support of reading competency and enjoyment. Because they serve the entire school community, librarians offer an articulated and cross-curricular perspective that helps all students develop life-long reading habits.

The moment that students walk in the door, they can be made to feel welcome and comfortable — and aware that they can experience a world of reading. Signs, reference sheets, student writing, displays, can all convey the importance of print. Both boys and girls need to be able to find nooks that appeal to them with interesting reading materials handy. The best libraries include areas for quiet, independent reading as well as group sharing of reading; also writing and other production areas, with supportive supplies and equipment, so students can act on their reading in meaningful ways. Ideally, staff includes both genders in order to model positive reading habits; at the least, other school community members ought to visit the library and have occasions to read there so students can see adults enjoying library resources.

Hopefully, the resources themselves support an inclusive curriculum and also address the out-of-school needs of youngsters: home life, hobbies, personal issues, and career exploration. Student writing can also be collected. Consider providing materials that offer a range of reading difficulty and a variety of formats, including books on tape and supportive video. Reading programs can remediate students in a neutral environment. Make assistive technology easily accessible, even to those students who are not formally diagnosed since some students may feel uncomfortable being labeled as "special" yet may benefit from technology that accommodates their reading differences. Manipulatives can also enrich reading; picture cards, games, puppets, and flannel boards are a few of the props that can help students interact or build upon their reading experiences.

Libraries today must consider the other "door" to its resources: the Internet. Digital resources can be stored, organized, and made accessible via intranets and extranets. Library web portals can include reading advisory service, online book clubs, a "chapter a day" feature, access to authors (e.g., http://childrensauthornetwork.com), and homework help. Electronic reference service can help students, particularly boys, who might be reluctant to appear needy face-to-face with their peers. Students can also contribute to this digital environment through online book discussions, evaluations of kid-friendly web sites, and even the design of the library web portal itself.

Programs and events also foster reading. Story hours and author visits are library mainstays, but consider other venues, such as: discussion groups such as Xtreme Readers, parent-child book clubs, poetry slams, read-ins, reading contests, writing/ literacy competitions, student reading award selections, media festivals, readers' theater, storytelling clubs, book reviewing groups, web design groups, anime/manga clubs, and teen parenting groups. For boys, reading promotion programs need to be lively, hands-on, and fun; themes that will interest boys in particular include transportation, the outdoors, adventure, science, monsters and science fiction, time warps, sports, humor, and survival. Most of these ideas can attract girls as well; in most cases, inclusivity is preferable to single-sex focus. Older teens will find real-life workshops attractive: how to get into college, find a job, live independently; all of these programs can weave in reading, seamlessly bridging school with the rest of life.

The greatest resource in the library, though, is the library staff. Sometimes the most effective way to support reading is via one-to-one conversations about good books. Librarians can provide individual and group advice about appropriate, high-quality reading through book talks, book lists and webliographies, displays, posters, announcements (including broadcasts), and publications. They can help students read critically and conduct research through graphic organizers, word charts, directional posters, reference sheets and handbooks, and web tutorials. They can also extend the understanding of the world of print by showing students how books and other resources are made; Aliki's web site offers elementary students a fun inside look at the process (http://www.harperchildrens.com/picture/features/aliki/howabook/book1.asp).

Importantly, librarians can collaborate with classroom teachers to provide rich reading experiences, both in support of the curriculum and to complement the curriculum. While teachers, especially elementary and language arts experts, can diagnose specific reading problems, librarians know the library's collections and can provide resources across the curriculum that address the problems. For instance, librarians can create booklists that align with phonics concepts or work well to stress listening skills. The library can also create a professional print and digital collection for teachers and parents, focusing on reading interventions and promotions. Here is a beginning list of good reading literacy web sites. Technology and Literacy (http://www.oswego.org/staff/cchamber/literacy/index.cfm) contains numerous tools to help teachers with language arts skills and instruction. Though slightly dated, The University of Connecticut's directory of web sites on literacy and technology (http://www.literacy.uconn.edu/littech.htm) is another good starting point. The International Reading Association's online publication (http://www.readingonline. org) includes research, articles, strategies, and a forum for discussing literacy issues. The Northwest Regional Educational Laboratory has a good white paper on using technology to teach reading (http://www.ncrel.org/sdrs/areas/issues/content/cntareas/reading/li300.htm). Schools of California Online Resources for Education: Language Arts (http://www.sdcoe.k12.ca.us/SCORE/cla.html) lists resources and lessons aligned with state standards. English Companion (http://www.englishcompanion. com) focuses on high school language arts help for teachers and students.

Reading Literacy Exercises

Note: Activities marked with an * are appropriate for elementary grades or include accommodations for younger students; unless otherwise noted, all the activities may be done by middle and high school students.

READING LIFE*

   What is each student's reading life? Students may be surprised how often they read or come into contact with reading. Class assignments, school signage, store signs, billboards, calendars, prescriptions, all involve reading. Ask students to list as many sources or kinds of reading material as they can. Then ask them to rate the texts in terms of how often the student reads them and how much the student values them. Pair students, preferably cross-gender, and ask them to compare their logs to find patterns within and across each person's writing. Find out if there is a class trend, and discuss implications, including the possible social implications of reading.

READING GRID*

   Create a class grid about student reading habits, and conduct a content analysis about the data relative to gender.

Student/ Gender	Title	Genre/ Format	Characters	Plot	Point of View

Does knowing the student and his/her background make a difference when looking for reading patterns? As an extension of this activity, students can explore reading patterns for older and younger students.

THE FUTURE OF READING*

   Students need to see the link between reading and employment. Ask them to shadow or interview a relative or neighbor in terms of the reading done on or for a job. Students can research the quantity and quality of text read, the skills needed to read the text, how text is read, and how the reading material is applied to the job. The class can discuss what reading skills they believe they need to develop now in order to be prepared for employment. In sharing their findings, students can explore possible gendered practices.

GENDER CONTENT ANALYSIS

   What gender patterns emerge in the reading material that students experience in and out of school? Do those patterns change from one context to another? For in-school texts, students can look at textbooks and student publications (e.g., newspapers, literacy magazines, web pages, and yearbooks). Students may brainstorm gendered features they can analyze; the list should include authorship, status/role of each sex, length and depth of coverage, and visual elements. What differences emerge across subject matter? Does student-created work reflect different patterns?

Students can also examine commercial trade periodicals (e.g., newspapers and magazines) in the same manner. Do different magazines carry different gendered messages based on their intended audience (e.g., *Seventeen* vs. *People* vs. *GQ* vs. *Rolling Stone* vs. *Sports Illustrated*)? How do educational texts differ from trade publications? What impact do these social messages have upon student education?

READING PORTRAIT*

Stories with strong characters and biographies typically show how a person changes over time, particularly due to of critical events in their lives. Ask students to choose a fictional or real person in a text, and then draw a portrait of that person at the start, at one or two critical points, and at the end. Accompanying the drawing can be quotations that substantiate the person's appearance. Compare boys' and girls' choices of persons, their drawings, and their choice of quotations. As a variation, males must choose female figures, and females must choose males to draw.

PICTURE READING

Dual-coding provides more cues for reading and helps students visualize what they read. Ask students to locate and analyze fiction and non-fiction graphic novellas or photonovellas in terms of the relationship between text and image. Are fiction and non-fiction publications approached differently in terms of visuals? What gender roles or stereotypes emerge in terms of the text, the image, or the production? What cultural differences arise? As an extension or variation, ask students to *create* graphic novellas or photonovellas. This activity works well for world languages.

READING IS FONTAMENTAL*

Visual and concrete poetry incorporate visual elements to reinforce their message. Have students find and analyze examples of these forms, and create their own visual poems. Even the nature of fonts can impact the reading experience. Have mixed-sex pairs each access or type a poem into a desktop publishing program, and each create two versions of the poem using different fonts and font features (e.g., color, size, word art) to express two different ideas. Have the pairs compare their process and products, noting their perceptions of their peer's altered message. Have each person compare his/her work with a peer of the same sex in the same manner. As a class, discuss how the visual element impacts concepts. Do gendered practices or perspectives emerge? A variation on this activity is a pyramid poem (Teele, 2004). The structure follows; students can still play with font features and even work in a strong pyramid visual effect.

1. one word for the character
2. two-word description of the character
3. three words for the setting
4. four words describing the conflict

5. five words describing a key event
6. six words describing a second event
7. seven words describing a third event
8. eight words to describe the event leading to the final resolution
9. nine words to describe the conclusion

SOUND OUT*

Sound effects can help students read, and they add another dimension to reading. Youngsters may already be familiar with board books that include sound-effect features. In this activity, however, they can be creating their own sound books. Have students augment a folk or fairy tale — or original story — with sound effects. After copying (with permission) or typing the story into a word processing program such as MS Word, students can insert sounds by locating them on the Internet or recording their own sound effects. This activity is best done in pairs, probably same-sex partners. Two sets of pairs could do the same story, and then compare their results. Alternatively, several pairs of students could create variations or parodies of the same story, such as *The True Story of the Three Little Pigs;* this approach works better with older students who understand the concept of irony and parody.

ORIGINAL AUDIOBOOKS*

Many students have listened to books on tape. However, few have tried to read a book aloud onto an audiotape for others to follow. The process is surprisingly difficult as students listen to their speech and realize that they need to improve their fluency, enunciation, pacing, and expression. The fact that the speaker can listen to her/his own efforts, erase them, and redo the oration until it sounds good enough, provides opportunities to practice and improve reading fluency. A good place to start is reading picture books, although copyright permission needs to be secured first. Students can create dialogues for wordless books, or create their own picture books or simple stories. Even older students feel comfortable reading these books if they know that younger children will actually use the tapes. Students with reading programs may find picture books less intimidating to read aloud. Students need choice in their reading materials. How they produce their audiobooks and the final products can be analyzed to determine if gender patterns emerge.

SPIN-A-PLOT*

Traditionally, stories feature characters, settings, plots, themes, and writing styles. Label two envelopes for each feature. Then give same-sex pairs one of these feature envelopes to brainstorm options for, one slip of paper per option (e.g., haunted house, Roman galley, 19th century New York City factory, etc.). Ask pairs to generate enough ideas so that each class member gets one slip per feature. Girls choose from the boy-generated slips, and boys choose from the girl-generated slips. Students then write a short story based on the features' slips. As a variation, same-sex or mixed-sex pairs can write the stories. In either case, the class can discuss process and results in terms of possible gender patterns. As another variation, students can create mathematics word problems based on these features.

HYPERREADING

Reflective thinking and contextualizing text result in deeper understanding. Students may already use Cornell note-taking or other commentary writing. They may have also researched the times, setting, or author of a story. Incorporating technology provides another dimension to reading commentary and context. Students can download, with permission, a text into a desktop publishing program. Tracking changes, students can put comments into the text. They can also insert images, sounds, and video clips, as they deem useful, to clarify or extend the text. They can also link a section to a web page or other type of document. Alternatively, students can save and modify the documents as a hypertext if they can generate a web page. In either case, they can define vocabulary, provide background information, question the text, relate it to their own lives, or connect it with other texts. This activity may be done several ways: (1) by structure—completely open, one type of change only, round-robin with students building on one another's work; (2) by content—all students augmenting the same text or each pair augmenting a different chapter or story; (3) by grouping—done individually or in pairs; or (4) by sex—same-sex or mixed-sex. In analyzing the results, ask students to report what they already knew and learned, and if gender patterns emerged.

Works Cited

Alloway, Nola, et al. (2002). *Boys, literacy, and schooling.* Canberra City, Australia: Department of Education, Science, and Training.

Blake, Brett, and Blake, Robert (2002). *Literacy and learning: A reference handbook.* Santa Barbara, CA: ABC-CLIO.

Block, C., Gambrell, L., and Pressley, M. (eds.) (2002). *Improving comprehension instruction: Rethinking research, theory, and classroom practice.* San Francisco: Jossey-Bass.

Brozo, W. (2002). *To be a boy, to be a reader: Engaging teen and preteen boys in active literacy.* Newark, DE: International Reading Association.

California Reading and Literature Project (2004). Los Angeles: University of California, Los Angeles. Retrieved February 3, 2005, from http://www.centerx.gseis.ucla.edu/CRLP/index.php.

Colvin, Carolyn, and Schlosser, Linda (1997, Dec.). "Developing academic confidence to build literacy: What teachers can do." *Journal of Adolescent & Adult Literacy,* 41, 4, 272–281.

Costa, Arthur (2001). *Developing minds.* Reston, VA: Association for Supervision and Curriculum Development.

Donalson, M. (1978). *Children's Minds.* London: Fontana.

Dresang, Eliza (1998). *Radical change: Books for youth in a digital age.* Bronx, NY: H. W. Wilson.

English-language arts content standards for California public schools (1997). Sacramento: California State Department of Education.

Everhart, Nancy (2004, Nov.). "Every child ready to read @ your library." *Knowledge Quest,* 33, 2, 77–79.

Frater, Graham (1997). *Improving boys' literacy: A survey of effective practice in secondary schools.* London: The Basic Skills Agency.

Goldberg, G., and Roswell, B. (2002). *Reading, writing, and gender.* Larchmont, NY: Eye on Education.

Herb, Steven, and Willoughby-Herb, Sara. (1994, Jan.). The importance of men as role models in literacy. *Catholic Library World, 64,* 3, 46–50.

Knuth, R., and Jones, B. (1991). *What does research say about reading?* Oak Brook, IL: North Central Regional Educational Laboratory.

Leu, Donald J., Jr., and Kinzer, Charles (2003). *Effective literacy instruction K-8.* Upper Saddle River, NJ: Merrill.

Ligamari, Joanne, and Goodwin, Katharine (2004, Nov.). "Boys, books and literacy." California School Library Association conference, Sacramento. Nov. 12–15, 2004.

Martino, Wayne (1998). "'Dickheads,' 'poofs,' 'try hards' and 'losers': Critical literacy for boys in the English classroom." *English in Aotearoa, 35,* 31–57.

Murdock, Maureen (1990). *Heroine's journey.* Boston: Shambhala.

National Endowment for the Arts (2004). *Reading at risk.* Washington, DC: National Endowment for the Arts.

National Institute of Child Health and Human Development (2000). *Report of the National Reading Panel: Teaching children to read.* Bethesda, MD: National Institute of Child Health and Human Development.

Newkirk, T. (2002). *Misreading masculinity: Boys, literacy, and popular culture.* Portsmouth, NH: Heinemann.

Noble, C., and Bradford, W. (2000). *Getting it right for boys ... and girls.* London: Routledge.

Pearson, P., and Taylor, Barbara (2002). *Teaching reading.* Mahwah, NJ: Lawrence Erlbaum.

Rainer, Lee, and Horrigan, John (2005). "A decade of adoption: How the internet has woven itself into American life." Washington, DC: Pew Internet and American Life Project.

Reach Out and Read National Center (2005). *Developmental milestones of early literacy.* Somerville, MA: Reach Out and Read National Center.

Resnick, L., and Weaver, P. (1979). *Theory and practice of early reading, Vol. I-III.* Hillsdale, NJ: Erlbaum.

Smith, M., and Wilhelm, J. (2002). *Reading don't fix no Chevys: Literacy in the lives of young men.* Portsmouth, NH: Heinemann.

Sousa, D. (2005). *How the brain learns to read.* Thousand Oaks, CA: Corwin Press.

Sullivan, Michael (2004, Aug.). "Why Johnny won't read." *School Library Journal,* 36–39.

Teele, Sue (2004). *Overcoming barricades to reading.* Thousand Oaks, CA: Corwin Press.

Willinsky, J. (1990). *The New Literacy: Redefining Reading and Writing in the Schools.* New York: Routledge.

Wolfe, Patricia, and Nevills, Pamela (2004). *Building the reading brain, preK-3.* Thousand Oaks, CA: Corwin Press.

Wollman-Bonilla, Julie (2003, Nov.). "E-mail as genre: A beginning writer learns the conventions." *Language Arts, 81,* 2, 126–130.

5

Information Literacy

"Information is power." This phrase has been bandied about for decades, but resonated loudly in the Information Age. Now in the Knowledge Age a more accurate truism would be "The *use* of information is power." Young people, especially females, who feel powerless need meaningful skills for knowledgeable decision-making to help them feel capable and in control.

Information literacy is, paradoxically, a "hot" topic and a misunderstood one. Some people consider it to be a subset of the more glamorous technology literacy, but a simple example of gathering data by face-to-face interview refutes that claim. Still, technology has become a cornerstone in information literacy, which is discussed.

As centers of information, librarians see information literacy as their core curriculum. Using gender issues as a content focus for gaining and solving problems, sample learning activities explore information literacy ideas.

The Information Cycle

Where does information come from? How does it originate? What role does gender play in this process? Few people think about the flow of information because they are too busy dealing with it. And yet examining the information cycle helps one understand its power — and the role that gender plays within that process.

Think about it. In order to create an idea *and express it in a permanent form,* one needs to be literate at some level. That person needs to have access to literacy tools and know how to use them, whether reading and writing instruments or imaging equipment. And someone needs to teach those skills, even if it is done passively where the learner watches the expert in action. Such access implies some degree of power and sense of value: to have the opportunity to access the resources and their application. Consider past centuries when girls were not encouraged to go to school or to work with scientific instruments; they were, in effect, out of the loop in terms of expressing their ideas formally.

Even when information is created, to enter the public domain, it needs to be published in some form. Publishers, then, serves as powerful gatekeepers or facilitators; they exert their power as they apply their own criteria for determining whether to support and publicize the proposed ideas. For centuries, patrons have served as the visual counterpart of publishers, backing an artist. Nowadays, producers back filmmakers. These publishers have financial and material resources and influence, and they have largely been male. They have tended to support "their own," in terms of ideology or sociological proximity (i.e., culture, economics, ethnicity, gender). Of course, one can say that in the Internet age, "anyone" can publish personal ideas; all that's needed is Internet access. However, even that "bar" requires access to an Internet service provider and technological skill, which until recently had been a male-dominated arena.

The receiver part of the information cycle can be subdivided into two levels: reviewers and consumers. Information may be examined by experts prior to its publication or upon its distribution. In either case, these reviewers have the influence to publicize and support new information — or to dismiss and disdain it. Furthermore, to be designated a reviewer or expert also entails judgment and bestowment by someone in power. True, anyone can be a critic — or reviewer — but their opinions are judged by others. So, in fact, they must be found worthy by a broad body to be accepted (although this body is likely to be more democratic than a pool of peer experts). Nevertheless, the same idea of supporting like minds can result in subpopulations being under-represented and unheard, and gender plays a part in this have/have not situation.

Consumers, which are comprised of a much larger and more diverse body, have power in terms of accepting and acting on information. Their sphere of influence, likewise, varies from themselves alone to whole nations; as a body, they are harder to control. However, if the information they receive is one-sided or limited, then they are more likely to follow that information than some intellectual void. To be more specific, if the only writing published is created by males in power, if the only paintings are done by males backed by men in power, then the populace will tend to think along those same lines of information. Those who reject the majority are called detractors, deviants, heretics, "odd," only to be vindicated when their point of view is corroborated by others.

Thus, the information cycle can seem closed or at least recursive. It does tend to confirm the status quo, if for no other reason than that those in power usually want to stay in power. To the extent, then, that power has been masculinized for centuries, information has also largely reflected a masculine point of view. On the other hand, as society has become more pluralistic and inclusive, more points of view have been introduced and discussed, and more people have become empowered to break through the information cycle.

Today's young people get involved in this information cycle as they learn to become literate and regard information with a critical eye. To do this, they need to have access to the varied tools of literacy so they can become information producers and facilitators themselves. As they learn about the information cycle, and experience it more critically, they can help broaden that cycle.

Defining Information Literacy

How do students become literate? One of the goals of education is to help individuals become functionally literate, which involves a continuum of skills that enables students to be able to *do* something. This is procedural knowledge. Students need to access, comprehend, and respond to information. In the United States, reading and writing ability are core competencies in that process. However, other skills such as numeracy and visual acuity are also implicated because knowledge can be represented in so many forms. Increasingly, in other countries, information and communication literacies are combined under the heading ICT (Information and Communication Technology).

The American Association of School Librarians (AASL) (1998) lists the following indicators of information literacy. The ability to:

1. Access information effectively
2. Critically evaluate information
3. Use information accurately and creatively
4. Seek information for personal interest
5. Appreciate literature and other creative works
6. Aim for excellence in information seeking and knowledge generation
7. Realize that information is important for a democratic society
8. Deal with information ethically
9. Collaborate in information-seeking and production

It should be noted that standards for information literacy do not equate exactly with the research process itself. Several models posit a step-by-step cognitive approach, which is more aligned with male learning tendencies (Marland, 1981; Eisenberg & Berkowitz, 1990; Loertscher & Woolls, 1999). McKenzie (1996) suggests a research cycle model. Kuhlthau's (1985) research model focuses on the affective domain of researching, which resonates with female information seekers. Pappas and Tepe (1995), who are both women, developed a non-linear model, contending that students should have a repertoire of strategies as they engage in information seeking and use; this approach fits the need of random access thinkers. In addition, only their model deals with literature appreciation. In short, researching is just one aspect of information literacy; the AASL information literacy standards describe knowledge, skills and dispositions *in situ*. In that respect, using a problem-solving construct provides a grounded basis for using information:

1. What is the problem?
2. What are the underlying issues?
3. What are the facts?
4. What are the options?
5. What are the consequences?
6. What is the best outcome?
7. How good was the decision?

This model can also help students confront gender issues because it acknowledges present perceptions and encourages a broader range of possibilities that can be acted upon. By approaching research skills as problem-solving techniques, students become empowered to make a difference, both intellectually and psychologically. It should be noted that teachers tend to intervene to solve girls' problems; boys are left to solve their own problems. Similarly, girls think themselves less able to solve problems, and are less likely than boys to argue with their teachers when they think they are right (American Association of University Women, 1992). These behaviors do not bode well for girls, 80 percent of whom report being sexually harassed at school. If for no other reason than to develop coping skills, girls need practice solving problems in safe and supportive surroundings.

In any case, information literacy transcends academic domains, aiming for students to successfully function autonomously in societal settings: as workers, as citizens, and as private individuals (Venezky, 1990). Moreover, as the concept of a learning society takes hold in the 21st century, the ability of students to learn independently and interdependently throughout their lives should constitute a core goal in K-12 education. In this scenario, libraries play a central role with their organized collection of resources and services, and with their blend of formal instruction and point-of-need guidance. Still, some students feel confused in the library, so extra effort is needed to address their fears even before tackling information literacy skills (Mellon, 1988). Thus, to optimize this process, rather than limiting information literacy to teaching one research model to students, librarians should consider a more inclusive approach by describing elements of *engagement* with information, offering some effective strategies, and then allowing students to discover their own paths to knowledge. The next section details these elements.

Task Definition

"What am I supposed to do?" "What is the problem?" These may be the hardest questions to answer. Young people naturally have questions, but they do not always know what action to take, if any, to answer those questions. In school settings, most questions are imposed by an adult — with the idea that answering the question will help the student learn the concept at hand (Gross, 1997). Unfortunately, students are less apt to value these questions — and more likely to plagiarize — unless the rationale for them is clearly articulated — and if students can participate in the questions' formation (Chelton & Cole, 2004). For these imposed questions, teachers need to have a clear idea what they want their students to accomplish, and they need to explain their expectations clearly. The easiest way to define the task or problem is to show an example of it or to concretize it contextually. While teachers sometimes object to the question "How long does it have to be?," they should realize that students usually are trying to get a handle on the assignment, and define the parameters. Students should be encouraged to ask clarifying questions; females, in particular need to feel safe asking for amplification. Information tasks are also made more meaningful if students have experienced similar activities before, so they should be encouraged to link the present project with past learning as a way to find defining connections.

Once students understand the task and have a model or goal to work for, they can determine what kind of information they need to complete the task or solve the problem. A simple, yet often overlooked, preparatory task is to have students list: (1) what information they know already, and (2) what they do not know. Another approach is to ask students to create concept maps of their existing knowledge base, a practice that appeals to non-linear thinkers and often results in more efficient searching (Gordon, 2002). In some cases, the content may assume gender stereotypes or ignore gender differences. A research project on same-sex relationships may be approached in entirely different ways, depending on students' gender or lifestyle. If students have prior experience with resources, they can focus on the specific task or new critical features more easily; otherwise, they may feel confused. For instance, in an assignment that requires students to analyze the different forces that make a motorcycle run, girls may have more difficulty than boys in identifying key factors. Thus, teachers need to be sensitive to possible gender-linked assignments. When those topics arise, then mixed-sex groups can inform their peers.

In addition, students need to select critical factors in the ultimate product in order to guide their thinking about choosing information sources. As with prior knowledge about content, students may also differ in their information communication skills. A project may call for small groups to develop a skit about the immigration experience. Girls may have more experience working in cooperative groups than boys, or they may have an easier time creating skits. In short, determining information requires that the teacher help students with those prerequisite skills of analyzing a task and linking likely sources of information to that task. Thus, teachers and students need to assess what preliminary content and information skills need to be taught before the lesson's main task can be accomplished and the problem can be solved.

Search Strategies

At this point students must figure out how to find what they need in order to do the task or solve the problem. Usually this requires exploring a series of processes to deal with the topic at hand. Teachers can help students develop this skill by providing them with sample strategies or frameworks. Teachers and librarians can discuss how one problem leads to another problem, just as one strategy can lead to another, ultimately generating a web of issues and consequences, both in terms of information and of process. Students can then document their efforts. Information mapping or webbing allows students to show how ideas relate. Drawings or diagrams can help student visualize the information and make it their own. Student recordings should include those resources and strategies that were not useful, as well as those that were; this encourages safe risk-taking which girls may need to experience more regularly. The underlying idea is that even a "wrong" strategy can provide valuable insights; the student knows one avenue not to pursue.

On their own, students tend to use a "convenience" model as their searching strategy: asking people, going through books at home, and consulting available dictionaries. As students mature, they seek a broader base of resources, but still think in terms of what is easy to find rather than what strategy might result in the best information. They tend to think in terms of quantity rather than quality. As a result, they may get information that is too hard to read, does not address the research question, or "doesn't have all the answers in one place" (Shenton & Dixon, 2004; Savolainen & Kari, 2004).

For major tasks or units, students may need several sessions to accomplish their searching if they use a recursive model whereby, as they search and use information, they find new information gaps that need locating. Ideally, at the end of each session, students should review and share their strategies. In this way, they can suggest ideas for others and receive new insights from their peers. Particularly if most work is done individually, this process time allows for group support, which is especially appreciated by girls. If research is done cooperatively, then the group needs to process their session's work as a means of evaluating their progress. Using the problem-solving image, students can share clues and set up more ways to dig into the "case." Students also benefit from discussing their initial search strategies and obstacles with the librarian.

Locating and Accessing Information

Locating and accessing information involves two subtasks: locating a source, and locating information *within* a source. Students may consult some kind of index or catalog in order to find the source itself. The research step use of key words is essential here since many indexes use a controlled vocabulary to organize the indexes sources; computerized access tools increasingly include metatags that provide pointers to subjects and other bibliographic information. Additionally, digital databases often combine searching features and full text so students do not have to go from one source to another. Still, students may need to be reminded that commercial indexes may refer to a document that the library might not own; fortunately, interlibrary loan has been improved with the use of email, fax, and digitization of documents.

Traditional research has concentrated on sequential, factual print material. Such narrowly defined resources do not address the learning style and interests of many students. Thus, teachers need to value and encourage the use of non-print resources (e.g., video, digital), human resources, and community centers. Multimedia sources can be harder to locate so librarians should create databases for these and other sources of information, such as local information and speakers.

Internet searching raises interesting developmental and gender issues. Generally, students do not know how databases and searching algorithms are constructed. Primary students tend to use trial-and-error methods when locating online information. As they get older, boys tend to be more active and confident on the computer: searching faster, reading less, and reflecting less on the process. They also tend to ask for help less and share their results less than girls. It should be noted that both sexes are equally successful in finding online information, although neither gender is likely to use advanced searching techniques (Large, Beheshti, & Rahman, 2002).

Physically accessing the information within the source is a separate procedure. For books, students need to look at the arrangement of the information (e.g., alphabetical, thematic, chronological) and both tables of contents (for broad topics) and indexes (for specific facts). Traditional videos require sequential scanning. In contrast, digital materials usually use random-access search engines or algorithms. Humans need to be interviewed or surveyed, which demands a separate set of information skills. Interestingly, girls may find themselves the experts in these non-traditional access methods since they are often expected to ascertain non-verbal or literal cues.

Another aspect of accessing information is intellectual. Students may find the information but not be able to understand it. Boys are better at retrieving information, but girls understand narrative and expository text better than boys (Smith & Wilhelm, 2002). This gap also exists when the student has little prior experience in the area, and so cannot link the new information to existing knowledge. As girls and boys differ in their upbringing and experience, the issue of intellectual access becomes something more than IQ. For example, some boys may not have much experience cooking so may lack skill in understanding certain chemical reactions. Teachers may need to take remedial steps to help students decipher the information place before them. In some cases, students do not have the requisite skills for reading in context (either textually or visually). Being able to "read" interviewees is a much more complex skill, for the student needs to hear the content and tone of the speaker as well as interpret the accompanying body language. Such interpersonal skills may be glossed over by some males—and relished by some females who may be well-versed in relational "data." Ultimately, educators need to appreciate the fact that locating a source does not equal accessing it, and they need to help students bridge that intellectual gap.

Nowadays, locating *too much* information poses as much of a problem as not finding *enough* information. Students frequently experience information overload, especially if they look for resources online. Interestingly, boys and younger girls tend to get irritable or angry, but older girls tend to get stressed and panicky, apparently internalizing their frustration. To handle that overload, students tend to filter out sources by some internal or external criteria, group similar materials together, or delay working on the project (Akin, 1998). These techniques link to the task of using information.

Using Information

Now that students have the information, can they understand it and use it? That is another step. The need to evaluate the source: what is the perspective, how accurate is it, how thorough is it, how useful is it for the purpose of solving the problem? Students sometimes do not give a critical eye to resources, and instead consider any piece of information as "holy script," particularly if it is found online. Teachers need to help students maintain an open approach to sources, which may be difficult for those who have been conditioned to accept whatever they are told by authoritarian people, a characteristic of girls more than boys. Again, using a problem-solving approach helps since most students would recognize that not all sources of information are equally credible or useful. Librarians and other educators need to emphasize that opinions may differ about a particular point of information and that the investigator needs to look at the background experience that the chronicler brings to the source material. For instance, how a single mother and an absent father look at childcare might be equally valid, considering their perspectives; one cannot automatically discount one viewpoint or the other. If a male doctor and a female doctor interpret symptoms differently, which expert might be regarded more highly? A useful subtask is content analysis, whereby students examine a source in depth by classifying, tabulating, and evaluating its key aspects.

Another significant task in information use is determining the important facts relative to the project at hand. Some students have trouble picking out the main ideas. Some intervention methods are simple; when examining a text, for instance, educators can usually help students by pointing out headings and topic sentences. The more subtle issue, though, is deciding what information is important in light of the topic being researched or the problem to be solved. Thus, documents on welfare reform need to be approached differently if the issue is child care or if the issue is tax rebates. In a way, those students who are field-dependent (usually associated more with females) will probably have an easier time because they can see the connotations as they impact their topic more readily than their field-independent learner peers.

Two gender issues are at stake here: the interplay of authority/acceptance, and the response to controversy. Young women may tend to accept the source's validity more than men, not necessarily because they think it is right, but because they see any chronicler as one in power. Girls may also see the relative validity of a person's point of view because their concepts of right vs. wrong may be situationally more sensitive than boys' ideology. That same sense of ambiguous "rightness" may lead to a feminine reluctance to challenge viewpoints; indeed, girls have been socialized to a great extent to harmonize varying opinions rather than to confront them. Boys, on the other hand, traditionally have been given more reign to fight and debate others. Controversy for them may be seen as an exciting challenge rather than as a nerve-wracking threat. Since both kinds of comparisons, finding similarities and differences, provide insights into ideas, boys and girls can teach each other different ways to engage with source material and move toward equity. Conflicting ideas can be viewed as a viable and healthy way to see other points of view and a means to create personally meaningful and valid solutions to gender-sensitive problems.

Synthesizing Information

The task of organizing and integrating information from those difference sources takes place as information is being gathered and analyzed. Too often, classroom teachers assume complete responsibility for this process, and believe that the concept of information literacy has been covered by their work. Librarians need to continue to work with them because locating and accessing information is, frankly, not very important if nothing is done with the information that has been uncovered. Students need to find patterns in their data; how do findings and sources relate? Naturally, students need to link their findings to the task definition, but they also need to look at the lateral connections between sources. In terms of problem-solving, students are comparing options to ultimately determine the best outcome. Synthesis is actually one of the most creative aspects of information skills, for it calls on a person's prior experience with trends and patterns, and encourages students to make intuitive, intellectual or psychological connections. Because male and female backgrounds may differ in terms of experience and interpretation of that experience, mixed-gender learning groups provide a way for all students to broaden their knowledge bases. Just as with note-taking, outlines are perfectly fine for organizing information, but ways of linking ideas should also be considered: mapping, webs, hypermedia, visuals, and so on.

Manipulation of information should align with considerations about how to communicate findings and conclusions. This latter task requires translating the synthesis into terms that others can understand. On a very practical level, this transformation of information ensures that students understand what they read and make it their own. Plagiarism is rarely an issue if meaningful presentations incorporate the transformation of gathered data into an original form. Students should be encouraged to explore alternative means of sharing their information via skills, debates, simulations, multimedia presentations, videos, "white papers," games, and other real life applicable modes. Often these presentations are team efforts, which reinforce feminine awareness of relational learning and group responsibility. Such collaborative results can be used to assess social tasks as well as academic ones.

Reflective Evaluation

Not just at the end but throughout the research or problem-solving process, students should be evaluating their efforts in terms of process and products. Girls, who have been traditionally associated with "doing things right," can have their efforts given greater weight relative to intellectual accomplishment. Rigorous and insightful evaluation should take into account both skills and attitudes, to mirror different students' abilities and to foster a broad repertoire of assessment methods for both girls and boys. Ideally, students and teachers would develop project-specific rubrics as the beginning of a unit and use it during the learning activity, modifying efforts through formative assessment.

A good model to use is an art critique whereby educators and students all comment on the project. Criteria for judgment are first agreed upon, in this case elementary criteria — such as content, composition, and technical aspects. The creators also explain their project, clarifying their intent and process as well as their self-assessment regarding relative success of the effort. This set-up is also an opportunity to delve into gender issues as they relate to process and product. For instance, gender expectations may influence the choice of subject matter; boys may feel that "still lifes" are sissy, and girls may not favor mechanistic artwork. Girls may feel more inhibited than boys about how they use a medium, afraid to make mistakes or look messy. These open critiques allow students to examine their assumptions about the quality of work, and broaden their criteria to embrace a variety of options.

Assessment tools can also take advantage of students' preferred learning styles. Ideally, students should be able to choose at least one aspect of their evaluation. For instance, they might write a learning journal, or share their findings verbally in a small group. They can construct timelines that show their process and forecast their next steps. Sharing those different styles also provides all students with a broader range of ways to respond to informational needs.

Another key factor in evaluation is authenticity. Does the assessment tool match the intent? The closer the assessment is aligned with the real world—and the research process also simulates or incorporates real world applications—the greater the chance for internalized and authentic learning. The assessment makes sense because it helps students predict how successful they will be when outside school walls. Thus, a student business plan can be assessed by actual business people, who could give their judgment about the feasibility of that business surviving. Especially as girls are sometimes protected from experimenting in real-world conditions, the safe environment of the educational world helps girls connect with the community, simulate life situations, and learn skills that will transfer to later life-dependent decision-making.

The incorporation of collaborative research complicates the assessment process, for students need to evaluate group social task skills as well as content/information literacy skills. They must look at both group and individual efforts. This approach reinforces the team approach that boys usually engage in through sports, and it recognizes girls' appreciation of supporting one another. Assessment may be holistic or detailed; it can pinpoint one or two unique, worthwhile issues to evaluate and not "grade" other factors. The approach frees both genders to try non-stereotypical behaviors without too much risk; boys can be reinforced for giving nurturing statements, and girls can be encouraged to speak out more.

Assessment not only proves a means to make self-corrections and reiterations during a research cycle but also signals the start of another learning activity. In other words, where do students go from here? Hopefully, the activity stimulates more questions that need answering or at least exploring, just as the solution to one problem often leads to another problem. The more students and educators can plan that learning journey together, the more meaningful the experience is likely to be. In addition, joint planning places more control in the hands of the students so they feel more empowered and respected. Furthermore, when skills build on one another naturally, as natural outcomes of prior learning, transfer of knowledge is easier—and more substantial. Especially for students who categorize or separate each learning experience (often boys), the skill of relating material is a valuable lesson in itself.

As students reflect on the processes they use, they can look at how they deal with obstacles and the unknown. In a way, research provides an abstract simulation of the personal quest that each person undergoes when growing up. The metacognitive aspect of research helps students transfer one experience or set of skills into other situations and problems, and also provides a means for students to examine their changing attitudes and knowledge about gender issues. Here are some starting questions they might use to analyze their work.

1. What am I learning about gender issues?
2. How have my assumptions or perceptions changed about gender issues?
3. Do I feel more comfortable thinking about and dealing with gender issues?
4. Do I value other people's perspectives more?
5. Do I feel more comfortable working with either sex than before?
6. Do I feel more skilled working with either sex than before?
7. How have I expanded my repertoire of information literacy skills?
8. How can I apply my knowledge about gender issues to my personal life?

The important point is that students become aware, both cognitively and affectively, of their efforts and their attitudes. They can then consciously plan and regulate their information work and perspectives. By continuous self-assessment, students become more responsible for and gain more control of their learning. It has more meaning, and thus becomes more powerful. It also fosters the information literacy skills needed to solve gender-sensitive problems in the real world.

Digital Instruction in Support of Information Literacy

In the digital age, librarians should seek alternative means to teach students information literacy skills. Increasingly, librarians have developed instructional web tutorials or, at the least, have created web portals that link to such learning aids. A good list of peer-reviewed online library tutorials, which may be applicable to high school settings, is found at http://www.ala.org/ala/rusa/rusaourassoc/rusasections/mars/marspubs/marsinnovativerefgeneral.htm. Other starting points follow.

1. ICT Literacy (http://www.ictliteracy.info)
2. Skovde University Library (Sweden): Information Literacy (http://www.his.se/bib/enginfolit.shtml)
3. Directory of Online Resources for Information Literacy (http://www.lib.usf.edu/ref/doril/)
4. Information Literacy for K-16 Settings (http://www.csulb.edu/~lfarmer/infolitwebstyle.htm)
5. Educator's Reference Desk: Information Literacy (http://www.eduref.org/cgi-bin/print.cgi/Resources/Subjects/Information_Literacy/Information_Literacy.html)
6. Information Skills Modules (http://ism-1.lib.vt.edu)
7. Library Research Guides (http://www.lib.berkeley.edu/TeachingLib/Guides)
8. OASIS: Online Advancement of Student Information Skills (http://oasis.sfsu.edu/)

Classroom teachers and librarians can use these resources in guided practice with an entire class, incorporate single sections of these materials into a learning activity, or encourage students to use them independently, individually and in small groups. Providing a choice of venues allows student choice and recognizes different learning preferences of boys and girls.

Another way for librarians to instruct digitally is through digital reference. In this online environment, students can ask for help through asynchronous email or real-time chat. While boys are less likely than girls to ask for assistance face-to-face, they like the relative anonymity and convenience of online reference. Indeed, users of digital reference service differ from traditional reference users in that they tend to be more self-motivated and independent, work non-traditional hours, dislike bureaucracy, like interactive online environments but may lack interpersonal skills; these characteristics seem to align with boys more than girls. On the other hand, girls who like to communicate online may well appreciate this service.

As students ask for reference help, librarians can take advantage of this learning moment to ask guiding questions that follow research process steps. Thus, they can help students clarify their informational needs and tasks, determine what students already know, identify a good list of key words, locate likely resources, and evaluate them. Particularly when the digital reference includes a mutual "whiteboard," both parties can see potential web sites together and even take turns navigating through the site, which helps the librarian see how the user interfaces with the site.

It should be noted that school librarians do not figure significantly in most digital reference services. Rather, academic librarians tend to host university-based digital services, and public and special librarians tend to support comprehensive online reference services. As a result, these online librarians often are not familiar with a school curriculum and may not know how to interact at the student's level (Bahremand, 2003). When an online interview does not go well because of communication difficulties or perceptions that the librarian is impatient or unresponsive, digital reference can backfire. For those reasons, school librarians should seriously consider participating in digital reference or collaborate with their peers to provide a K-12 focused digital reference service instead. If adequate infrastructure or support cannot be guaranteed, however, it is better to provide high-quality, face-to-face reference service that incorporates information literacy instruction instead of dysfunctional technology-based reference "help."

Contextualizing Information Literacy

Sometimes librarians consider information literacy as "their" curriculum. This set of processes, though, is more accurately considered a vital learning tool *across* the curriculum. Thus, librarians should think of information literacy as an educational *lingua franca* that helps the school community communicate and learn together. In this spirit, information literacy is best taught within the context of subject matter; providing true informational needs.

For this reason, beside the fact that good teaching often arises from a community of practice, librarians and classroom teachers should collaboratively design learning activities that foster both subject matter competency as well as literacies. Ideally, librarians understand all curricula so that they can identify appropriate research processes in light of specific academic disciplines. For example, discerning fact from opinion, which is typically addressed in social studies, is part of the comprehension and evaluation process within information literacy. Frankly, many content frameworks include information literacy components, but they are not always explicitly labeled as such. Therefore, librarians and classroom teachers need to look at content standards and information literacy standards simultaneously, together, taking into consideration students' prerequisite information literacy skills and available resources.

On a more systemic level, the entire school community can examine information literacy standards alongside subject matter standards in an effort to develop an interdependent matrix of learning activities that ensure student information competence. In this model, developing a hypothesis or a thesis statement exemplifies the process of identifying a task. If the science teacher introduces this concept prior to the language arts teacher, then the latter can build upon the students' recent learning, thus deepening understanding and offering more opportunities to practice that skill in other contexts. Similarly, just as each grade level builds on the prior year's knowledge set, so can information literacy skills build upon prior experience that is contextualized to optimize meaningful engagement.

Using this approach, classes can also focus on one information literacy skill, such as working cooperatively toward a goal, which can be implemented in a physical education or music class as well as in a science class. Similarly, if students are comfortable evaluating print resources, they can concentrate on evaluating web-based resources for the moment. Having a school-wide scope and sequence across curricular areas provides a venue for meeting specific information literacy standards *and* linking them to the overall intellectual framework. In terms of gender issues, this method allows girls to serve as experts in generating key words, for instance, during one learning activity, and boys model numerical analysis skills in another project without having to go "tit-for-tat" in every class session. In other words, not every learning activity has to consist of a full-blown research project. Like eating an elephant, students can become information-literate bite by bite.

Information Literacy Exercises

Note: Activities marked with an * are appropriate for elementary grades or include accommodations for younger students; unless otherwise noted, all the activities may be done by middle and high school students.

CONCEPT MAPPING*

Within an academic domain, specific topics can have different connotations for, or be experienced differently by, each gender. Concept mapping offers a visual way to demonstrate these differences. This process can be contextualized several ways. Students can draw a concept map, at the beginning of the year or at the start of a unit, which can be used as a diagnostic tool to discover their prior knowledge. Students in same-sex and mixed-sex pairs may compare their concept maps, and look for overlaps and gaps in knowledge. As a class, discuss what gendered knowledge exists and brainstorm ways that students can teach each other in those areas where learning gaps exist. Likewise, students can create concept maps for specific topics, and discover whether those topics have gender connotations. Over time, students can compare different topics to see what patterns, if any, exist. For instance, in social studies, migration patterns may exhibit gender-neutral treatment, but war-time topics may reveal that boys know more about that area. If topic coverage seems to favor one sex's knowledge, the class can also brainstorm related issues that could address the other sex's interests; using the war example, learning how daily life is impacted by war offers more gender-neutral or girl-favored opportunities for learning. At the end of a unit, students can make another concept map to see if gender differences decline because all students have has increased their knowledge equitably.

UNLOCKING THE KEY*

Prior experience and vocabulary knowledge impact the choice of key words in research. Ask students to individually write down as many key words as they think relevant for a unit. Next, instruct them to categorize these words in terms of broader, narrower and related terms. Students may want to use a concept map or tree graphic organizer to help them organize their thoughts; alternatively, students may be given a graphic organizer at the start to prompt their thinking. In same-sex pairs, students can compare their lists and categories. Then, match a girls' pair with a boys' pair to compare results. As a class, discuss the results, and look for possible gendered patterns. As a variation of the activity, when students pair, they can modify their lists at each point. In a class discussion, students could also share their reasons for making changes; gendered behavior can also be explored at that point.

SEEK AND FIND

Even though most Internet searches result in about the same quality of information for girls and boys, the process by which they reach the end can differ significantly. Arranging for students to see how peers conduct online searching can help them consider different searching strategies. Have mixed-sex pairs search for an assigned topic using the Internet (the entire class can have the same topic, or two to four pairs can have the same topic). One sex can serve as the recorder for the other; ideally, an equal number of girls and boys should serve as recorders. For the next search, the two sexes can switch roles. In each case, the searchers talk aloud about their strategy, revealing their decision-making process. Students can brainstorm what elements to record. Hopefully, the following factors: the search terms used, the length of time spent looking at each site, the number of sites visited, and the final list of relevant sources chosen. Ask same-topic pairs to compare their processes and results, noting possible gender differences. If the entire class searches the same topic, findings can reveal whether gender or personality differences are more significant.

Interviewing

Interviewing involves a number of skills: developing a sense of trust, asking relevant questions, drawing out an interviewee and guiding that person's responses. Interview success also depends on the interviewer's prior knowledge. Have mixed-sex pairs conduct an interview. They should develop a set of questions collaboratively; if done by using MS Word, each student's contributions and changes can be recorded separately. As a practice activity to hone interviewing skills, and an additional opportunity to explore the impact of gender, students can conduct a mock interview of their peers. For this purpose, the same topic should be used for both pairs (e.g., interviewing senior citizens about local history); ideally, at least four pairs would have the same topic so comparisons can be made between small groups. In this scenario, it's best for students to compare process and information with same-sex interviews and mixed-sex interviews. While one member of each pair can serve as an observer, the interviews can also be videotaped. The interview can then be critiqued by the active participants, the observers, and then the whole group in response to watching the videotape. At the end, the entire class can debrief the process, and determine what gender patterns arise. Hopefully, students can learn from each other's approach and thus make the actual interview process more successful. During that real interview, students should consider taking turns asking questions and recording the interview.

Data Mining

Rich data sets offer students latitude in deciding what kinds of hypotheses to develop, what information to use, and what interpretations to make. The process can also reveal subtle gender differences. Students can start with print almanacs, look at different tables and brainstorm what kinds of information and implications can be gleaned. For instance, they may see occupation differences by region or gender. Students can then posit reasons for these differences and locate other tables that might explain the reason for these differences, such as geography or education. As students have free rein in choosing data sets, they can compare their choices afterwards to determine what patterns—including these gender-linked — emerge in their choice of the original data set as well as possible correlative data sets. Students should document their decision-making process and results in order to facilitate class analysis.

In the first go-around, students can examine the data visually and make a rough estimate of the trends. Creating graphs from the data can be time-consuming, but if students use online almanacs, such as Information Please (http://www.infoplease.com), they should be able to export the data tables into a spreadsheet for easier manipulation. Alternatively, students can progress from print almanacs and quick assessment to rich online data sets (e.g., government statistics, industry surveys, sports figures) that are already created in spreadsheet form; Math Forum provides a good collection suitable for K-12 settings (http://mathforum.org/workshops/sum96/data.collections/datalibrary/data.set6.html). Students benefit from examining the data both in table form and in graph form. This activity may be done individually, in same-sex pairs, or in mixed-sex pairs. Ideally, each of these groupings should be present so that the class can examine how groupings impact the process and results, and how gender enters into the picture.

VIDEOTAPING INFORMATION*

Knowledge can be represented in many forms and captured using a variety of tools. Videotape offers an insightful way to not only capture an audio-visual reality, but also to capture individuals' perceptions of that reality. Because the camera lens enables the machine to record only a section of the entire environment, the viewer can control and select what s/he considers relevant features. As students videotape their perceptions of an environment, they can compare their recordings along a number of dimensions: time frame, camera angle, framed image, recorded sound, scope of shot (e.g., long shot, general shot, close-up), camera movement. The raw footage offers an unscripted data gathering process that can be analyzed in terms of point of view. Students can brainstorm other ways to analyze content: choice of images, choice of sound, presence and quality of voice-over commentary, presence of gender-sensitive data (e.g., action vs. talking heads, people vs. objects).

Video editing exemplifies the organizing/synthesizing step of the research process. Making sure that the original footage is write-protected, students can make three copies of the master. Single- and mixed-gender pairs can take the same original material and edit it to communicate a message. The original video recorder can also edit the footage as a baseline product. As they work, students can document their decision-making process, or a third student can act as a recording observer. Students can then compare the editing process and product. Criteria for comparisons may be predetermined, or students can develop their own set of criteria. Both the criteria-determination process and the actual content analysis can reveal gendered approaches to evaluation.

PARALLEL UNIVERSES

Depending on prior experience and learning preferences, students choose a wide variety of resources when they research a topic. Each step along the way influences the next decision point. As a variation on the traditional I-Search project, have students create a decision flowchart of their efforts. At each decision point, they must list at least two alternatives. For instance, they might posit two thesis statements that differ in scope or critical features. The students then indicate which thesis statement they chose and the reason for that decision. They continue their research flowchart in a similar way. At the point of identifying key terms, they can list those sources that generated the term and also list the sources they found as a result of using a key word. Where key words prove unfruitful, the flowchart can so indicate because few or misleading sources would be listed underneath, and the flow in that direction would stop. As students evaluate and use their resources, they may find that they have to change their thesis statement, choice of terms, or strategy of accessing sources; the flowchart can reflect that change in direction. At the end of the process, students compare the charts in terms of choices made, the decision-making process, changes in direction, and final results. Typically, the entire class starts with the same topic; yet, if the project is rich enough, each flowchart differs—even if the final list of resources is the same.

As a variation, a variety of topics can be researched, and decision flowcharts compared. Students can determine if different tasks and topics lend themselves to different types of flowcharts. They can also discover what influence, if any, gender plays in the process. In another variation, each student can begin the decision flowchart and research process. When a decision is made, individuals give their flowcharts and notes to another person to continue through the next decision point. Students keep passing their work at each point. At the end, they can compare flowcharts, and also share their experience of building on their peers' decisions. The transmission can be kept to the same sex or switched alternately between sexes, with a debriefing noting any difference in experiences.

PATHFINDERS AND PATHMAKERS

Bibliographies are very helpful starting points for student research as well as a reflection of the results of their endeavors. Sometimes students do not realize the work that is done to develop those bibliographies. One way to gain appreciation for this work is to deconstruct and reconstruct such bibliographies. Request that students locate relevant bibliographies, including Webliographies, on a topic. Then have them use key terms, locational tools, and evaluation sources to reconstruct the same bibliographies—or improve them. Some of the factors they might consider include the kinds of reviews and awards each source has, citations to the source, related bibliographies, and bibliographer's background and expertise (e.g., a female subject specialist librarian).

Alternatively, students can create narrative webliographies that guide the reader through the main points of a topic or concept, hyperlinking to supporting sources such as dictionaries, images, and in-depth information. These Webliographies can be critiqued in terms of possible gendered content, perspective, and information structure.

SEARCHING BY ROLE

Each person brings his or her own perspective to the research process. Thinking in terms of another person's viewpoint can help students become more sensitive to different information processing approaches. Students can brainstorm factors that might impact research strategies: prior experience (impacted by culture, age, gender, locale, schooling), learning preference (subject matter, learning style), language competency (English language learner, illiterate, avid reader), physical condition (visually impaired, deaf, dyslexic, mute, motor constrained), family conditions (homeless, resource-rich, no study area, DSL cable with state-of-the-art computer, presence of siblings and other adults), access to resources (nearby bookstores, neighborhood library, local university, no Internet connectivity, Internet cafes). Create several slips of paper for each factor, making one pile per category. Ask each student to pick one slip each for three categories, take the opposite gender role, and develop a research strategy that would reflect those factors. For instance, an English language learner boy with a high-speed computer with Internet who is a visual learner would probably look for visually rich web sites and streaming video sources in his primary language. Students can then critique each other's strategies in terms of plausibility.

As a variation, students can assume different roles in society by profession (e.g., professional business person, artist, farmer, performer, etc.), socio-economic status, gender, and age, and generate a plausible research strategy on the same topic. This activity helps students project their assumptions about different lifestyles.

CROSS-CURRICULAR INFORMATION LITERACY

Particularly in high school, students use "silo thinking" about their courses, not seeing, for instance, the connections between mathematics and social studies. Information literacy can serve as a "translator" between subject domain processes, and help students transfer their learning to new contexts. After providing an overview of a research process, focus on each step. Ask students to identify tasks they do in each course that speak to that step. An easy way to accomplish this is to post one newsprint sheet per step — or designate one section of a black/dry board to write the task and the associated course. Divide the class into small groups, one per step. Ask each group to write the task and course on the board. When all the groups are done, do a gallery walk, asking students to add to each list as they think of additional related tasks. To focus on gender issues, the class can be divided into two main groups, each with a full set of steps. After generating lists, the two groups can switch sites and add to the opposing group's lists. In either case, the entire class analyzes the lists and makes deductions about information literacy across the curriculum and possible gender influences.

Works Cited

Akin, Lynn (1998). "Information Overload and Children: A Survey of Texas Elementary School Students." *School Library Media Research, 1.* Retrieved on February 3, 2005, from http://www.ala.org/ala/aasl/aaslpubsandjournals/slmrb/slmrcontents/volume11998slmqo/akin.htm#research.

American Association of School Librarians and Association of Educational Communications and Technology (1988). *Information power: Partners for learning.* Chicago: American Library Association.

American Association of University Women. (1992). *Shortchanging, girls, shortchanging America.* Washington, DC: American Association of University Women.

Bahremand, V. (2003). *24/7 Digital reference services: Does it work for students?* Unpublished master's project. Long Beach, CA: California State University.

Chelton, M., and Cole, Colleen (Eds.). *Youth information-seeking behavior: Theory, models, and issues.* Lanham, MD: Scarecrow, 2004.

Eisenberg, Michael, and Berkowitz, Robert (1990). *Information problem-solving: The Big Six approach to library and information skills instruction.* Norwood, NJ: Ablex.

Gordon, Carol (2002). "Methods for measuring the influence of concept mapping on student information literacy." *School Library Media Research, 5.* Retrieved February 3, 2005, from http://www.ala.org/ala/aasl/aaslpubsandjournals/slmrb/slmrcontents/volume52002/gordon.htm.

Gross, Melissa (1997, Spring). "Pilot study on the prevalence of imposed queries in a school library media center." *School Library Media Quarterly, 25,* 3, 157–163.

Kuhlthau, Carol (1985). *Teaching the library research process: A step-by-step program for secondary school students.* Englewood Cliffs, NJ: Prentice-Hall.

Large, Andrew, Beheshti, J., and Rahman, T. (2002, May). "Gender differences in collaborative web searching behavior: an elementary school study." *Information Processing and Management: an International Journal, 38,* 3, 427–443.

Loertscher, David, and Woolls, Blanche (1999). *Information literacy: A review of the research.* San Jose, CA: Hi Willow.

Marland, Michael (1981). *Information skills in the secondary curriculum.* New York: Metheun.

McKenzie, Jamie (1996, March). "Making WEB meaning." *Educational Leadership, 54,* 3, 30–32.

Mellon, C. (1988). Attitudes: "The forgotten dimension in library instruction." *Library Journal, 113,* 14, 137–139.

Pappas, Marjorie, and Tepe, Ann (1995). "Preparing the information educator for the future." *School Library Media Annual,* 37–44.

Savolainen, Reijo and Kari, Jarkko (2004). "Placing the Internet in information source horizons." *Library and Information Science Research, 26,* 415–433.

Shenton, Andrew, and Dixon, Pat (2004). "Issues arising form youngsters' information-seeking behavior." *Library & Information Science Research, 26,* 177–200.

Smith, M., and Wilhelm, J. (2002). *Reading don't fix no Chevys: Literacy in the lives of young men.* Portsmouth, NH: Heinemann.

Stein, N. (1999, Dec.). "Listening to—and learning—from girls." *Educational Leadership,* 18–20.

Venezky, Richard (Ed.) (1990). *Toward defining literacy.* Newark, DE: International Reading Association.

6

Numeracy

The numbers are clear. New scientific and technology advances lean heavily on mathematics. This is our students' world, their future. Success in math leads to success in other fields. However, as the Trends in International Mathematics and Science Study (TIMSS, formerly known as the Third International Mathematics and Science Study) (Mullis, et al., 1999) reports make clear, today's students are not performing at grade level in terms of mathematics. The 2004 Nation's Report Card of the USA found that two-thirds of fourth and eighth grade students performed at the basic or above level, but less than a quarter were considered proficient.

In examining the reasons for student achievement, the TIMSS report studied the impact of teachers and curriculum. While no one instructional approach outperformed another, still the impact of having just 41 percent of eighth-grade USA math teachers majoring in mathematics in college (30 percent lower than the international average) is sizeable. (USDE, 2003) Additionally, as mathematics education itself has changed, teachers outside the academic mathematics arena may not be aware of those new approaches. Fortunately, as project-based learning and cross-curricular collaboration increasingly occurs, numeracy can be systematically addressed by incorporating it across the curriculum. The issue is how.

One answer is the infusion of information literacy skills: that is, effective access, selection, evaluation, and use of information. The 1991 USA SCANS Report (Secretary's Commission on Achieving Necessary Skills) identified the need for thinking skills and the productive use of information. Mathematics teachers can collaborate with librarians to map problem-solving techniques onto information literacy processes, and then work with other subject teachers to incorporate mathematical thinking into the rest of the curriculum. As students think about mathematics contextually through research topics of interest to them, they are more apt to form a positive attitude toward math — as well as respect it.

What Is Numeracy?

Surprisingly, a clear definition of quantitative literacy, or numeracy as it is called in British English, is hard to find in professional literature. Dr. Lynn Steen describes it this way: "Numeracy is to mathematics as literacy is to language." A useful working definition is provided by Kay Whitehead of Flinders University, who reports on the South Australian Curriculum Standards and Accountability Framework Committee: "[Numeracy is] the ability to understand, analyze, critically respond to and use mathematics in different social contexts."

National standards for mathematical competency for K-12 students (National Council of Teachers of Mathematics, 2000) offers some operational delimiters. Basic mathematical content includes numbers and operations, algebra, geometry, measurement, data analysis, and probability. Mathematical processes include reasoning and proofs, problem solving, representations, connections, and communication. They posit six guiding principles in supporting numeracy: equity, coherent curriculum, effective teaching, active learning, supportive assessment, and technology.

Steen (2001), who offers a more gestalt perspective on numeracy, asserts that the quantitatively literate person has confidence in understanding and applying numerical ideas, and has a cultural appreciation for the nature and history of mathematics and its role in scientific inquiry and technological progress. Such a person has number and symbol sense; and can intuit numerical meaning, estimate, and realize numbers as a measure of things. Steen lists the following mathematical processes: interpreting data, logical thinking, decision-making, and the use of mathematical tools in specific settings.

By now, the concept of learning *how* to learn has become as important as *what* to learn; the word "literacy" is used to capture this idea. Most educators in the "hard" areas realize that mathematical thinking permeates all curricular areas. The rest of the school community needs to understand the richness of numeracy as students gather numerical data from a variety of resources and try to create meaning from that information. At their fundamental basis, word problems exemplify this practice. A real world situation is posited, and students need to solve the problem given certain data. Could today's students figure out how much carpet to buy? Could they estimate college costs, and how to plan to meet them? More sophisticated scenarios provide students with opportunities to engage in a variety of mathematical and information processing strategies. Indeed, quantitative literacy is most powerful when linked with information literacy, whereby students learn how to access, evaluate, manipulate and communicate information critically.

For students to be numerically literate, teachers need to design, implement and assess learning activities that enable students to learn and apply those numeracy competencies. Certainly, those teachers credentialed in mathematics should have a deep understanding of these concepts. However, to provide meaningful context for mathematical thinking, math teachers need to collaborate with their professional colleagues to design cross-discipline learning activities. In the process, all teachers can gain numeracy competency — and all can better appreciate the impact and incorporation of mathematics throughout life.

Gender Issues in Numeracy

Primitive number sense and reasoning ability are actually hard-wired in the brain, mainly in the left parietal lobe. Mathematics is linked to areas of the right brain dedicated to music because of patterning processes (notes vs. numbers), and the visual cortex on the right side for processing geometric and graphic analysis. The left side of the brain is used for sequencing and analysis. Thus, both genders have the potential to succeed in mathematics. However, mathematical achievement by the time of high school graduation still strongly favors males. What happens?

Girls and boys perform equally in elementary grades. Then, interest in mathematics declines for girls in middle school, even before their mathematics grades drop. Perception of mathematics is a strong predictor of career choice, and girls are less likely to follow that path. Several factors contribute to this disappointing situation. Parents and teachers often convey lower expectations for girls. Societal messages about femininity strike girls when they enter puberty. Simultaneously, girls become less confident and attribute failure to their own inferiority rather than to curriculum or instructional limitations. In upper grades, mathematical instruction becomes more competitive and closed in nature. Girls prefer a more open and collaborative approach where they can discuss and reflect on the meaning of mathematical processes. Boys do not like the pressurized atmosphere either, and actually have more anxiety about math than girls at age twelve, but they adapt to the rigor better than girls (Furner & Berman, 2004).

Boaler (2002) insightfully suggests that mathematical instruction, rather than girls' attitudes, should change. Several strategies can provide more equitable learning experiences, starting by incorporating social aspects into the activities. Students can be provided opportunities to question mathematics and to conjecture, encouraging original thinking rather than rote learning. Using gender-neutral real-life problems helps all students ground their understanding. Educators can "tease out" the quantitative aspects of various subject areas, such as physical fitness figures, scientific data analysis, demographics, artistic proportions, and literary content analysis. Using collaborative study groups appeals to girls, and using mathematical manipulatives (including online ones, such as the National Library of Virtual Manipulatives at http://matti.usu.edu/nlvm/nav/vlibrary. html) appeals to boys. Writing about math processes is easier for girls, and using technology is easier for boys; both sexes can teach the other these valuable skills. Students should also have input on alternative assessment methods such as observations, writing samples, and portfolios. To deal with math anxiety, educators need to provide a learning environment that encourages intellectual risking, which is often harder for girls, and separates mathematical success and self-esteem. Ideally, students begin math study at their current skill level, are responsible for their own attitude and learning, and ask for help when needed (Furner & Berman, 2004). Librarians can help ease math anxiety by sharing stories that have fun with math concepts (e.g., *Math Curse* and *The Phantom Tollbooth*), introducing recreational math books and web sites (e.g., http://www.counton.org and http://www.cut-the-knot.com), and providing print and non-print resources that can help students learn mathematics via their preferred learning styles, and at their own pace.

The Impact of Technology on Numeracy

Technology has comprised an integral part of numeracy for decades. Digital drill programs increasingly offer accurate diagnostics, increased interactivity, and specific record-keeping. Spreadsheet programs can now quickly generate graphs that help students visualize data as they analyze it. Digital manipulatives offer even more flexibility than physical ones, and help students link concrete and symbolic representations of mathematical concepts (American Association for the Advancement of Science, 1999). Handheld calculators have become sophisticated graphing instruments; handheld devices offer microcomputer capabilities. With the incorporation of multimedia, graphic interface, and broadband capacity, the Internet now has thousands of high-quality mathematical web sites that foster numeracy, even for young children. Since technology comprises a part of daily life for most occupations, students need to use technological tools in K-12 education so they will be adequately prepared. No wonder the 2000 *Principles and Standards for School Mathematics* deems technology essential in teaching and learning.

Has technology made a difference in student qualitative literacy? Yes, if used appropriately. Potentially, technology can help students focus on concepts rather than on rote calculations, and can facilitate inquiry-based learning through simulations. However, technology requires student and teacher training as well as changes in current teaching and learning practice. These issues require extra time and effort at the beginning. As mentioned in other chapters, technology offers a rich repertoire of teaching and learning tools. Math digital tutorials, while sometimes not very exciting, do help students with basic math skills because of their targeted interventions and specific feedback. They actually impact student learning more than digital simulations, mainly because teachers do not always know which programs to use, when to use them, or how to use them effectively; digital tutorials are more highly structured and easier to use independently (Kulik, 2002).

Most students today have grown up in a technological world so they expect technology to be present at some point in their education. Boys, in particular, like to engage in technology-based learning activities, and spend more time in that arena. Because of their closed nature, web tutorials are probably more popular with boys, while girls prefer the open-ended features of spreadsheets and exploratory math software programs such as Geometer's Sketchpad. Both sexes can enjoy simulations, manipulating data to achieve different results. Both can use rich data sets (e.g., government statistics on population, health, economics, education; online almanacs; election information) to make predictions and then test their hypotheses using calculators and spreadsheets. Collaborative efforts, which girls favor, can be facilitated through email, instant messaging, and groupware. In short, educators can avail themselves of several technology options to meet the differentiated numeracy needs of students.

Some beginning web sites that help the entire school community address numeracy follow. Math Forum (http://www.mathforum), out of Swarthmore College, is the most well-known center for K-12 math education. The Eisenhower Clearinghouse for Mathematics and Science (http://www.enc.org) lists more than 7000 educational resources and includes research information. The National Council of Teachers of Mathematics (http://illuminations.nctm.org) provides lessons and activities aligned with math standards. The Center for Technology and Teacher Education for Mathematics (http://www.teacherlink.org/content/math/home.html) focuses on technology-infused learning activities. S.C.O.R.E. (http://score.kings.k12.ca.us) has teacher-developed lessons and resources. NASA (http://www.nasa.gov) offers many interactive mathematical activities. Figure This (http://www.figurethis.org) provides math challenges for families. The California Learning Resources Network (http://www.clrn.org) includes a database of video and digital math resources reviewed by state standards.

What Can Librarians Do to Facilitate Numeracy?

Numeracy is ultimately the responsibility of the entire school community. Therefore, all constituents should be involved in assessing the present situation, and planning effective interventions to improve the system. As teachers learn together, and develop action plans together, they model active learning for their students and the rest of the school. As a side note, it's recommended that math teachers not work in isolation, but, rather, collaborate with difference disciplines and partner with support personnel such as library media and reading specialists to apply mathematical concepts across the curriculum. As curriculum linker and model for learning communities, librarians have several tools at hand to optimize student learning and teacher collaboration.

Know the curriculum and the concepts. On the national level, two organizations shape content and outcome standards for mathematics: the National Council of Teachers of Mathematics (http://www.nctm.org) and the American Mathematics Society (http://www.ams.org). Both groups have developed standards for K-12 students as well as mathematics teachers. The National Council for Accreditation of Teacher Education uses NCTM's guidelines (http://www.ncate.org/standard/ new%20program%20standards/nctm%202001.pdf). Each state has its own set of mathematics standards and curriculum framework (http://www.edexcellence.net/ standards/math.html and http://dir.yahoo.com/Science/Mathematics/Education/ K_12/Curriculum_Standards/). It should be noted that state standards might not be aligned with national standards, so librarians need to be sensitive to possible conflicts in mathematical pedagogy philosophies. In some cases, the emphasis is on articulated conceptual strands such as measurement and relations. In other cases, math standards reflect grade-by-grade student outcomes based on demonstration of specific skills. Particularly in light of high-stakes standardized tests, some faculty may feel conflicted about "teaching to the test" vs. constructivist learning.

Know the environment. Librarians have the responsibility to collaborate with mathematics teaching and learning. As such, they need to look at several factors that support learning. What *curriculum* are teachers following? Does the curriculum reflect the latest trends in mathematical thinking and pedagogy? What *resources* are used to deliver the curriculum? Are high-quality electronic resources, videos and manipulatives readily available in sufficient amounts for teacher and student use? What *instructional strategies* are used? What kinds of learning activities are used to provide students with opportunities to practice and demonstrate mathematical competence? How do teachers *work together* to plan curriculum and learning strategies collaboratively? What background, experience, skills and dispositions do *students* bring to the classroom? Librarians need to assess students' current numeracy competency in order to optimize learning experiences.

Facilitate a Cycle of Inquiry. By looking at the total learning system, librarians and classroom teachers can identify critical factors that impact achievement. What is happening relative to the total math achievement system and its components? What is *not* happening, but should be? What discrepancies exist relative to student learning? Why do such discrepancies occur: student demographics, scheduling, experience, teaching practice, assessment instrument? What interventions show promise?

Assessment instruments and procedures should be developed at the time that interventions are designed. By analyzing the results, and using that data to drive decision-making and planning, the school community demonstrates reflective practice, which is likely to facilitate student learning.

Using Information Literacy Research Steps to Foster Numeracy

The information literacy research process provides a useful framework for learning activities that encompass numeracy. Each step of the research process can be applied to numeracy:

1. What is the problem to be solved?
2. What data are needed to solve the problem? Subtasks include:
    a. Are the data available, or does the student need to locate them?
    b. Where are the data?
    c. Are the data reliable and valid?
3. How should the data be manipulated? Subtasks include:
    a. How should the data be analyzed?
    b. How should data be structured to be analyzed?
    c. What conclusions can be drawn from the analysis?
4. How should the conclusions be shared? Subtasks include:
    a. What is the most effective method to represent the data and the analysis?
    b. How should the conclusions be presented?

A concrete example makes the process more accessible:

1. What is the optimal way to package products within a defined space?
2. What are the dimensions of the product? What are the dimensions of the container? Are the dimensions of either package subject to change?
3. What algorithms apply in this problem?
4. What is the most effective way to represent the solution to the problem: visually, orally, a combination of approaches?

Professional development provides an efficient way for librarians to optimize curriculum development and collaboration efforts within an information literacy framework. A sample workshop follows:

Objectives: Teachers will identify numeracy concepts within their curricular areas; describe a research process that incorporates numeracy.

Grouping: Teachers sit at tables according to their subject matter, with one math teacher joining each subject table; ideally, each table consists of same-grade teachers to facilitate cross-curricular coordination.

Activities:
1. Each table brainstorms numeracy concepts that arise in its curriculum area. Each table reports its list in order to identify possible patterns, particularly across disciplines.
2. The school librarian traces the information literacy research process using numeracy as the guiding principle (as noted in the above description). The librarian also shows how the research process can be assessed (e.g., information literacy rubrics of process and product).
3. Each table develops a research project that links numeracy and its subject area, reporting its efforts.

4. Each table brainstorms how to assess numeracy within the concept of the research project, reporting its approaches.

Resources: Lesson plans and learning activities from the Internet and professional reading, curricular frameworks and course outlines. Ideally, a math/subject matter/library media teacher team locates high-quality lessons ahead of time so the documents can be consulted during the brainstorming session.

Follow-up: Teachers share their students' work from the proposed research projects that are implemented.

Reaching Out

Mathematics is a human endeavor. As such, it must be taught as a language that organizes and communicates valuable information. Numeracy needs to be linked with the larger community to provide a reality check for mathematics applications and a validation of its worth. Students and educators can visit business and agencies that use mathematics daily. Librarians can facilitate these experiences, getting information about community agencies and service organizations. These networking efforts result in career exploration opportunities for students and community support for numeracy. When both girls and boys see successful adults using mathematics, they become more motivated to become numerate.

Numeracy Exercises

Note: Activities marked with an * are appropriate for elementary grades or include accommodations for younger students; unless otherwise noted, all the activities may be done by middle and high school students.

Numeracy Around the House*

Ask students to look for mathematics in their homes. They can record their findings by taking photos, drawing pictures, videotaping, or writing about their evidence. They can also interview another family member to compare perceptions about mathematics. As the students share their findings, see if gender patterns emerge in terms of perceptions.

Topology of Clothing

Topology can be made more understandable and intriguing when contextualized in terms of clothing. For instance, the classic doughnut shape in topology is equivalent to a tube top. Have students find examples of different topological shapes and clothing. Does gender enter into the picture in terms of clothing identification, number of items identified, or accuracy of mathematical thinking?

NUMERACY AND CULTURE*

Culture reflects mathematical thinking in various ways: music, art, clothing, architecture, literature. Ask student pairs, one boy and one girl, to independently find examples of mathematics for a culture. Then ask each pair to compare their findings. Next, ask the class to compare different cultures in terms of mathematics, noting possible gendered contexts.

DIGITALLY SPEAKING*

Numerical systems are typically based on natural phenomena, such as body parts or cycles in nature. Students can investigate different number systems (e.g., Mayan, Chinese, Egyptian, Roman, computer-based) in terms of their development. See if the students can determine the culture and governmental structure (e.g., matriarchical, military, etc.) that prevailed at the time of the system's development. As a way to organize their findings, the number base can be listed ordinally in order to see if some number bases are more popular (e.g., base ten) than others.

NUMERICAL NOTES

A strong correlation exists between music and mathematics. Small cooperative groups can each research one musical feature that reflects numeracy (e.g., ratios and harmonics, fractions and rhythm, sets and keys). The following two web sites provide a number of relevant links: http://cnx.rice.edu/content/m11638/latest/ and http://www.math.niu.edu/~rusin/papers/uses-math/music/. Alternatively, student pairs can investigate the mathematics of different musical instruments, comparing their findings afterwards.

DIGITAL DIGITALS

CGI (computer-generated image) has become a popular film-making technique. In small cooperative groups, students can research how numeracy is involved in each step of creating a CGI film, from idea to DVD. See if students can also determine the gender balance of employees in each phase of the development. Alternatively, students can trace the mathematics involved in making different types of film (e.g., claymation, CGI, traditional, videotape-based), and compare their findings.

MATHEMATICIANS

Girls tend to eschew mathematical careers. To some degree, this decision reflects the meager number of well-known female mathematicians in history. To raise awareness, the class can brainstorm the names of famous mathematicians, and then classify those names by sex and ethnicity; note if boys and girls identify different names. Based on their conclusions, students may be more motivated to find information about mathematicians who are under-represented in general literature. The class can generate a database template, noting important facts to find:

vital dates, ethnicity/nationality, gender, area of mathematics, family/personal life, possible mentors or supporters. Each student inputs her/his findings into the class database. In pairs, students can develop hypotheses about the mathematicians, and then sort the database accordingly to analyze the data. The class can then share hypotheses and conclusions, and see if any gender issues arise (e.g., female mathematicians tended to have positive relationships with their fathers, etc.) or if there had been change over time (e.g., more women mathematicians exist now). A good web site for finding female mathematicians has been developed by Agnes Scott College (http://www.agnesscott.edu/lriddle/women/women.htm).

MATH IN YOUR FUTURE

Even through the heroine in the movie *Peggy Sue Got Married* asserted that she really didn't need algebra, most jobs actually do involve numeracy. Students can interview employees and employers about the use of mathematical thinking in their work. What kind of mathematics is involved? What critical math thinking approaches are needed? What kind of mathematical thinking is needed to enter and succeed in the field? Students can compare their findings to see if gender patterns emerge.

CONSUMER MATH

Ask students to brainstorm consumer issues related to numeracy: comparison buying, online purchasing, credit ratings, banking, insurance, investments. Ask small cooperative groups to each focus on one issue, sharing their perceptions, noting possible gender differences. Then request that they research numeracy-related factors for the issue, identifying sources of information and impact of gender on consumer decisions (e.g., who is more likely to get a bank loan or who is charged more for car insurance). Students can generate graphs to facilitate comparisons between issues.

STATISTICAL LIES

How numerical data is presented can impact an audience's acceptance of those figures as well as their interpretation. The classic book *How to Lie with Statistics* and the newer title *Innumeracy: Mathematical Illiteracy and Its Social Consequences* show how numbers can be misrepresented. Ask student pairs (either mixed-sex or same sex) to create a presentation that tries to convince someone by lying with statistics. Then have the pairs exchange their presentations, and look for logical holes in the arguments. In the class debriefing, see if gender patterns emerge in the process or product.

Works Cited

American Association for the Advancement of Science (1999). *Dialogue on early childhood science, mathematics, and technology education.* Washington, DC: American Association for the Advancement of Science.

Boaler, Jo (2002). *Experiencing school mathematics.* Mahwah, NJ: Lawrence Erlbaum.

California Commission on Teacher Credentialing (1997). *California Standards for the Teaching Profession.* Sacramento: California Department of Education.

California State Department of Education (1997). *Mathematics framework for California public schools kindergarten through grade twelve.* Sacramento: California Department of Education.

Conference Board of the Mathematical Sciences (2001). *The mathematical education of teachers, part I.* Washington, DC: Mathematical Association of America.

Department of Education, Science and Training (2004). "Your Child's Future — Literacy and Numeracy in Australia's Schools." Canberra: Australian Government. Retrieved February 3, 2005, from http://www.dest.gov.au/schools/publications/2002/yourchild/english.htm.

Furner, Joseph, and Berman, Barbara (2004, Summer). "Building math confidence for a high-tech world." *Academic Exchange Quarterly, 8,* 2, 214–220.

Glenn Commission (1999). *Before it's too late.* Washington, DC: United States Department of Education

Kulik, James (2002, Nov.). "School mathematics and science programs benefit from instructional technology." *Infobrief.* Retrieved February 3, 2005, from http://www.nsf.gov/sbe/srs/infbrief/nsf03301/.

Mullis, I., et al. (1999). *TIMSS 1999 international mathematics report: Findings from IEA's repeat of the third international mathematics and science study at the eighth grade.* Chestnut Hill, MA: Boston College.

National Center for Educational Statistics (2004). *The nation's report card.* Washington, DC: Department of Education.

National Council of Teachers of Mathematics (2000). *Principles and standards for school mathematics.* Washington, DC: National Council of Teachers of Mathematics.

National Policy Board for Educational Administration (2002). *Instructions to implement standards for advanced programs in educational leadership.* Alexandria, VA: National Policy Board for Educational Administration.

Steen, Lynn (1999, Oct.). "Numeracy: The new literacy for a data-drenched society." *Educational Leadership, 57,* 2, 8–13.

Steen, Lynn (2001). *Mathematics and democracy.* Princeton, NJ: National Council on Education and the Discipline.

U.S. Department of Education (2003). *The facts about good teachers.* Washington, DC: U. S. Department of Education.

U.S. Department of Labor (2001). *Secretary's Commission on Achieving Necessary Skills.* Washington, DC: Government Printing Office.

7

Visual Literacy

As the United States becomes more pluralistic, society uses visuals — a universal language — to communicate and teach. Now technology and gender issues have put a new "spin" on visual literacy. This chapter explains the principles and concepts of visual literacy, and notes current trends in teaching these skills. Libraries need to embrace visuals, in terms of resources as well as instruction. Exercises explore issues of visual literacy, particularly from a cultural perspective.

Within a week of their birth, babies can recognize their parents, and they respond accordingly. By age three, children can draw and explain their drawings in terms of what they are trying to express. Walk into a museum and immediately one is drawn to some artwork and unimpressed with other pieces. "I don't know great art, but I know what I like." Is visual literacy something to be taught or is it hard-wired?

Historical Perspectives on Visual Images

Is the world becoming more visual? It appears so. What with television, film, advertisements, colorful web pages, and constant signage, people are inundated with visual images all day long. As societies become more diverse, images that can be understood universally have become increasingly more important. And yet timely and appropriate response to visual stimulants was as important to Neanderthals as to 21st century man.

While it is not explicitly stated, visual images often refer to human-made images, not those that exist in nature. There is an underlying assumption that human consciousness has to "name" a visual for it to be considered a formal visual image. This kind of approach reminds one of the koan "If a tree falls in the forest and no one listens, does it make a sound?" For that reason, the earliest visual images have been subscribed to prehistoric drawings found in ancient French caves of Chauvet-Pons-d'Arc and Lascaux that date 30,000 years ago. Recently, paint-grinding equipment dating back to more than 350,000 years ago was found in Zimbabwe. Even then, visual images were used to represent and document things and events, as well as to express human consciousness. Lines on a stick were precursors to numbers; the first writing was pictographic. Still, many pre-historic vessels were not only functional, but also decorative. For millennia, religions have used visual images as teaching tools (e.g., stained glass windows) and means to worship. The creation *and sale* of visual images strictly as an esthetic experience is a fairly modern concept (usually the Renaissance is considered the turning point), dependent on the ability of a society to have the disposable income to purchase the visual and the time to enjoy contemplating it. At first, photography seemed to threaten one of the functions of original visual art: to document. However, "traditional" artists came to realize that photography freed the creator to be able to visually express human inner feelings. Thus abstract art came into its own. Now the digital world enables visual artists to choose from a wide range of tools to express a variety of realities. One substantially new factor of digital images is the capacity to modify and repurpose them. Nevertheless, visual images continue to be both concrete and abstract, depending on the artist and the objective of the creative expression.

Is the visual image a public or private endeavor? If it is to be considered a means of communication, then it might be considered a public effort. Does an artist need a viewer? Probably not, but for a visual image to endure, it must have the imprimatur of expert opinion; it becomes public by default. While one could say that a single artistic creator is reflecting a self-identity, many visual images have been created to reflect a group identity or purpose, whether religious or political. Public architecture, for example, is generally a group endeavor and upholds a public purpose, as do the Sphinx and the Vatican. Still, the idea of museums for public viewing of visual images is, again, a recent concept: just a couple of centuries old. Museums were based on social responsibility to educate the masses culturally.

In that social realm, another question arises about visual images: do they influence society, or do they reflect society? The simplistic answer is: both. Ancient goddess sculptures reflected societal ideals of womanhood. The flat icons of the middle ages reflected the belief that religious images carved in the round are idolatry. Perspective started about the same time that the scientific method and instruments were invented. Photography and digital art existed because the corresponding technology was available. On the other hand, the importation of Japanese art into Europe impacted fashion and instigated interest in Oriental Eastern thinking. Picasso's painting "Guernica" influenced war attitudes. Certainly, the visual aspects of advertisements, war photography, and film documentaries have influenced society. Digital images, particularly those that capture realities never before seen — microscopic or cosmic — have changed the way that humans think about their world and their place within it.

What about the future? Will the world be visual? Probably, particularly as globalization forces international societal "intimacy." Even though visual images have cultural connotations, they are easier to deconstruct than aural or written language. However, those same visual images can be easily manipulated, so people need to evaluate visual images carefully to determine their authenticity as well as their message. While the issues are complex, students need to learn about them so they can deal with visual images more effectively.

Defining Visual Literacy

The most basic definition of visual literacy is "the ability to understand, create and use visual images." A more thorough definition was generated by consensus of visual literacy experts:

> A group of acquired competencies for interpreting and composing visible messages. A visually literate person is able to: (a) discriminate, and make sense of visible objects as part of a visual acuity, (b) create static and dynamic visible objects effectively in a defined space, (c) comprehend and appreciate the visual testaments of others, and (d) conjure objects in the mind's eye [Brill, Kim, Branch, 2001].

The International Visual Literacy Association developed the following visual literacy indicators in 1996:

1. Interpret, understand, appreciate meaning of visual messages
2. Communicate more effectively by applying visual design principles
3. Produce visual messages using technology
4. Use visual thinking to conceptualize solutions to problems

Visual literacy is a learned set of skills and knowledges, not an innate ability. Interestingly, when teachers have students create visual images as part of a learning activity, they seldom evaluate the effectiveness of the visual image, and instead comment on the image's neatness. Such an attitude devalues visual literacy.

In the United States, formal educational interest in visual literacy began in the late 19th century as photographs and stereographs became recognized as effective means to document reality. Concurrently, educational theory advocated the use of teaching materials that closely approximated the real, concrete world rather than focusing on abstract lectures. The term "visual education" was coined in 1906 by William Bagley to emphasize this concrete approach to instruction. The visual education movement of the early 20th century saw the rise of museums with educational changes, the production of visual teaching materials, and visual education services within school districts and universities. In the late 1940s, to some extent due to audio-visual advances in wartime training methods, audio-visual materials and instructional media broadened the field from its visual roots. More emphasis was also placed on communication and feedback. With the advent of digital technology, this once specific field has become very complex (Saettler, 1998).

Along the way, particularly with the burgeoning impact of mass media, visual literacy became construed to mean media literacy. That is, the viewer was cast as a consumer, with the need arising to educate the visually gullible. Vance Packard's book *The Hidden Persuaders* (1957) and Marshall McLuhan's book *Understanding Media: The Extensions of Man* (1964) pointed out the subliminal ways the media shape messages. Nevertheless, the International Visual Literacy Association was formed in 1969, and coined the term "visual literacy" to encompass the idea of understanding, creating, and appreciating visual experiences. Media literacy almost overtook visual literacy, but the latter has regained its niche and is focusing more on visual aspects of instruction and design.

The Visual Process

The process for comprehending visual images differs significantly from learning to understand textual information. At the most basic level, visual elements are manipulated simultaneously unlike words or music, which must be accessed sequentially. That is, the eye normally sees the entire visual image at once. The right brain dominates this process; in fact, 30 percent of the brain cortex is devoted to visual processing, in contrast to 3 percent of the cortex devoted to hearing. The brain registers a full-color image (megabyte of data) in a fraction of a second, much faster than the processing speed for deciphering text. Still, when visual images are linked with text, the messages are dual-coded and easier to comprehend and remember. This dual coding is very important for children who read picture books and who then find it difficult to transfer to text-only literature.

Brain processes for visual literacy are slightly related to gender differences. Females perform better at sequencing images and identifying specific features of an object. Males tend to perform better on spatial tasks and spotting shaped within a complex image. To some degree, females favor the brain's left hemisphere, which is typically linked to verbal and sequential learning; boys prefer the right hemisphere, which can help them succeed in school environments where visual literacy is valued. However, cultural and social experiences for boys and girls are more likely to impact how visual images are seen — and responded to— than any brain differences (Sousa, 2001).

Try this exercise. Draw an elephant. Then draw a wombat. If the word "wombat" is unknown, it will be hard to draw. Now use this written description to draw a wombat: "A wombat is a stocky, short-legged furry badger-like animal up to 4 feet long, that weighs 30–75 pounds." While a written description of a wombat helps one draw it, a photograph of a wombat would make recognition immediate.

If one knows about Australian marsupials, and is told that wombats belong to that family, then more information might be culled when looking at the photograph. Likewise, if that photograph includes background information and a sense of scale, then more associations can be made about a wombat, which demonstrates that knowledge is contextualized. The double-coding process is associated with gender in that some textual information is more commonly known by one sex than another. For example, boys probably have an easier time identifying and drawing a "Hemi" than most girls because this aspect of the car world is considered more "muscular," of more interest to males than females. In the final analysis, combining textual language and visual imagery can help both genders learn more effectively and equitably.

Visualization: From Thought to Symbol

One aspect of visual literacy is the ability to visualize an idea or process. One obvious approach is to draw a picture — or, on a more abstract or general level, one can draw a sign or symbol of the idea. A sign is an object that represents something else in a straightforward way, such as a road sign; it serves as a one-to-one correlation. Symbols are signs that have an additional, more profound meaning, such as a cross that represents Christianity. Signs and symbols try to capture critical features of an idea so that it can be understood quickly by many people across disciplines or languages, for whoever needs to know. Representative symbols include flags, zodiac signs, and heraldry, among others. Maps are a good example of the use of symbols in that they serve as shorthand representations of specific ideas.

In the case of visualizing a process, one can draw a series of pictures. and draw connecting lines to show the direction of a process. Likewise, a complex idea may be comprised of numerous sub-ideas or related concepts, which can be mapped visually. This kind of visual diagramming is sometimes referred to as concept mapping, and represents one type of visual tool. The basic definition of visual tools is "symbols graphically linked by mental associations to create a pattern of information and a form of knowledge about an idea" (Clarke, 1991). He asserted that three kinds of visual tools existed: brainstorming webs, task-specific organizers, and thinking-process maps. Brainstorming webs are sometimes called mind maps or webs, and are used to help students visualize what they already know and link to new information needs. Graphic organizers tend to fall into the second category, particularly when students are given a visual structure to "fill in the blanks" such as a means to solve a math problem or track a plot line:

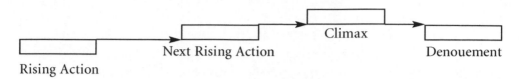

Rising Action

Thinking-process maps can be used across disciplines to show cause and effect, sequencing and decision-making (such as flowcharts); classification (such as branching); comparison (such as Venn diagrams); contexts for frames of references (such as circles within circles); and whole/part thinking (such as pie charts). One can use words, symbols, or pictures to describe each distinct idea. It is the linking aspect that involves the particular visual symbolism. Each visual tool needs to be explained and demonstrated to students, even though most are intuitively understood once exemplified.

In all cases, visual symbolism offers an alternative way to formulate an abstract concept, and to show relationships between ideas. Where outlines foster a sense of sequence, concept maps and other visual tools take advantage of non-linear thinking. (It must be noted that Inspiration software can transform a concept map into an outline, thus providing an instant visual instructional aid to explain the basis for outline form. This process works particularly well with boys and students in some cultures who do not instinctively process information in a sequential manner.)

Typography as Visual Image

Going back to the idea of visual images and written language, typography reflects the power of visual "language" because the letters are abstractions of sounds, but their visual variations can be used to reinforce or contradict the meaning of the word. The following exercises illustrate some of the visual principles.

The word "information" by itself has the meaning "communication of knowledge." When the word is used in a sentence, it gains more meaning, such as "The spy gave his superior classified information" as opposed to "What information do you have about the poetry contest?" Likewise, the visual aspect of the word "information" can also contribute meaning:

1. Color can denote urgency or importance.
2. Italics can imply movement.
3. Size can be equated with importance.
4. Script is sometimes associated with femininity or formality.
5. Novelty fonts can connote informality or youth.
6. Some type fonts are linked with history or culture.
7. Density of type font can be associated with power or masculinity.

The same word can evoke different meanings because of its appearance. For example:

1. Which "no" seems more serious?

2. What kind of "theater" is associated with the following?

3. What kind of "dog" comes to mind?

4. Which "Sydney" looks like a girl's name as opposed to a boy's name?

No or **NO**

THEATER   or   **Theater**

dog or dog

Sydney or SYDNEY

Typography varies according to several elements, each of which is used to convey a specific message. By understanding these elements, students can interpret communication more fully.

1. *Font:* the "style" of the alphabet; Times New Roman is considered a formal font, and Comic Sans is considered an informal font. If one wants to show stability and high reputation, then a formal font is normally used.

2. *Size:* usually size is equated with importance; however, small type size of type is often associated with detail, which can be very important (i.e., in contracts).

3. *Readability:* hard-to-read fonts, such as Fractur, may be skipped over — or comprehended only on a visual level rather than encouraging focus on the words and their meanings.

4. *CAPS vs. lower case:* letters in ALL CAPS are harder to read, but some people use them to draw attention to their words; CAPS in email is equated with screaming.

5. *Weight:* if a topic is **serious**, the type face might be weightier; likewise, thin letters might be used to communicate airiness.

6. *Proximity:* related text should be close enough physically to enable the reader to connect the elements.

7. *Alignment:* centered text is usually used for headlines; left-justified text is usually the easiest to read, and full-justified text is considered more formal.

8. *Emphasis:* these two techniques are often used to emphasize meaning — *underlining* and **bold facing.**

These typographical conventions help the reader decipher textual meaning. Even when these "rules" are broken, their existence proves the rule because the reader is usually meant to see the inconsistency of the word meaning and the typography, usually to communicate an inside joke or sense of irony, as these examples show:

QUIET   *elitism*   𝔐𝔒𝔇𝔈𝔯𝔫   *drug abuse*   **tragedy**

Typography offers a gender-neutral venue for examining visual "language." Everyone uses letters. Black and white type, in particular, is gender- as well as color-neutral; most texts are written in a font style that does not elicit gender-linked response. However, the appearance of different fonts and their use can generate gender stereotypes. For instance, a pink script might be considered feminine, while a bold Futura type font might evoke a sense of masculinity. Thus, librarians and other teachers can help students see how such gender-specific messages are communicated in advertisements, for instance. Students can also use the elements of typography to create their own messages that reinforce or contradict textual information, and thus take control of their gendered environment.

Visual Elements

Discussion about typography provides an easy lead-in to the formal elements of visual images as developed by artists over the centuries. These universal elements constitute the vocabulary of visual art, which one uses to create an image. While these elements may be sensed intuitively or viscerally, viewers must learn this language to comprehend and interpret a visual image.

Definitions of Visual Elements

1. Dot: establishes a central focus or location; constitutes the basis for digital images (most commonly associated with a pixel)
2. Line: establishes boundaries and movement; can be used to define shapes or textures
3. Space: usually discerned in terms of geometry; squares usually connote stability while triangles connote action and circles connote cycles and organisms
4. Direction: shows movement from one element to another (i.e., pointed shapes); diagonal movement is usually associated with energy
5. Texture: the "feel" of a surface; this element links visual and tactile sensations
6. Hue: usually associated with the sense of color
7. Saturation: the amount of grey in a color; the more saturation, the more brilliant the color

8. Value: the lightness of, or darkness of, an image; usually light value is associated with good and airiness

9. Scale: shows the relative size of objects; when two objects are shown together, the larger one is considered more powerful or important

10. Dimension: the sense of three dimensions and perspective

11. Motion: links time and space, so in 2D art this element is illusionary although significant (Stonehill, 1998).

Color

Hue, or color, is probably the most significant and most observed visual element.

1. Color visuals increase willingness to read by up to 80 percent.
2. Color enhances learning and improves retention by more than 75 percent.
3. Color accounts for 60 percent of object acceptance/rejection.
4. Color ads outsell black-and-white by 88 percent.
5. Color makes presentations look more professional (Eiseman, 2000).

Color impacts mood. For example, prisons use pink to decrease aggression, feng shui artists incorporate color in their analyses, yellow is linked with violent behavior. Blue is used:

1. To show respect by banks
2. To calm people in therapy
3. As an appetite suppressant
4. For presentation slides
5. For most important persons in Renaissance painting (ground from the precious stone, lapis lazuli).

It should be noted that the connotations of color are culturally determined, not universal. For instance,

1. White is used for purity in European cultures, and associated with death in Asian cultures.
2. Red is used for Asian weddings and celebrations, and for violence and energy in Europe.
3. Yellow means cowardice in Shakespeare, but denotes royalty in China.
4. Green means fruition, but is used for medieval brides' gowns.

Other visual elements are also culturally defined. For instance, the "protocol" for distance differs by culture. In European cultures, things that are farther away are smaller; in Hindu cultures, these same items are placed higher in the picture to show distance. As students access resources from other countries, they need to know the connotations of visual images in order to interpret information accurately.

Color can also connote gender, although it is tempered by culture. For instance, in the United States, pink is typically associated with baby girls, and blue is linked with baby boys. On the other hand, in Japan, both sexes like pink. To a degree, girls prefer warm colors and pastels, while boys prefer cooler shades and more vibrant colors. Still, color preferences of children in general, of bright colors, overshadow preferences based on gender. Interestingly, the most popular color scheme for web pages targeted to teenage girls is green-orange-purple (Farmer, 2004). Implications about color seem to be more emotionally based than gender-based. For example, until age ten, boys and girls use color in the same ways, but after that point, boys use color less because emotional inhibitions begin to impact behavior. It should be noted, though, that about 8 percent of males are color deficient, while only .5 percent of females are, so a significant number of males will miss some of the connotations of color altogether (Vandergrift, 2003).

Visual Principles

When creating a visual image, certain principles are used, intuitively or consciously, to produce a specific impact. These principles reflect universal consensus on how images affect humans. At the basic biological level, humans and forty other animal species prefer symmetrical, well-proportioned partners (Moller & Thornhill, 1998) because they tend to be better reproducers. In the same way, a regular rhythm indicates healthiness, so regular visual rhythm and pattern are also associated with positive feelings. Humans strive for equilibrium, so visual balance is more pleasant than visual imbalance. Humans like stimulation, so variety in an image attracts the eye. Thus, the following seemingly abstract principles are mere collations of human nature.

These principles are briefly defined here. Students and teachers/librarians can locate and produce examples of these principles in many different sources: art books, photos, posters, advertisements, web pages, and so on.

1. *Balance:* equal "weight" on both sides of an image, either through formal symmetry, informal symmetry (different but equal), or radial symmetry (as in a sunburst)

2. *Contrast:* two elements that differ greatly, e.g., light and dark color, thin and thick lines, large and small shape

3. *Proportion:* the relative size or shape of an element relative to another; a

three-fifths proportion (the Golden Mean) is considered the most pleasing proportion

4. *Pattern:* a repeated element, such as stripes, polka dots, or gingham

5. *Rhythm:* related to pattern, in that it often uses repeated elements; bridges and waves are often used to convey rhythm

6. *Emphasis:* a focal point, center of interest

7. *Unity:* a sense that every element fits together, typically through comparable elements or subject matter

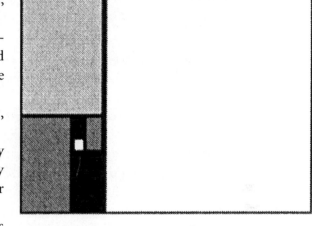

8. *Variety:* different elements or subject matter that provide a variety of interest points (Study art, 2005).

Another good web site to use as a means to help students decipher visual elements is the University of Arizona's Center for Creative Photography page "Learning to Look" (http://dizzy.library.arizona.edu/branches/ccp/education/guides/aaguide/lookguid.htm).

The benefits of laying forth these principles is that students can consciously realize how these principles impact their visceral responses to a visual image, and also surmise the creator's intent. Students can also explicitly use these principles when creating their own visual images in order to elicit a desired response. For

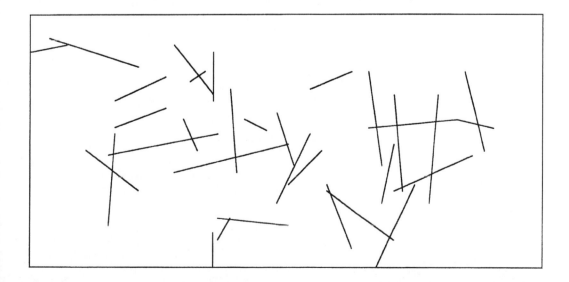

example, if a student wants the viewer to be uncomfortable about a subject, such as war, then he might draw an image that is disproportionate, unbalanced, chaotic.

The Digital World of Art

The fact that in 2004 The Walt Disney Company closed down a traditional animation department and wanted to join forces with Pixar, a digital production company, is just one example of the impact of digital technology on visual images. Today's high-end technology can produce images with resolution and subtlety that surpass any paint brush or traditional film camera. Technology enables the artist to modify an image quickly in order to create a final product that satisfies the creator's inner vision. Technology also enables the artist to disseminate the image throughout the world — and to manipulate and repurpose the image to meet different objectives for different audiences. For example, the image of a U. S. President can be changed so that he is placed digitally in a situation that is patently false, such as stabbing a baby, in order to persuade some targeted audience not to re-elect him. Thus, viewers need to be able to ascertain the verity of visual images more than ever before because such techniques can be performed so expertly. Likewise, as sophisticated technology becomes more accessible to a broader spectrum of the population, the ability of students to create, manipulate, and distribute visual images grows exponentially. Thus, students need to learn about the ethical use of these technologies relative to visual images both as consumers and as producers.

Thanks to mass media and telecommunications, students can access many more visual images than at any other time in history. Certainly, television shows billions of visual images daily. Even if one limits visual images to two-dimensional static images, television transmits photographs, illustrations, diagrams, and other 2D images frequently, particularly in documentaries. Still, for sheer number of documents, the Internet is the most obvious broadcasting channel. Students can virtually visit museums, examine rare primary documents, see exotic landmarks, study science concepts, and chat with artists. Live cameras enable students to see sites in real time. Videoconferencing enables students to interact with remote experts. It should be noted that many museums now have educational web pages with fascinating learning activities about visual literacy.

Examining how images can be manipulated demonstrates the processes behind creation and the factors to consider when examining these images. What is a typical process for manipulating visual images?

1. Decide what message to be conveyed — and to whom.
2. Decide which images to use.
3. Locate and evaluate possible images.

4. Select appropriate images.
5. As applicable, edit/manipulate images.
6. As applicable, sequence images.
7. As applicable, match images with text or sound.

An image may stand alone, such as a photograph or digital drawing. Many times, however, a sequence of images is called for. (Traditional film is actually a series of still images, which the brain processes as smooth movement.) A sequence of visual images might constitute the entire message, such as a wordless book. In other cases, the text or sound might be chosen before the images are. In graphic novels and photonovellas, text is interwoven with the image, while in other publications, the text and image are more separate.

Regardless of the process, the creator uses a series of images to communicate an idea: to describe, to show a point of view, to persuade, to gain power. The more that the creator understands visual language, elements and principles, and has a clear sense of objective and audience, the more effective that visual communication can be.

Gender Issues and Visual Literacy

Looking at visual arts over the centuries, one finds a preponderance of male artists and females as sexual visual objects. Art as a vocation has been overwhelmingly male-dominated, while folk art has been relegated to a minor art form, more likely to be created by women. Thus, students are more likely to see the visual expressions of males than females.

The painting process itself may reflect an artist's life style. An interesting example of this process is the case of Berthe Morisot. An outstanding 19th century painter, Morisot's style changed dramatically after she started having children; her brushstrokes became broader and her images, more abstract. One explanation for this stylistic change is that she no longer had hours of interrupted time to paint, but had to "dash off" paintings when not taking care of her offspring. In contrast, Rubens' majestic room size renditions of historical events illustrate his sizable patronage and the amount of time he had to execute such works. Indeed, it was thought during the 18th century that women were not capable of this genre of painting (Nochlin, 1999).

What are acceptable roles for each gender? Male artists tend to reflect societal mores. Men are more associated with movement, and women are seen more as static objects (Berger, 1977). Women are more likely to be lying down, and males are more likely to stand. One of the reasons that Artemisia Gentileschi was so controversial, beyond her gender, was her portrayal of powerful active women. Even in modern Nepal, women are identified principally in terms of passive mother and wife (Ranjit, n.d.). Other visual "codes" indicate attitudes about gender:

1. Subservient women in the background
2. Submissive expression by women
3. Grasping men vs. women with light touches
4. Accessories of power (e.g., globe, telescope) vs. accessories of virtue (e.g., prayer book)
5. Mainly young women vs. a broad age spectrum of men (Nochlin, 1999).

For students to understand visual images more accurately, they need to know about those gender-linked elements.

Universal design is one approach to providing equitable visual experiences for all students. The original concept of universal design was to address the physical differences of users: for example, speech recognition would enable persons with limited motor ability to input data on the computer; captioned pictures would provide information for the visually impaired. However, universal design also addresses different learning and communication preferences of individuals. One could extend that way of thinking by saying that gender differences should also be considered in designing visual learning activities. Thus, visual images should be comprehensible to both genders. Gender-specific images should be balanced so all students can see a variety of positive role models.

The three topics that follow demonstrate how gender impacts visual literacy.

Architecture

Are buildings gender biased? According to Betsky (1997), architecture has helped define gender lines and sexual roles. In primitive cultures, during menses women were housed in a separate building so they would not contaminate the rest of the population. Betsky asserts that interior design reflects the inner spaces of child-bearing women, and constitutes a way for women to "make a place for themselves in a male-dominated environment." Men, on the other hand, traditionally dealt with the outside world, so their values are reflected in the exterior design of buildings. From "muscular" constructions of civic buildings to the Freudian connotations of skyscrapers, architecture reflects a sense of masculinity, particularly in cities. Even the broad boulevards of major cities are designed to help the military march and conquer. Betsky continues, saying that suburbia is women's "revenge" in that the low-lying homes, winding little streets, and comfortable shopping malls mirror a woman's nurturing persona. Spain (1985) noted that businesses usually put women in open space working environments, and place men in private offices. Even schools are gendered spaces as public and private spaces separate gender-specific activities.

Students can start to think about architecture by considering their own homes and their own rooms. Students can take a photo of their room, and develop a classroom database for content analysis. Then students can take pictures of their homes, and compare the visual images to see if gender-linked patterns emerge. Ask boys to design interiors, and girls to design exteriors. How do students envision their community? Are there environments that girls seldom see, such as skate parks, or that boys don't see, such as nail salons? Have them list those locations, and then get pictures in order to help them see the other side of life.

Children's Literature and Visual Literacy

One of the first formal educational experiences with visual literacy, particularly in libraries, is with children's picture books. For many children, picture books constitute their first "formal" experience with fine art, although the Internet now offers an immediate way to visit art museums and other artistic venues virtually. Librarians and classroom teachers can help students understand story and text by "reading" and interpreting images. Children can learn about the interdependence of textual and visual content, and can appreciate artistic style on its own visually aesthetic terms. The physical structure of the picture book itself also reflects visual elements.

Pre-readers have unique visual literacy learning needs. Image and reality can get mixed up in children's minds. They are likely to think that a realistic (e.g., photographic) image indicates that the image is real; an abstract image implies fantasy. Thus, style gets confused with reality/fantasy. Television producers know this factor, and take advantage of it as they create realistic effects such as talking toys so children will believe in the object and want it for their own. For that reason, adults need to help children distinguish between artistic approach and subject matter. Eric Carle's collage abstractions of butterflies create a whimsical mood but the intent remains to show how butterflies develop. On the other hand, "realistic" renditions of dragons, as in Peter Dickinson's *The Flight of Dragons*, do not make those imaginary subjects authentic. This task actually affirms children's own artwork, which may not be very realistic or technically accurate, but does portray real things (Lacy, 1986).

Other pre-reader visual literacy challenges arise from children's mental development. Children can see visual details very early, which is one reason they delight in Margaret Brown's *Goodnight, Moon,* and the numerous *I Spy* books. On the other hand, children have a hard time discerning the main concept in a visual image, confusing detail with importance. Likewise, they may confuse scale with importance. They may also think that a naturalistic image is "good" and a simplified image is "bad" or poorly done, regardless of compositional or stylistic expertise. Thus, adults should explicitly draw children's attention to each visual element, and show how it contributes to the overall visual experience. Molly Bang's *Picture This: How Pictures Work* (2000) provides a wonderful introduction to visual elements and how they evoke different feelings and connotations. The Art Sense web site (http://www.artsense.net/level2_content.htm) lists picture books that exemplify each art element. Wolf and Levy's Analysis of Art Elements web site (http://www. uwstout.edu/lib/irs/art.htm) provides a detailed list, by art element, of features to look for in picture books.

The physical structure of a picture book itself exemplifies visual elements and principles. How the artist sequences the visual images impacts the story line; indeed, having children predict the image of the following page helps them learn how to read and extrapolate information from a visual image. The Picturing Books web site (http://picturingbooks.imaginarylands.org/) offers a good explanation of each part of such books, and includes visual examples so children can see how structure impacts meaning.

Because picture books comprise children's first reading experiences, the images found therein influence children's perceptions of the world and their own gender roles significantly. Creany's (1990) analysis of the appearance of gender in award-winning children's books found much sexual bias in early titles. Books written in the 1970s featured male characters more often, and both genders were portrayed in traditional, stereotypical roles. Although more females were shown in 1980s books, gender roles remained stereotypical. By the 1990s, the two genders were portrayed more equitably, and folktales, in particular, deviated from stereotypical character portrayals. Thus, adults are encouraged to check copyright dates as they select picture books, and to examine images carefully in light of these gender stereotypes. While older titles should not be dismissed, they ought to be balanced with more current offerings to ensure a balanced picture for youngsters to experience. Older students can conduct visual content analyses in picture books as well as textbooks to discover for themselves what kinds of stereotypes are portrayed over time.

Clip Art

Clip art, ready-made, that can be used without copyright restrictions, has been in use for decades. Dover Publications produces books and digital collections of them. Advertising companies and print media have incorporated clip art, particularly when they cannot afford in-house or contract artists. Now digital collections of clip art exist in basic applications. Students routinely insert them in their papers and presentations. So what's the problem?

On the most basic level, using clip art limits students to the role of consumer, locating and selecting images. Few libraries of clip art have a consistent style, so students often have to mix visual approaches, thus producing a discordant or inconsistent visual product. In effect, these images control student expression rather than enhance it.

Binns and Branch (1995) studied computer clip art images, and found that they include stereotypical signals and gender themes, such as male scientists and female teachers. On the basis of their findings, they made several recommendations relative to using clip art in instruction:

1. Use non-gendered images and labels
2. Create original images
3. Scan images from other sources
4. Look for a broad variety of clip art portraying males and females
5. Contact software companies to advocate for gender-equitable clip art

The most effective solution is creating one's own clip art library. Students then become producers, and make more of their own decisions. Students' own unique styles emerge as they develop a collection of visual images. They develop a sense of ownership and pride in their creations. They also improve observational skills as they try to capture the critical features of a visual stimulus. While some students may decry their lack of artistic skill, especially in comparison to commercial artwork, they can feel good that they are using their own talents and that increased practice can result in better products. This mindset can be applied to the more general issue of plagiarism. Developing clip art can also improve students' technological skill (Meltzer, 2000). With the use of digital drawing and editing tools, students can refine their work more easily than they could have done with traditional drawing tools. Not only can they scan their first mechanical efforts and then manipulate the image, but they can also capture an image using a digital camera, and then edit it into their own clip art.

Libraries and Visual Literacy

The library's environment can set a tone for visual literacy. The general ambiance of the facility needs to entice the user to "see" the library and its resources. Visuals such as posters, plants, and clean lines of furniture ought to model art principles. Displays signal what librarians value in their collections, and can help students link visuals with reading. Lighting itself helps users see and comprehend visual images better. If possible, libraries need desktop lights, wide-spectrum ceiling lighting, and ambient outdoor lighting; these differentiated lighting sources can then support close-vision reading, screen viewing, and long-distance gazing. Likewise, clear, high-profile signage can help users find their way in the library and help them understand the link between signs and content. Production areas for developing visual projects also benefit the library.

Of course, a core function of the library is collection development and management, so students can access and use a wide variety of visual resources: illustrated books, periodicals, videos, 2D art (e.g., photographs, slides, art reproductions), and digital visuals. Libraries can provide equipment (e.g., still cameras and camcorders) and software (e.g., computer-aided design, paint/draw) for students to create their own visuals. Likewise, technology can help students manipulate visual images: video recorders, scanners, and image editing programs.

As a hub of information technology, the library provides visual digital resources as well as aids for becoming visually literate. Visual messages can even be disseminated via the library's computer screen savers, such as an animation version of the Dewey Decimal Classification system (http://www.oclc.org/dewey/resources/screensaver/ default.htm/) Library web portals can promote visual literacy through pictures of the library, staff, and students. Links to visual literacy sites can also stimulate students to learn more about visual literacy on their own.

Librarians can introduce visual literacy issues as early as kindergarten as they share books and digital images. Indeed, traditional book talks can incorporate visuals in several ways:

1. Book jackets can form the basis for a bulletin board "book talk."

2. Scanned illustrations and digitized jackets (copies from web sites such as http://www.amazon.com) can be incorporated into flyers and multimedia presentations.

3. Student-made book "posters" can be the basis for book talks.

4. Images from books can be used to create a card game.

5. Visual "props" can be used in book talks: articles that remind the reader of the story (e.g., rubber duckies for *Make Way for Ducklings*), a flashlight aimed up under the face to create a spooky mood, puppets that tell the story.

6. Paper folding and paper cutting related to stories add another dimension.

7. Book talks can be in the form of mobiles of the characters and significant objects (e.g., *What I Saw on Mulberry Street*).

8. Book talks can be videotaped, broadcast, and "streamed" on the library or school web portal.

Still, visual sources and tools are relatively useless unless students know how to understand and use them. Thus, visual literacy should be part of the library's curriculum — and integrated across the academic domains. Moreover, when librarians instruct — to expressly teach visual literacy or to demonstrate other skills— they can use visual teaching aids such as overheads, posters, and multimedia presentations. In the same vein, librarians can provide students with visual learning aids such as guide sheets, graphic organizers, and visually oriented software programs such as Inspiration or spreadsheet applications with graphing options.

Not only do these aids reinforce visual literacy tools, but they also help the visual learner understand otherwise difficult concepts. Instruction on the presentation end of the research process can include sessions on video production, multimedia assemblage, and web design. Librarians need to make sure that boys and girls take turns with different production roles: camera person, director, editor, layout designer. Particularly since these visual communication channels help students apply their visual knowledge to teach others content in attractive and creative ways, attention to gender optimizes *all* students' opportunities to learn how to communicate fully.

Visual Literacy Exercises

Note: Activities marked with an * are appropriate for elementary grades or include accommodations for younger students; unless otherwise noted, all the activities may be done by middle and high school students.

DO YOU SEE WHAT I SEE?*

Have students each take a photograph of the same setting, such as recess. The images constitute a data set of information. Ask students to describe their own image in terms of what they were trying to convey and how they chose their image. Next, ask students to analyze another person's image; they can also analyze a set of images, in either case, according to their own preferences. Alternatively, the teacher can specify what to look for. Their analyses may be written or shared orally, either at this point, or at the end of the entire activity unit. The intent is to show how personal perspective impacts the images collected, and the images viewed.

Students can then sequence the images, again according to their schema. Ask them to share their thought processes. If their sequencing processes are written in the form of directions, ask students to exchange their directions, and see how well those directions are followed and the extent to which the resultant sequence matches the original sequence. As with the single image, these activities demonstrate how each person develops a storyline differently, and how words work with image. See if chosen images, their analyses, sequencing, and directions differ along gender lines. A good web site that demonstrates how this activity can be developed into a high level pictorial essay is: http://www.readingonline.org/newliteracies/muffoletto/

WISH YOU WERE HERE!*

Send students to a drug store or gift shop that has local postcards, and ask them to decide to what degree the images represent their locale. They can imagine being a tourist: what kind of history, values, and lifestyles are reflected in the images?

Next, ask students to locate images that capture the essence of different locales, and produce postcards with narrative information on the back. Ideally, small groups will develop a collection of narrated postcards for each location. To see if gender enters into the decision-making or writing, create both single and mixed gendered groups; see what differences arise.

HISTORIC ALBUMS*

Ask students to brainstorm how images impart historical information. For a particular time in history, the can list different aspects of those times that might be captured in visual images. The list might include: transportation, clothing, shelter, food, occupations, recreation, human relationships, politics, religion, gender. Pairs of students can find several images for each category. This step may be done in a couple of ways: (1) students have to come to consensus on the images chosen, (2) each student chooses images and then compiles them, comparing the results. Consider single and mixed gender pairings. As they collect their images, they need to describe each one, state its significance, and cite its source. Ideally, students will digitize their images (if the image is from the Internet, that step is simple; otherwise, they can scan the image or take a digital photograph of it) so they can create a digital "album" of their images. The entire class's image collections can be combined to create a single album, multimedia presentation, or web page. An interesting variation is to share the images without the textual information, and find out how much information can be culled from the image alone. A good web site to visit to start this activity is: http://www.csuohio.edu/history/exercise/vle-home.html.

VISUAL AND MATERIAL CULTURE*

Visual culture refers to those images that give information about another culture. In some cases, the images might be considered art by an "outside" culture but be considered a functional tool by the original culture (e.g., basket, Kachina doll, umbrella, boomerang). The analysis of such items also constitutes the term "material culture." Using the following web site on Japanese culture, http://www.culture-at-work.com/jpnlinks.html, request that students draw conclusions (in written or visual format) about Japanese culture. Can any conclusions about gender be drawn? Ask them to determine which artifacts might be defined as art and which might be termed functional tools. Tell them to locate images to capture the essence of other cultures, describing and classifying them, and to create a web site or multimedia presentation of this virtual cultural collection.

YOU ARE WHAT YOU HAVE*

Ask students to identify personal artifacts that reflect a culture and/or time, and to research background information about those artifacts. A good source of information is *Material World,* which is available in print and CD-ROM format.

They can also create simulated rooms (e.g., drawings, models, computer-aided design), either from a public or private sphere, that include images of those artifacts. Ask students to consider how gender impacts what objects are included and how they are placed.

NORMAN ROCKWELL

Suggest that each student locate an image at http://www.nrm.org/eyeopener/. Then, (1) discern what is fact, fiction, opinion for the image; (2) write a justification for his/her stance; (3) write a narrative based on the image. Alternatively, suggest that students conduct a content analysis on how Rockwell portrays females and males. What stereotypes are noted? How do those images change over time? To what extent do the images reflect the values of their time? Ask students to research the period in which the illustrations were done — or the era that Rockwell was trying to represent.

PORTRAITS*

How do male and female features and values display themselves in visual images? Students can conduct content analyses on portraits throughout history. The critical features can be identified by era (e.g., clothing, stance, coloring, etc.) or across time or cultures. Ideally, students will develop a list of features. Some of the leading questions include:

1. Where are they positioned?
2. What is their environment?
3. What objects are associated with them?
4. What clothing are they wearing?
5. What is their expression?
6. What body language is communicated?
7. What gender is the artist?

If different periods of time or different cultures are examined, students can compare their findings across those dimensions.

SHAKESPEAREAN PORTRAIT

Ask each student to choose a character from *MacBeth* or other Shakespeare play. It's best if there are no duplications of characters, although it is possible that students will present different interpretations. Each student will create a portrait of the character for each act, accompanied by quotations that support the rendering. Ask students to discuss visual interpretations of Shakespeare. Discover how Shakespeare describes men and women. It should be noted that some students have difficulty visualizing text, and thus have a hard time comprehending the words, while other students can visualize a character but may have difficulty comprehending the text. Thus, a good approach to this activity is to pair textually and visually proficient students.

MANIPULATING IMAGES

Ask students to locate images of career people, such as dancers, politicians, lawyers, scientists. Alternatively, ask them to locate images of public figures. Using image editing software, ask students to distort the image in order to communicate a point of view. Then request that they exchange their images, with their peer interpreting the visual message.

STYLISH IMAGES

Ask students to locate different visual expressions of the same type of object (e.g., flowers, cities) or concept (e.g., war, loyalty). Production differences can include: style (e.g., photorealism, impressionist, pointillism, expressionist), medium (e.g., collage, serigraph, watercolor, digital photograph), and art technique (e.g., intaglio, spattering, sponge, wax resistance). How does each approach impact the visual's content and connotations?

Next, suggest that students create their own impression of an object or concept, one that they think aligns with the medium, and one that contradicts it. Image editing software works particularly well for this activity. Then ask students to exchange their images so that their peers can interpret the images in light of the production. See if any of the styles have gender connotations.

MORPHING

Ask students to find a variety of male and female faces of different ethnicities and ages. Tell them to morph the faces digitally, noting how features change, and to experiment with different combinations, such as:

1. Old to young female with same skin tone
2. Male to female of different ages
3. Anglo to Asian male of same age

Where are changes most startling — or least noticeable? Which features change the most? What conclusions might one draw when the image is half-way between the two ends? What do these changes reveal about age, gender, ethnicity?

Signal/Symbol Flags*

National flags symbolize a country. Students will research the history and symbolism of national and organizational flags. Pool the information to see which symbols/symbolism (including color) are unique to that country or those that cross borders. To what extent do similar flags (e.g., Paraguay and Netherlands) reflect similar cultures or values?

Next, ask students to create flags that symbolize their family, their class, their grade level, their ethnicity, their gender, their personality.

Maps

Ask students to compare different maps (e.g., political, topographical, historical) of the same area. How do the keys / legends compare? Not only do these keys help the viewer understand the drawing, but they also indicate what is important. Thus, ask students to identify what information is *not* included in the legends, and brainstorm how the critical keys were determined. Alternatively, suggest that students use existing keys / legends — or create their own keys / legends — to produce their own maps of real or imaginary places. The following web site is a good place to start: http://www.k-8visual.info/maps.html

The concept of maps can also be applied to non-geographic entities, such as the human body, a career, or one's mind. What kinds of keys / legends would be appropriate in each case? Ask students to locate and create these non-geographic types of maps. In so doing, see if gender differences arise.

Color and Mood

Color has long been associated with mood, if for no other reason than biology: blood rushes to one's face when one is angry, so red is associated with anger. In medieval history, the "four humors" (sanguine, melancholy, choleric, phlegmatic) were associated with color and moods. The following web sites demonstrate contemporary approaches to color and mood. Select small groups to investigate each site, and report their findings, including whether gender impacts color and mood.

1. http://www.colorgenics.com
2. http://brightworld.com/Cool/Mood_Light.html
3. http://www.weprintcolor.com/moodofcolour.htm
4. http://www.webdesignclinic.com/ezine/v1i3/mood/
5. http://houseandhome.msn.com/decorate/decoratingwithcolor0.aspx
6. http://www.yourneighborhooddoctor.com/color_therapy.html
7. http://www.kiradesign.com/colors.htm
8. http://www.icolormyworld.com/

Works Cited

Bang, Molly (2000). *Picture This: How Pictures Work.* New York: SeaStar Books.

Berger, John (1977). *Ways of seeing.* New York: Penguin.

Betsky, Aaron (1997). *Building sex: Men, women, architecture, and the construction of sexuality.* Arlington, TX: Quill.

Binns, Jane, and Branch, Robert (1995). "Gender Stereotyped Computer Clip-Art Images as an Implicit Influence in Instructional Message Design." 315–324. In Beauchamp, Darrell, Braden, Roberts and Griffin, Robert. (Eds.). *Imagery and visual literacy.* Sugar Grove, IL: International Visual Literacy Association.

Brill, J., Kim, D., and Branch, R. (2001). "Visual literacy defined: The results of a Delphi study: Can IVLA (operationally) define visual literacy?" *Selected Readings of the 31st Annual Convention of the International Visual Literacy Association.* Ames, Iowa.

Clarke, J. (1991). *Patterns of thinking.* Needham Heights, MA: Allyn and Bacon.

Creany, Anne (1990). "The effect of sex role stereotypes on the gender labels children apply to picture book characters." Indiana, PA: Indiana University of Pennsylvania. *ProQuest Dissertations and Theses.* (AAT 9034352).

Eiseman, Leatrice (2000). *Pantone guide to communicating with color.* Cincinnati, OH: North Light Books.

Farmer, Lesley (2004, Jan.) "Using Internet metasites to foster teenage girls' interest in technology." *School Librarianship Worldwide, 10(1–2),* 92–100.

Griffin, Robert, et al. (Eds.) (1996). *Eyes on the future: Converging images, ideas and instruction.* Sugar Grove, IL: International Visual Literacy Association.

Lacy, L. (1986). *Art and design in children's picture books: An analysis of Caldecott Award-winning illustrations.* Chicago: American Library Association.

Meltzer, Bonnie (2000, Mar.). "Cheating the kids." *Library Talk, 13,* 2, 31–32.

Moller, A.P., and Thornhill, R. (1998, Feb.). "Bilateral symmetry and sexual selection: A meta-analysis." *American Naturalist, 151,* 2, 174–193.

Nochlin, Linda (1999). *Representing women.* New York: Thames and Hudson.

Ranjit, S. (n.d.). *How to design attractive and appealing literacy materials for girls and women: Comparisons of successful cases and inadequate cases in terms of visual literacy.* Kathmandu, Nepal: Participatory Rural Appraisal. Retrieved February 3, 2005, from http://www.accu.or.jp/litdbase/pub/dlperson/96SRW/96SRW_03.pdf.

Saettler, Paul (1998, Jan.). "Antecedents, origins, and theoretical evolution of AECT." *TechTrends, 43,* 1, 51–57.

Sousa, David (2001). *How the brain learns.* 2d ed. Thousand Oaks, CA: Corwin Press.

Spain, D. (1985). *Gendered space.* Chapel Hill, NC: University of North Carolina Press.

Stonehill, Brian (1998). *The on-line visual literacy project.* Claremont, CA: Pomona College. Retrieved February 3, 2005, from http://www.pomona.edu/Academics/courserelated/classprojects/Visual-lit/intro/intro.html.

Study art (2005). Rockford, IL: Sanford. Retrieved February 3, 2005, from http://www.sanford-artedventures.com/study/study.html.

Vandergrift, K. (2003). "Color preference and gender research." Princeton, NJ: Rutgers University. Retrieved February 3, 2005, from http://www.scils.rutgers.edu/~kvander/gender_project/bibliography/bibliography1.htm.

8

Aural Literacy

Some literacies are so natural and enduring that they may be overlooked. Consider. What literacy predates written history — and birth? Aural literacy, the ability to identify, interpret, and create meaningful sounds. Being able to tell from which direction a stalking tiger was coming could mean the difference between life and death. Even at day one outside the womb, a child can distinguish between two different songs, and show a preference for one over the other.

Based on such examples, one might conclude that aural literacy is an instinctive skill, like breathing. Parents talk and sing to their children from birth, and teens spend hours chatting and listening to music. However, identifying an action by critical aural features such as pitch, intensity, and tone typically requires explicit training. Students who consider themselves "tone deaf" usually can be taught basic musical skills. English is not a very tonal language, as opposed to Mandarin or Vietnamese, but it still requires the speaker to intonate phrases to communicate accurately, and the listener needs to know those tonal inferences as well. Teachers spend years helping students read with expression; this too constitutes part of aural literacy. Indeed, hearing-impaired students experience difficulty learning to read because orthographic literacy largely depends on orality.

If anything, one might be tempted to say that today's students are less aurally literate than their ancestors. How many students can identify bird calls or sing a ballad? On the other hand, they may distinguish between motor engines and can classify rock music selections into several subcategories. Technology offers many more possibilities for accessing a world of means and means of creating sounds.

About 30 percent of students prefer to learn by listening; in contrast, about 65 percent prefer to learn visually and 5 percent learn kinesthetically. Howard Gardner lists musical intelligence as one of eight or nine multiple intelligences. Much teaching is still conducted orally through lectures and other oral presentations. Aural literacy, as it applies to phonetics, comprises a significant foundation for reading, so all students need to learn this skill set. Additionally, audio is a participatory medium, which requires active attention and imagination, especially as the listener has to "fill in the blanks" mentally. The skills needed to form mental images again helps in reading. Because music listening and performance improves aural and visual memory and improves critical thinking, music as part of aural literacy should be included as a vital part of education in general.

Even though the library is usually considered a print environment, librarians often instruct and share reading orally. More fundamentally, the role of sound can be instrumental in children's reading habits and enjoyment, and deeper understanding and training in aural literacy broadens students' academic foundations and personal life skills. In short, the library can provide a rich "soundscape" and the means to understand its nuances.

What Is Aural Literacy?

How do people make sense out of the cacophony of sound surrounding them: the variegated soundspace? Basically, aural literacy may be defined as the ability to distinguish, process, and deduce meaning from a variety of sounds as well as use them to produce meaningful communication. One may further distinguish between oral literacy, which refers to speech, and aural literacy, which is more closely associated with listening. Auditory skills are usually associated with reading skills, although their elements also apply to non-linguistic sounds, such as auditory awareness and attention, sound localization, auditory memory, and auditory closure (Project Slate, 2002). Musical literacy overlaps this definition since it also deals with non-aural elements of music notation. In contrast, aural literacy can exist independently of the visual world, although visual elements sometimes provide clues to a sound's meaning.

It should be noted from the start that hearing is not listening, and listening is not aural literacy. Hearing is basically a physical phenomenon while listening is a psychological process. Chion (1983) posits four modes of listening, from the most basic to the most complex. He also suggests that a tension exists between concrete experience and abstracting from it, and between subjective and objective response.

1. Hearing: physically being aware of a sound (concrete/subjective)
2. Listening: trying to identify a sound (concrete/objective)
3. Listening actively: choosing to listen, and selecting what to pay attention to (abstract/subjective)
4. Comprehending: finding meaning in what one hears (abstract/objective).

At the least, listening requires mental effort because the sound needs to be remembered long enough to process and interpret it. Particularly as one often needs to discriminate a "relevant" sound from a plethora of other, ambient sounds, active listening is part of aural literacy.

Sounds

Sounds may be categorized in terms of quality, source, and type of information. For example, Brazil (2001) categorizes sound as speech, music, or environmental.

The quality of sound itself may be delineated into specific properties, based on physics and musicology:

1. Frequency or pitch
2. Tempo
3. Pulse and meter (beat)
4. Intensity or volume
5. Texture: complex interaction of sounds
6. Timbre: quality of sound, usually based on how sound is produced

The ElectroAcoustic Research Site at de Montfort University in Leicester (UK) links sound to meaning:

1. Silence: lack of sound
2. Noise: random, chaotic, meaningless sound (although one person's noise may be another person's music or language)
3. Abstract sound: sound which has value as it reflects a quality of sound, such as pitch or tonality
4. Referential sound: sound which refers to another entity, such as the sound of wind or a motor
5. Harmonic: sound that has meaning or value in terms of its musicality or harmonious nature
6. Semantic: sound that conveys information, usually linguistically

Focusing on non-verbal sounds, Laurel (1991) and Loge (1993) suggested five categories of information that can be obtained from listening to sounds:

1. Physical activities (e.g., a passing car, a falling tree)
2. Invisible structures (e.g., a blind person hearing rain hitting different types of plants, a heavy knock on a door)
3. Dynamic changes (e.g., a plane taking off, a runner's breathing over time)
4. Abnormal structures (e.g., an irregular heart beat, engine trouble)
5. Events (e.g., a series of actions such as a fire or a parade)

These categories of sound emphasize the temporal and special nature of sound. In terms of time, sounds start and stop, compose patterns (or lack of them), and can produce a narrative sequence. In terms of space, sounds may be far away or close, stationary or moving through space, isolated or a conglomeration.

In 1969 the Alpha-Numeric System for Classification of Recordings (ANSCR) was introduced to public libraries as a way to classify recordings based on users' information-seeking behaviors; the four major divisions are art music, commercial music, spoken word, and children's material. (Sound effects are listed in a separate class.) This classification reveals the importance that people place on music as a positive listening experience.

Aural Processes

Auditory literacy involves both internal processing of outside sound as well as the ability to create meaningful sound. Aural acuity begins before birth; even fetuses can hear sounds and distinguish them. Developmentally, younger children are more likely to be aural "readers" than visual readers, picking up phonetic cues through active listening.

Clinically, central auditory process skills include:

1. Auditory discrimination: isolating and identifying distinct sounds (phonemes)
2. Auditory figure-ground discrimination: separating significant sounds from background noise
3. Auditory memory: short-term and long-term storage and recollection of sounds
4. Auditory sequencing: reconstructing the order in which sounds occur
5. Auditory blending: putting together phonemes to form words

This set of skills generally applies to linguistic sounds.

Phonetics is the specific study of the production and perception of speech sounds. It is concerned with the sounds of language, how these sounds are articulated and how the hearer perceives them. Phonetics is related to the science of acoustics in that both use the same techniques in the analysis of sound. There are three sub-disciplines of phonetics:

1. Articulatory phonetics: producing speech sounds
2. Acoustic phonetics: studying how speech sounds are physically produced and transmitted.
3. Auditory phonetics: studying how speech sounds are perceived.

Fessenden (1955) developed a seven-part aural processing model, which handles sound more globally.

1. Isolation: giving attention to a specific sound isolated from competing sounds

2. Identification: comparing the sound to past sounds, and identifying it
3. Integration: contextualizing the sound (e.g., hiking, school yard)
4. Inspection: determining more specific characteristics of the sound (e.g., volume, pitch, tone)
5. Interpretation: giving the sound specific context and meaning (e.g., a barking dog may signify that a stranger entered the house)
6. Interpolation: "filling in the blanks" about the sound and its implications (e.g., the stranger is an expected water meter reader)
7. Introspection: deciding whether to act on the sound-based information.

Halle and Stevens (1962) proposed a model based on active listening. Listeners bring their relevant predispositions, their past experiences, their knowledge about the sound's perceived subject matter, and their knowledge of language to the sound event. Based on those factors, listeners make decisions and apply rules to derive meaning quickly. Isolated sounds are combined to form ideas that then constitute a message.

In communicating aurally, students need to use the tools of sound critically. They have to have a message or objective in mind, know the content, determine an effective aural delivery mechanism, locate or produce appropriate sounds (speech, music, or environmental), organize the components, and share the results (Ferrington, 1994).

Bhogal (1996) asserts that oral literacy, by necessity of communication channeling, is always contextualized in terms of real-life situations. Oral communication is also considered a public (or at least social) act. Orality may be considered an ephemeral, dynamic experience; recording of the same constitutes a way to preserve it but does not equal the original transition. Recording decontextualizes the communication.

Gender Issues

Aural literacy is not sex-linked *per se,* but specific factors contributing to its overall competency do correlate with gender. For example, boys prefer aural work to writing, yet girls develop verbal ability earlier than boys. Boys are more likely to speak up in class (mainly because of greater assertiveness), but girls are encouraged to talk more about themselves (Davies, Marsh, & Millard, n.d.). Boys learn more kinesthetically than girls, and tend to learn to play music on their own; girls are more apt to take formal lessons (Olsson, 1997). Another aspect of risk-taking is boys' musical compositional ability, which is reinforced by adults.

Biologically, brain development impacts aural competency. For instance, children with dyslexia (more likely boys) have more difficulty recognizing sounds quickly. When two sound pitches are less than 100 milliseconds apart, boys have a harder time processing the sound (Holmes, 1994). Girls have better directional hearing than boys, and can differentiate sounds better than boys. Girls also process music using both hemispheres of the brain, in contrast to boys who use mainly the right brain. Interestingly, children in general develop music and language ability in the same hemisphere, unlike adults, which points to the significance of the musical features of speech in aural literacy (Koelsch, 2003).

Socially, gender seems to have the most impact in terms of music if for no other reason than perceptions that exist about musical instruments and musical activity. Musical instruments sometimes have gendered connotations, the drum being the most "male" instrument and the flute being the most "female" one. Girls are more likely to be involved in music as children, with boys sometimes perceiving music to be "sissy." However, gender bias against female composers has also been found (Colley, North, & Hargreaves, 2003). Adult musicians are more likely to be male. the underlying assumption is that girls do not take music seriously or do not persevere in their musical training. Sloboda (1993) asserted that the development of musical talent requires practice, support by caring parents and teacher, and intense affective experiences; formal music education often overemphasizes assessment leading to performance anxiety, both of which affect girls more negatively. He also noted that music teachers pushed high-achieving boys more than high-achieving girls.

In terms of "consuming" music, young people spend significant time listening to popular music, which includes strong societal messages about conventional gender role models. Musical "taste" is somewhat gender-linked as well. While studies assert that social gender identification helps form musical tastes (e.g., North & Hargreaves, 1999), the aural characteristics of music can also be said to form taste. Music's texture and tonality can, for instance, invoke different emotions and moods; consider the difference between heavy metal and Christmas carols. Teens use music to enhance their moods, mainly to feel good (Tarrant, North, & Hargreaves, 2000). Interestingly, lonely female teens seek love music while lonely male teens avoid that music (Zillmann & Gan, 1997). In a study of American adolescents' perceptions (North, Colley, & Hargreaves, 2003), jazz was the most sex-typed musical genre, with boys preferring it more than girls; boys were also found to downplay female jazz musicians while girls favored them. Other studies reinforce the jazz gender link, and reveal that girls prefer classical and folk music, while males prefer rock (Zillman & Gan, 1997).

Based on these gender issues, librarians and teachers can provide several interventions to facilitate equitable aural literacy. Additional attention and sensitivity need to be paid to quiet learners' oral skills. Girls, in particular, need to learn assertiveness skills. Free aural expression of emotions should be incorporated into learning activities. Libraries need to provide access to and opportunities for exploration of a wide variety of music genres, musical instruments, composers and performers.

Technology Supporting Aural Literacy

Several technologies are available to help students become aurally literate, via extended access to sounds, means to record sounds, programs to help process aural information, and methods of producing and/or editing sounds. From AM radios to specialized scanners, both commerce and government sources can help students.

Telegraphs, telephones and radios have transmitted sound signals for over a century. Almost all families own some sort of radio, which can cost just a couple of dollars, and telephone (even the homeless often have a cell phone). Thus, children have easy, cheap access to these technologies as a means to listen to—and transmit—meaningful sounds. Libraries circulate audiocassettes, which can be played on machines available for a dollar. For less than $10, mini-recorders can capture thirty seconds to five minutes of sound, offering a portable means for students to identify sounds in their environment as well as tape-record their own voices. Most current computers have built-in recording devices and applications to read text aloud. In short, audio literacy is within the reach of every child, and technology can extend a child's access to sounds worldwide as well as enable everyone to produce and preserve original sounds.

More expensive, MIDI technologies can help students develop auditory skills by creating and editing computer-based music. Music composition also offers a creative outlet for students. Having a keyboard available helps students explore musical sounds. Girls, in particular, need encouragement in this area, especially when such compositions are MIDI-based. At the same time, MIDI technology helps the musically challenged through its pre-set software options, such as quantization, which corrects for sounds that are not input on the beat. At the same time, MIDI technology can help advanced, musically inclined students to edit and orchestrate complex pieces (Ohler, 1998).

For children with special needs, audio technology can compensate for disabilities. The Library for the Blind and Physically Handicapped at the Library of Congress can provide special audiocassette players and audio materials (recordings of selected books and periodicals) free to local libraries, including school libraries, that have eligible users. The organization Recording for the Blind and Dyslexic records and disseminates required textbooks for students. Likewise, federal funding for special education finances state-operated centers that produce and distribute instructional materials to public schools for use by students with disabilities. For example, the California Department of Education's Clearinghouse for Specialized Media and Technology (http://www.cde.ca.gov/re/pn/sm) provides state-adopted textbooks, workbooks, and literature books in Braille, large print, on recordings, and in American Sign Language video books. In addition, several commercial companies sell assistive technology devices that scan and read aloud text. Classroom FM amplification systems consist of a presenter microphone and speaker system so the entire class, or individual students with hearing problems, can hear even soft sounds.

Library Resources

Libraries can provide resources in various formats to help students increase their aural literacy. Here is a beginning list.

1. Non-fiction books: physics, biology, music, speech, broadcasting
2. Audiocassettes; books: unabridged literature; oral/speech performances, music, sound effects
3. Sound CDs
4. Software: This site describes a variety of auditory training and music theory software (http://www.palatine.org.uk/directory/index.php/Music/soft/aur/); ECS Media produces several software programs on music theory and ear training (http://www.ecsmedia.com/products/prodmusic.shtml); Lentine provides trial downloads of more than twenty companies' aural and music training software (http://www.lentine.com/Download%20Page.htm)
5. Internet web sites:
    i.   The University of Washington's web site "Neuroscience for Kids" provides several fun learning activities to help a child build aural acuity. The site also has a tour of the ear, appropriate for high school students (http://faculty.washington.edu/chudler/chhearing.html) http://library.thinkquest.org/3750/hear/hear.html)
    ii. A thinkquest by fifth and sixth graders explains each sense (http://library.thinkquest.org/19537/?tqskip1=1)
    iii. The Soundry, another thinkquest, has several sections covering the process of hearing, the physics of sound, the role of sound in daily life, a timeline about sound-related technology, and an interactive sound "lab" http://kidshealth.org/kid/body/ear_noSW.html
    iv. "Let's hear it for the ear" is a series of articles from Kids Health (http://www.up-to-date.com/saitwebsite/computergames.html)
    v.   This site offers free computer games to build auditory skills (http://www.jpda.net/proj_aural.html)
    vi. Aural Urban Fabric Project provides interactive exploration of spatial narrative through aural perception (http://www.jpda.net/proj_aural.html)
6. Equipment: audio players and recorders, MIDI systems, microphones

Practices To Foster Aural Literacy

Across the curriculum and throughout the library program, librarians can incorporate practices that facilitate aural literacy for all students. The earlier that aural literacy can be introduced, the more impactful that intervention will be on student success.

1. Create a positive soundscape that enables students to focus on their tasks at hand without distraction. While constructive noise can indicate active learning, having a quiet atmosphere or corner can be a welcome respite for some learners.

2. Use chants, song, and raps to build auditory memory and a sense of rhythm; both educators and students can create them.

3. Use rhymes to facilitate memorization — and to build up phonetic awareness.

4. Use different voice timbres, including animal "voices," for recitations or reading out loud.

5. Encourage children, especially boys, to move to sound.

6. Encourage students to check each other's understanding by asking each other questions.

7. Ask students to gather information by interviewing experts.

8. Offer aural-based events such as read-alouds, poetry slams, readers' theater, dramatizations, speeches.

9. Enrich book talks with complementary or reinforcing sound effects and music.

10. Record and archive students' presentations and music performances.

Aural Literacy Exercises

Note: Activities marked with an * are appropriate for elementary grades or include accommodations for younger students; unless otherwise noted, all the activities may be done by middle and high school students.

I Hear You *

Show students diagrams or simulations of the hearing process (e.g., http://www.neurophys.wisc.edu/animations/, http://www.innerbody.com/anim/ear.html). Recreate the hearing process by asking each student to act out one part of the ear. Alternatively, students can recreate the ear drum by following the directions at http://biology.about.com/c/ht/00/07/How_Simulation_Ear_Drum 0962932481.htm

No! No?*

Ask students to practice sound qualities by expressing the same word or phrase in different ways. As starters, try these words:

- No — yes — maybe
- What a surprise — oh, really
- What a doll

Discuss how expression shapes the meaning of words, and ask students to suggest other phrases to try with each other.

Linking sound with linguistics, remind students that punctuation marks serve as notations for expression. Likewise, musical notations help musicians perform expressively.

Seeing Through Your Ears*

Sometimes the familiar can become the unfamiliar when experienced through a single sense. In pairs, have students go to areas in the school where they can pick up distinguishing sounds (e.g., science lab, gym room, cafeteria). One student is blindfolded, and a sighted student guides her/him to the spot, recording the blindfolded student's experiences. Alternatively, the blindfolded student can record distinctive sounds using a mini-recorder. Ideally, two sets of pairs (one male, one female) will explore the same areas so they can compare experiences afterwards. With the total class, ask pairs to share their sound experiences, and identify the critical sounds that capture the essence of each area.

Guess The Sound*

Sounds gain meaning when contextualized. On the other hand, an event or location can be captured by a single sound (e.g., fire engine or ambulance siren). Suggest that students use mini-recorders to record distinctive sounds in their homes or neighborhoods. Afterwards, they can play the sound in class and ask the rest of the students to guess the sound and surrounding. Find out if boys and girls choose different kinds of sounds, or have different abilities in identifying sounds.

News Broadcast *

Assign students the job of analyzing news broadcasts on different radio stations; they can also analyze television broadcasts with the monitor screen off. Students can brainstorm what features to listen for. Sample lists should include:

• Content: topic, length of coverage, point of view, sequence, gender of newscaster
• Commercial elements: advertisements (content and length), transitions between stories
• Sound qualities: pitch, timbre, tempo, dynamics/volume, articulation, texture.

Whenever possible, analysis should be done in light of the sound qualities. That is, how does the newscaster's voice and other ambient sound impact the listener's perception of the news story? How do different stations cover news? What differences emerge between radio and television sound treatment? What role does gender play in news broadcasting, such as the choice or placement of story; do newscaster voices have a lower pitch or different timbre than typical males and females?

This activity may be done in same-sex or mixed-sex small groups, preferably of four students. One group member should act as an observer to check group dynamics and participation relative to gender.

As an extension, students can research how newscasters are trained and hired. To what extent is voice training part of the process?

Class Radio*

Ask students to develop a radio show or news broadcast using an audiocassette or computer to record their production. Encourage students to try out different voice qualities and dynamics, and to tape each time they try so they can review their efforts. While it is a good idea for students to keep track of their work, they may want to erase their efforts until they achieve broadcast quality. One option is to keep a master tape, and edit a final version. Remind them to consider what role gender plays in terms of content or process.

Experimenting Aurally*

One of the best ways for students to understand sound and its transmission is to conduct their own experiments. To increase their sense of responsibility, ask them to locate student-appropriate experiments about hearing, speech, and sound. Ideally, each small group will focus on one aspect of the total topic at hand. Students will conduct the experiment, and then demonstrate the findings to their peers. Students might consider presenting information using *only* sound — or any sense *except* sound. They can also set up the experiment for their peers, which helps them crystallize their own learning.

Recording, Recording

Sound production has become much more complex and varied with advances in technology. Students can research and compare different technologies used in sound processing (e.g., digital recording, Dolby, computer-based sampling, synthesizers, sound mixers). Alternatively, each student can research one stage of sound production, and then jigsaw findings to create a multimedia presentation on creating audio products (e.g., CDs, DVDs, film, audiotapes, digital sound files).

Story Sounds*

Ask students to identify sounds to accompany picture books, and then locate or produce the appropriate sounds. Optionally, students can share their sounds for their peers to identify in the referenced story. Ideally, one boy and one girl will find and incorporate sounds independently, and then compare their work.

ORAL HISTORY*

Interviews are an excellent way to help students listen actively and responsively. Teach the class basic interviewing skills, and request that they develop a set of relevant interview questions. Next, let them practice these skills in interview simulations, and critique their peers' efforts. Teach students how to use audiotape recorders correctly, and then ask them to tape an interview with their family or community members, asking questions about local history. Alternatively, students can interview in pairs, taking turns asking questions and taking notes; ideally, students will interview in mixed-sex pairs. In class afterwards, they can compare their experiences and conclusions. As always, ask them to reflect on possible gender impact: interviewing process, content dealing with gender, gender-based interpretations of history or the interviewing process.

AURAL DIARY*

Students can create sound diaries of a typical day, either a school day or weekend. Then they can conduct a content analysis of their sounds, preferably asking both a girl and a boy to analyze the same content independently. Each pair can compare their analyses, and then share their findings with the class.

POETRY SLAM

Poetry offers a unique opportunity for expressive writing and reading. Follow the guidelines at http://www.poetryslam.com/. To lower anxiety, ask students to perform in class. Audiotaping the slam can help students critique their own efforts. Also ask students to reflect on the role that gender potentially plays in terms of content choice and delivery style.

Works Cited

Berman, S. (2003). "Alpha–Numeric System for Classification of Recordings (ANSCR)." Vancouver, CA: University of British Columbia. Retrieved February 3, 2005, from http://www.slais.ubc.ca/courses/libr517/03–04-wt2/projects/TP/website/alpha.htm.

Bhogal, B. (1996). "Discussion about orality and literacy based on Murray Jardine's *Sight, sound, and epistemology: The experiential sources of ethical concepts.*" JAAR, 44(1). Retrieved February 3, 2005, from http://cedm.derby.ac.uk/multifaith/images/content/seminarpapers/discussionaboutorallityandliteracy.htm.

Brazil, E. (2001). *Cue points: An examination of common sound file formats.* Limerick: University of Limerick.

Central auditory processing skills. (2004). "ThinkQuest for Tomorrow's Teachers." Retrieved February 3, 2005, from http://t3.preserve.org/T0300887/page3.html.

Chion, Michael (1983). *Guide des objets sonores.* Paris: Buchet/Chastel.

Colley, A., North, A., and Hargreaves, D. (2003, April). "Gender bias in the evaluation of new age music." *Scandinavian Journal of Psychology, 44,* 2, 125–31.

Davies, Julia, Marsh, Jackie, and Millard, Elaine (n.d.). "Differently literate: Some ways of working in schools to promote equal access to the language curriculum for boys and girls." Sheffield, UK: University of Sheffield.

Ferrington, Gary (1994, Autumn). "Keep your ear-lids open." *Journal of Visual Literacy, 14*, 2, 51–61.

Fessenden, Seth A. (1955). "Levels of Listening — A Theory." *Education, 75* (January 1955), pp. 288–291.

Green, Lucy (1997). *Music, gender, education.* New York: Cambridge University Press.

Halle, M., and Stevens, K. (1962). "Speech recognition: A model and a program for research." *IRE Transactions on Information Theory, IT-8*, 155–159.

Holmes, Bob (1994, Aug. 27). "Fast words speed past dyslexics." *New Scientist*, 1010.

Koelsch S. et al. (2003 July 1). "Children processing music: Electric brain responses reveal musical competence and gender differences." *Journal of Cognitive Neuroscience, 15*, 5, 683–93.

Lamb, R., Dolloff, L., and Howe, S. (2002). "Feminism, feminist research, and gender research in music education." In Colwell, R. and Richardson, C. (Eds.). *The new handbook of research on music teaching and learning.* New York: Oxford University Press.

Landy, L., and Atkinson, S. (2004). "EARS: ElectroAcoustic Research Site." Leicester, UK: De Montfort University. Retrieved February 3, 2005, from http://www.mti.dmu.ac.uk/EARS/

Laurel, Brenda (1991). *Computers as theater.* Reading, MA: Addison-Wesley.

Loge, Kenneth P. (1993). *Audio: More than meets the eye*, AECT conference presentation, New Orleans.

Mulvaney, Eileen (1998). "Learning to be audio-literate." 1998 Conference Proceedings. Northridge, CA: Center On Disabilities Technology And Persons With Disabilities Conference. Retrieved February 3, 2005, from http://www.csun.edu/cod/conf/1998/proceedings/csun98_037.htm

North, Adrian, Colley, Ann, and Hargreaves, David (2003). "Adolescents' perceptions of the music of male and female composers." *Psychology of Music, 31*, 139–154.

North, Adrian, and Hargreaves, David. (1999). "Music and adolescent identity." *Music Education Research, 1*, 75–92.

Ohler, Jason (1998, March). "The promise of MIDI technology." *Learning & Leading with Technology, 25*, 6, 6–10.

Olsson, Bengt (1997). "The social psychology of music education." In Hargreaves, David and North, Adrian (Eds.). *The social psychology of music.* New York: Oxford University Press.

Project Slate (2002). *Listening, aural reading, and live reader skills.* Lubbock, TX: Texas Tech University. Retrieved February 3, 2005, from http://www.educ.ttu.edu/slate/Braille%20Framework/Listening.htm

Sloboda J. (1993). "Musical ability." *Ciba Foundation Symposium Proceedings, 178*, 106–13.

Tarrant, M., North, A., and Hargreaves, D. (2000). "English and American adolescents' reasons for listening to music." *Psychology of Music, 28*, 166–173.

Zillman, Dolf, and Gan, Su-lin (1997). "Musical taste in adolescence." In Hargreaves, David and North, Adrian (Eds.). *The social psychology of music.* New York: Oxford University Press.

9

Media Literacy

Every day young people encounter mass media, sometimes without their conscious awareness, as radios and televisions blare their messages at home and in public. Mass media, on the other hand, are very conscious of their messages; they are trying to influence their public in order to gain power or profit. When one considers that today's children spend more time watching TV than attending school, there it is little wonder how mass media influence what they know and do.

Mass media inform and uncover. They entertain and challenge. So they should not be blackballed as the enemy. However, their audience needs to be aware of their intent in order to understand that information accurately and know how to respond to it.

Librarians play a key role in helping young people learn how to experience mass media, or mass communication as it is sometimes called, in a critical manner. Librarians can help youth develop the skills to produce their own messages as they seek to build their own influence.

What Is the World of Media for Today's Students?

Television, film, radio, newspapers and magazines, and commercial electronic sources are ubiquitous for today's students, who seem to have been "born with a chip." The obesity crisis among youth in the United States arises at least partly from hours of sitting with electronic gadgets. Parental guidance in mass media viewing generally fades by the time adolescence hits. And what do those young people watch, particularly on television? Girls tend to favor teen-centric soap operas. Boys tend to prefer sports, comedy, and "shows with shock value" (Marlo, 2004, 42). Poker shows have become a major hit for this audience. Reflecting teens' love of music, music videos remain popular with both sexes. Along with adult Americans, youngsters get most of their news from the media. Although the Internet now outranks television as the preferred source of entertainment for teenagers, this age group constitutes a vital market niche for television and film producers; of course, it should be noted that U. S. and European teens now outspend adults on the Internet: $10.6

billion predicted for 2005, according to Jupiter Corporation. For this reason if for no other, students need to be savvy media consumers. Mass media can have even more serious personal repercussions though; young people who watch television shows containing sexual activity *or even "just" sexual talk,* are more likely to become sexually active themselves at an earlier age. Researcher Collins (2004) recommends that youth learn about the risks of sexual behavior from parents and other knowledgeable, caring adults.

What Is Media Literacy?

Media literacy can be easily confused with multimedia literacy: the ability to understand a variety of media. In today's parlance, mass media has been defined as "a new expanded view of traditional literacy which acknowledges and includes the role and impact of mass media." (Aspen Leadership Conference on Media Literacy, 1992) The Center for Media Literacy has developed core concepts relative to media messages:

- All media messages are constructed.
- Media messages are constructed using a creative language with its own rules.
- Different people experience the same message differently.
- Media have embedded values and points of view.
- Media messages are constructed to gain profit and/or power.

The critical features are the purposeful means and end of the production.

Even though young people "get" the messages that mass media send, they may be unaware of the underlying agendas. Youth respond to the *language* that mass media use: arresting images, fast-paced scenes, clever word play. They may get so caught up in the delivery of the message that they may miss the message itself *on a conscious level,* but may fall prey to the underlying objective, which is to buy a product or support a cause.

How to Interpret Media Messages

When examining media messages, people need to consider:

- The process by which the message is made
- The content of the message
- The framework of the message
- Production value of the message

These factors work together to create a strongly contextualized message. Often messages are so seamlessly interwoven that the audience is not aware of them at all, and may be unwittingly influenced by them. When those messages encourage children to smoke or to exploit others, then the harm done by ignorance can be significant.

All mass media follow a general communications model, which differs significantly from interpersonal communication. However, each medium has unique features that distinguish how that process is implemented.

COMMUNICATIONS MODEL

The classic communication process model flows thusly:

1. A person creates an idea.
2. A person expresses that idea explicitly using...
3. ...a communications channel (e.g., voice, writing, photo).
4. Another person receives the idea via the communications channel. (Silverblatt & Finan, 1999)
5. The other person *may* communicate back to the idea's originator.

When the cycle is completed, the original person may modify the idea based on the receiver's feedback. Communication is said not to have occurred if no one receives the idea / message. Indeed, some communications experts assert that communication does not occur until the process comes full circle. A dialog or conversation may be considered the epitome of communication, particularly when each person is building on what the other person is saying.

Mass communication's process differs in a couple of significant ways. The flow begins as follows:

1. A communications channel is created (e.g., radio, newspaper) by an individual or corporate body.
2. The owner of the channel looks for ideas/content to "fill" the channel. Typically, the owner looks for people who have ideas.
3. The idea is shaped so it can be transmitted using the communications channel.
4. Another person receives the idea via the communications channel.
5. The other person *may* communicate back to the idea's originator.

When the cycle is completed, the original person may modify the idea based on the receiver's feedback. This last part can be very problematic, depending on the goal of the owner of the communications channel. If the goal is to make a profit, then the idea/message itself might be less important than selling space or airtime. As long as the *buyer* likes (or doesn't object to) the message, *and* the audience/

receiver buys the product or message, then the owner of the channel may well be satisfied.

What happens when the receiver does *not* like the message? If the receiver links the message with the buyer, and decides not to buy the product, then the buyer may decide to stop paying for access to the communications channel. Then the channel owner has to decide whether to change the idea/message or look for another buyer. Simultaneously, the receiver may give the channel owner feedback about the idea, which the owner may act upon or not. The deciding factor is usually the buyer, not the receiver.

This latter scenario plays out in another way. If the buyer doesn't like the message, but the receiver *does*, chances are that the channel owner will either: (1) find another buyer, or (2) find another message. In either case, the channel owner will consider the buyer seriously. Where advertising is involved, audience/receiver satisfaction *alone* is usually important but not sufficient; the advertiser is often the lynchpin. In terms of movies, profit-making typically drives decision-making, so, again, if audiences like a movie but few view it, then the film company might try to market it better or distribute it more widely — or the company might decide not to make that kind of movie again for a while and look for a more lucrative genre. Thus, the most important type of receiver feedback is often financial. Money talks.

In sum, the idea might be less important than the motive. An idea or message might die, the originator of the idea might be tossed out, but the communications channel needs to survive.

To give mass media their due, other goals besides profit-making exist. They may want to express an idea, describe a condition, instruct, exchange information, persuade, or perform.

As youth get involved in the mass communication process, they need to ascertain that media's intended goal or function. What makes that task difficult is that a particular medium may have both an overt and a covert agenda. For instance, televising a beauty contest may recognize outstanding young women, but that broadcast is likely to include advertisements for beauty products and communicate an underlying message about the importance of body image, which can subtly affect girls. In other cases, the message may be unclear, as in a movie that has a confusing plot. When tobacco companies show anti-smoking public service announcements, their reason may be based more on complying with a legal decision (as when a diseased smoker successfully sues them) than on discouraging youth from starting a smoking habit; the message in that case may actually be competing or conflicting.

MEDIA CHARACTERISTICS
    As youth examine each mass medium, they need to consider the format itself: its critical features, its influence on communication strategy, its effect on communication style, and on content.

Print. Print is a tangible, relatively permanent medium. It can be considered quite efficient because, while it is portable, it allows in-depth textual and visual information that can be accessed quickly and flexibly. It also can describe internal states of consciousness. Print is a primary, direct experience for the reader. It requires interactivity, which also offers some user control (e.g., pacing). Its dissemination is deliberate, and may involve several layers of review and editing.

Photography. Photography is essentially a visual experience that is relatively "instant," particularly relative to digital photography. It often has a lifelike quality, and may be evocative because the images remind the viewer of other experiences. That same feature demonstrates that both creator and viewer may have different perspectives, and, thus, may interpret the image differently. Photography is disseminated in a variety of ways: informally among a group during some event, displayed formally at an exhibit, reproduced through the print dissemination process, stored and shared via optical disc, and broadcast via telecommunications. Likewise, quality control varies greatly.

Radio. Radio is an aural experience that is nearly ubiquitous these days, serving as background atmosphere. It requires hearing, listening, and imagination. The creator of radio controls the pacing, and dissemination centrally from a separate space; still, the process can be accomplished in real time, instantaneously.

Film. The critical feature of film is movement. Thus, it is most effectively used to capture movement and processes. Film is primarily a public experience that may require a public space. Because it usually requires a dark room to see it, film tends to evoke a quiet communal spirit. While a product of collaboration, film exhibits a certain unrelenting nature because the creator controls the image and determines the pace. And, even though some audiences decry the quality of some productions, film usually undergoes great review and is deliberately disseminated.

Video. Video resembles film in terms of its ability to capture movement even though it is physically different, utilizing magnetic or electronic signals. Today, video is used both in film and television. In its digital form, it is also incorporated in telecommunications. Video may be created instantly, capturing a fleeting personal moment, or it can be constructed professionally using a large team of specialists. Likewise, review and dissemination may be accidental or very deliberate.

Television. TV, like film and video, combines sight and sound. Indeed, film and video are transmitted via television. In the U. S. television has become the main leisure activity, although 21st century teenagers rate the Internet higher than TV. More families own TVs than refrigerators, and, like radio, television is nearly ubiquitous. Both television and radio are often turned on to provide subliminal background sound as much as to serve as an information or entertainment source. Unlike first-run movies, though, television is basically an in-home experience where there is a sense of intimacy. Moreover, viewers sometimes develop a personal dynamic with television characters (e.g., Lucille Ball's pregnancy, *M*A*S*H* fan clubs, furor over who killed J. R.). Even though schools introduced television in the 1960s and cable stations are required to have an educational channel, television has not become a mainstay in most classrooms. On the other hand, *The Simpsons* has become *lingua franca* for teachers to use in explaining some universal quality.

Telecommunications. The most critical feature of telecommunications is digital communication, both one- and two-way, in private as well as public environments. With the advent of the World Wide Web, graphical, sound and video elements can be easily transmitted synchronously and asynchronously. Accessing telecommunications messages requires Internet connectivity and a service provider, along with the personal ability to receive the information through the senses. This communication channel can be disseminated with little review or quality control, although the established mass media industry goes to great lengths to provide high-quality and convincing content.

MEDIA COMMUNICATOR

In tracing the process of mass communication, young people need to look at the originator of the communication.

• Who owns the communications channel? Is it a profit or not-for-profit group? To whom or what do they owe their allegiance or financial support?

• Who owns the production? Is it a public or private institution? Is the production subcontracted or done in-house? What influence does the producer have on the owner?

• What are the demographics of the producers? What interest groups do they represent?

• How does the originator affect the content and perspective of the message? To what extent do originators foster their own values—can they offer alternative views in support of larger issues?

THE AUDIENCE

Mass media know the importance of their audiences, and try to find out as much as possible about them in order to impact them to the greatest degree possible. Youth would do well to make a conscious effort to learn as much about those efforts to ascertain the needs and desires of audiences.

As they create a message, mass communicators usually have an audience in mind. They shape the message to impact their audience on both an intellectual and emotional level. Young people can learn about both the originator and the audience when they evaluate a message. That identified audience is expected to respond to that message in a predictable manner, which young people should also discern. Because those responses are usually shaped by the audience's values, perspectives, and experiences, young people should try to decipher those attitudes in order to understand the message they too are experiencing. The choice of audience impacts the strategy, style, and content of the information. Particularly with controversial issues, messages are carefully constructed. Take, for example, birth control, gun control, and legalization of marijuana. How might the mass media craft their message about abortion if they target a Catholic father as opposed to a teenage girl rape victim?

THE CONTEXT

Ultimately, all information is contextual. Is a "1" good or bad? If you are #1 Hertz, that's good; if you're 1 on a scale of 1 to 10, that's bad. For both the originator and the target audience, context is vital, and helps shape the experience and the reaction.

Messages may convey an historical moment or value. As young people look at this information, they need to decipher what the message says about that period in time, and the degree to which that message is accurate. Obviously, the more that youth learn about history, the better equipped they are to critique those messages. They can also look at historical messages to determine the extent to which these messages represented the values of those times and how they impacted their contemporaries, such as Leni Riefenstahl's film about the 1936 Olympics or Thomas Paine's broadside *Common Sense.*

Messages are also culturally defined. They may reflect, reinforce, inculcate, or shape culture's values, attitudes, behaviors, and myths. How does the Super Bowl reflect the values of manhood, sports, and the United States, for instance? In addition, each message comes from a particular world view or perspective. How does that mind set reflect a specific demographic? Does it reinforce stereotypes, attitudes, and hierarchies? Does it foster certain psychological or physical controls, particularly as they relate to gender, ethnicity, age, or class? What world view did the late TV series *Sex and the City* demonstrate? How does that contrast with the TV series *Married with Children* or *The Bill Cosby Show?*

Structure also impacts the context of a message. For instance, the ownership pattern is likely to determine how messages are produced: top-down, collaboratively, by specialization. Moreover, when communications channels are owned by conglomerates, the variety of messages may be limited. Such ownership patterns can impact the context, particularly if products are being cross-promoted. The government also impacts the context. Regulations about "fair and balanced treatment" and the requirement to provide public programming in television broadcasting can offer more open communication. The Patriot Act, on the other hand, might limit coverage of certain topics. Issues of obscenity also impact messages. How people view these regulations may well depend on their own agendas.

THE FRAMEWORK

Most mass media use an operational "language" to communicate. These protocols become expectations on the part of the audience. Children are taught these predictable norms when introduced to print. Most literature, for instance, is expected to have a title, a beginning, a middle, and an end, with an underlying plot. Genre writing, such as romance and mystery, typically follows conventions in character, plot, and setting. This framework applies to film and television almost directly, although the "language" is largely visual. Newspapers and magazines have their own protocols of layout and content, including advertising. For instance, the right side of the page and the top half of the page get more attention than the left side and bottom half in English publications. An article is more likely to be read if placed first or last rather than towards the back. Color attracts more than black-and-white. Television news and variety shows visually repeat the same placement values.

Realizing the power of these frameworks, or conventions, mass media can exploit them to persuade their audiences. For example, Rod Serling wanted to explore social issues, but found it hard to get financial backing or mass media support. However, when he couched those social concerns in the language of science fiction or horror, then he was able to convey his message, albeit indirectly. Trekkies assert that the world would be a much better place if the ideals reflected in *Star Trek* were implemented in contemporary society. Increasingly, advertisements are using formulaic storylines to sell their products: romance — or sex — blossoms in coffee and beer ads, for example. Even though the conclusion may be illogical — e.g., that Coca-Cola will bring world peace and harmony — mass media can use such frameworks to "set up" the audience, have them suspend disbelief, and maybe, just maybe, buy the message.

PRODUCTION VALUES

Words are value-laden, and the creator of an idea should choose them carefully to convey the intended meaning clearly. Values play a significant role in the use of mass media as well as the channel for the message. Each process can, in effect, promote a certain perspective or bias.

These values are most clearly understood when considered in light of film production. Even though film is the result of complex collaboration and coordination, the final product needs to present a unified message for it to be effective. How visual and sound elements are edited together reflect careful decision-making. When one considers how much more footage is shot than is finally used, what is ultimately omitted may say as much about a film's message as the material that was included in the final version. How each scene is directed and shot impacts the total picture. Moreover, the sequencing of each scene shapes the final message.

Within each scene are several elements of filmatic language, each of which conveys an idea and a value.

• *Color.* Warm colors (e.g., yellow, orange) draw the audience in and excite them, as opposed to cool colors (e.g., blue, purple) that distance them. Contrasting colors, such as black and white, add drama and intensity. Nowadays, a black-and-white film may convey a sense of the past or a sense of seriousness.

• *Lighting.* What is the source of light: natural or artificial, above (sun) or below (fire), a single candle or the sun? Is there a single source of light — suggesting a single source of inspiration? Each of these components shapes the message. How bright is the lighting? While light usually connotes good, and darkness connotes evil, harsh light can connote rigidity and soft candlelight can conjure a sense of romance.

• *Shapes.* Cartoons are a great way to examine shape for meaning. Villains usually have rigid, sharp angles and edges; the hero is usually more defined by curves. Artificiality is typically conveyed through angular shapes (think of science fiction), while natural settings use rounded, softer shapes.

• *Scale.* Want to make a woman look vulnerable? Show her as a small figure in a big setting. Want to show a person in power? Have the face fill the screen. Epics are easy to identify: they use a cast of thousands and huge, open stage sets or open country. In contrast, an intimate story may be told within the confines of a small room.

• *Relative position.* How people are positioned in a setting can show their relationship; enemies often face each other from across the room or screen while buddies stand next to each other far away from the rest of the crowd. People in the background are considered less important than those who are "stage front." Typically, a "chick flick" will feature the women and the guys will stand in back or off to the side; a teen film will push the parents back into a corner.

• *Angle.* When the camera is positioned high, looking down on the scene, the character seems insignificant. When the camera looks up to a person, it visually mirrors the psychological idea of respecting a person. A camera angle that is off to the side may connote distance or deceit.

• *Movement.* Contrast a car chase to a stroll in the park; one focuses on action, and the other probably focuses on human relationships. The pace of a film likewise cues the viewer about its genre, comic or dramatic. Movement may be said to have a rhythm as well, usually perceived in terms of scenes or episodes. The film *Babe* presents a good example of a rhythm that reminds one of a series of chapters, something out of a children's storybook. Movement also has direction. "Normal" movement usually reflects the direction of writing, so when a character in an English movie moves left, the viewer can expect something out of the ordinary. On a broader scale, when a film's movement is inconsistent or illogical, the audience tends to feel uncomfortable, such as in the film *Memento*.

• *Point of view.* Who is telling the story? That perspective influences how the audience reacts. *Rashomon* is the classic example of the significance of viewpoint. A message about drugs from a parent's viewpoint probably differs from a message using a teen's perspective. When slasher films started to be shown from the viewpoint of the murderer, audiences became unnerved — or shockingly engaged.

• *Sound.* In a thriller, one expects music that is played in a minor key as well as sharp, sudden noises. Comedy usually has light, "sparkly" music and sound. Whenever the shark in *Jaws* was about to attack, ominous music cued the audience just in time. So accustomed are audiences to music in film that they often do not even realize that it is playing in the background. Other ambient sound conveys the film's atmosphere — a bustling city or a restful country home; sound can also provide subtle information about the setting, such as whether we are in medieval Japan or contemporary Rio. Even the sound of dialogue provides cues about the message and its values; quiet conversation may connote intimacy while formal diatribes may connote power struggles. Some filmmakers use those conventions to mislead the audience, playing lilting music just before a murder, for example, to heighten the unexpected nature of the event.

• *Performance.* Each character exemplifies a set of ideas and values through costume, make-up, gestures, voice, and style of delivery. Contrast Carol Burnett and George Burns, Clint Eastwood and Jim Carrey, the Wicked Witch of the West and the Good Witch. A strong performance demonstrates how the whole is greater than the sum of its parts.

When these elements are integrated seamlessly, they can convey a powerful message and a strong value. Commercials serve as connotative "jewels" of filmatic language, and their influence can be measured by the millions of viewers who watch the Super Bowl in order to see the latest commercials. It is amazing how strong a message can be conveyed in just thirty seconds! It has been said that Nixon lost the 1960 election because of his poor "performance" in the televised debates — in stark contrast to charismatic Kennedy. Thus, the values that under-gird mass media messages should not be under-estimated.

Teaching Media Literacy

Mass media play a significant role in today's society, influencing millions of people daily. Even when one is not searching for information or looking for a message, mass media permeate our environment. Young people need to consciously and critically analyze and evaluate mass media messages, and then decide their response step. This reflective process helps youth stop the stimulus-impulse cycle so they learn to think before they act.

The Center for Media Literacy posits five key questions that people should ask when examining a mass media message:

• Who created the message?
• What techniques were used to attract your attention?

• How might different people experience the message differently from you?
• What values, lifestyles, points of view are represented or omitted?
• Why was this message sent?

It should be noted that gender issues arise in the context of each question.

• Who owns the media channels; it is usually men; what functions are done primarily by women and by men?
• What media images have sexual overtones? What message might attract one gender over another?
• How might the experience of media differ between boys and girls?
• What values, lifestyles, and points of view favor one gender over another, or restrict the acceptable images for men or women?
• What gender-linked agendas might the media have?

In short, gender comprises a significant factor in the production and dissemination of mass media messages as well as in reception and actions on the part of the audience. The more that students can explore these issues, and see each other's point of view, the better able they will become to interpret and act upon media messages in a critical fashion. Their own creative expressions can also become less gender-biased and more gender-enriched.

Library media specialists have unique skills to help young people in this process because they evaluate and work with all kinds of information in various formats. While media literacy might first be considered out of the range of school libraries because that skill is usually linked with TV and film not found in most library collections, librarians need to remember that print is a mass medium. In terms of elements of motion, video has been part of school library holdings for decades. Moreover, the web brings a whole new dimension to the concept of mass media. It might be more accurate to say that mass media have not been integrated well into traditional curricula, but have certainly had an impact on political decision-making, controversial issues in science, creative expression, and physical and mental well-being.

The easiest way to start teaching media literacy is to show a well-known commercial image and ask students to explain it and share their feelings about it, guiding them with questions. As they provide answers, librarians can fill in conceptual gaps. This first activity can be used as a diagnostic tool to determine what students know and perceive about mass media. At that point, critical media analysis can be demonstrated so students can see how to become critical media consumers.

As much as possible, librarians need to provide a learning structure for inquiry-based learning so students can become aware for themselves how media work and influence them. They should also be given opportunities for creating their own messages.

Mass media literacy fits well under the umbrella of information literacy.

• *Identifying a purpose.* Students can identify media's purpose, and also identify their own informational tasks.
• *Developing a strategy.* Students can identify media's strategy, and also identify how they will research media-based messages.
• *Locating sources.* Students can find sources that match their needs—or media's objectives.
• *Evaluating sources.* Students can assess the quality and relevance of media sources, and discern how media assess what sources to use to create their message.
• *Comprehend and interpret sources.* Students can identify main ideas, accuracy, authenticity, point of view, facts vs. opinions, and strength of argument.
• *Use information.* Students can use media for their own purposes, and analyze how media use information.
• *Share information.* Students can use media to communicate information, and observe how media disseminate their information.

Teaching media literacy is more powerful when linked with curriculum. Here are some examples:

• *Language arts:* different vocabulary and tone in alignment with an intended message and target audience; alignment of text and visual messages; use of language in propaganda; journalistic approaches and objectives
• *Social studies:* use of propaganda in history; use of media in politics; businesses' use and impact of mass media; psychology and sociology of mass media; cultural connotations of media; use of media to portray history
• *Science:* use of media to teach science; science used in media production
• *Mathematics:* statistics related to mass media; mathematics used in media production; mass media economics
• *Health/physical education:* impact of mass media on body image, physical fitness, health, and sports; use of mass media on sports and health-related businesses
• *Arts:* esthetics of mass media; visual language; mass media's use of art; use of photo and video editing software to share and modify media messages

As librarians collaborate with classroom teachers to design learning activities, they can draw upon a rich collection and access to sources worldwide.

Librarians can also help students become media literate in other ways as well:

• Create annotated posters or advertisements showing media elements
• Develop pathfinders and bibliographies on mass media
• Lead group discussions on books dealing with mass media (e.g., *The Locust,*

The Amazing Adventures of Kavalier and Clay, Where the Girls Are, Nothing but the Truth)
   • Lead group discussions about mass media as it is portrayed in film (e.g., *The Front Page, Broadcast News, The Player, Day for Night, Groundhog Day, Medium Cool, The Candidate, The Truman Show, Network, Quiz Show, Zelig, Tunnelvision)*
   • Host guest speakers from the media industry
   • Advise video and anime/manga clubs, particularly as they create products.

One of the key concepts in media literacy is the idea that people experience media differently. Librarians must make it a point to help students see how mass media address issues of gender — and how gender shapes the experience of mass media. Topics need to engage both girls and boys — and also underline possible preference for either gender. The language of media should be examined to see if it has different connotations for boys than for girls. Librarians need to incorporate different learning styles as they introduce mass media concepts: active, reflective, concrete and abstract. They need to provide opportunities for both individual and collaborative learning. Groups can be arranged sometimes by gender so students can become more aware of how gender affects learning processes. In each case, librarians need to make sure that students are aware of those gender issues, that they process their own experiences, and draw conclusions that they can transfer to everyday life in their own decision-making.

Media Literacy Exercises

Note: Activities marked with an * are appropriate for elementary grades or include accommodations for younger students; unless otherwise noted, all the activities may be done by middle and high school students.

THE FLOW OF INFORMATION*
   Students draw a flowchart tracing the creation of a mass media product. Then pairs compare their flowcharts. Elementary students can watch a "behind the scenes" television program that shows how a movie is made; then discuss how media literacy elements are addressed. As an extension activity for high schoolers, students locate organizational and personnel information about a representative company in that industry, and find out if gender is correlated to positions or hierarchy.

SOUND OFF*
   Students view a television show without the sound. They listen to a television show without the picture. Ask them to describe the message, noting the impact of a missing medium. Note if gender impacts the interpretation.

MIXED MESSAGE*

Students choose video or television footage that includes sound. Then they replace the original soundtrack with a conflicting/contradictory soundtrack. For example, use ballet music to accompany a football play. Another student can experience the modified media, and describe the reaction and analysis. Elementary students can identify a contradictory type of sound or music, and play it while the video is on mute mode. Note if gender impacts the choice of soundtrack.

THE INTERNATIONAL LANGUAGE*

Ask students to examine periodicals written in languages that the students do not know and extract as much information as possible, stating how they discerned content. Note if gender impacts the interpretation.

SNAKE OIL*

Each student can locate an historical advertisement from the Library of Congress's American Memory collections (http://memory.loc.gov/), and analyze the advertisement without consulting the bibliographic description. Older students may analyze the resource in light of the collection information. In addition, students can research other documents from the same period of time, or the same producer or type of product, in order to contextualize the advertisement and garner more information. As another extension, students can identify advertisements that they think are targeted for one gender, explaining the basis for their assessment; note how male and female choices differ, if at all.

MUSEUM OF HOAXES

What is true? What is a hoax? The reality may surprise you. In this era where images can be easily modified, determining what is true becomes increasingly difficult. The Museum of Hoaxes is a great vehicle for critical viewing (http://museumofhoaxes.com). It includes a series of gullibility tests, and also showcases hoaxes over time, all of which reveals how media have tried to fool the public for hundreds of years.

ALL IN THE FAMILY

Students can research a conglomerate to determine its related corporate entities (e.g., AOL-Time Warner or Disney). Next, have them locate an advertisement for each entity, and explore possible connections in terms of message or value. See if gender enters into the picture.

SELLING ENTERTAINMENT*

In small groups, students may track six hours of television and/or radio. Each student chooses a different channel for a different period of time, as follows:

	3 a.m.–9 a.m.	9 a.m.–3 p.m.	3 p.m.–9 p.m.	9 p.m.–3 a.m.
NBC				
FOX				
ESPN				
History Channel				
Etc.				

Ask each student to log each show and advertisement (targeted audience, content, context, framework, production values). Then they can compare their analyses along both dimensions: channel and time. Another dimension can be gender. The class as a whole then can uncover overarching trends. Elementary students can compare two programs, and focus on answering the five key questions posed by the Center for Media Literacy.

GENDER CHANNELS*

Mixed-gender pairs can watch a television show separately, each answering the five key questions posed by the Center for Media Literacy, and then compare their findings. Students may examine a variety of shows and channels: e.g., soap operas, comedy, sports channels, detective shows, talk shows with male and female hosts, and history programs. Students can compare findings across the different genres of TV programming.

PLAYING TO THEIR AUDIENCE*

Ask students to describe their ideal video game. Compare boys' and girls' ideals, and request that students conduct a content analysis of a video game in terms of media messages.

IS THE NEWS GENDER-LINKED?

Who writes the news? Who manages it? Who is the subject? As students see males and females making news, they may identify with the players. How representative is the news relative to gender? This exercise makes students more aware of gender in the mass media, and helps them think about the origins of societal expectations relative to literacy.

1. Who writes the news? Have students identify the gender, if possible, of a newspaper's by-line reporters and also the general news staff. In some cases, students may need to research more about reports to discover their gender.

2. Who manages the news? Have students identify the gender, if possible, of a newspaper's editors and managers. Here, too, students may need to research more deeply to uncover gender.

3. Who makes the news? By type of news (e.g., world, national, state, local, business, sports, entertainment), ask students to identify the gender of key newsmakers.

Also note if the person identified has a power position (e.g., winner, office, star) or is on the receiving end of power (e.g., victim, loser, supporter). In some cases, where names may be male or female, students may need to research further to reveal their gender.

4. Ask students to discuss what gender-linked patterns emerge in this content analysis. Do they tend to dominate in certain roles? Does one gender dominate "in the front" positions, and another dominate in "behind-the-scenes" roles? What impact does that have on students?

5. Students can also compare local, regional, and national newspapers for possible gender role differences.

6. Alternatively, request that students do content analyses on other mass media outlets: television, radio, movies. Do different outlets generate different gender trends?

THE CANDIDATE

In this exercise, students download campaign commercials. Divide students into pairs. For each piece of footage, one student edits to support the candidate and the other edits to either counter the candidate or support the opposing candidate. Students then explain the production techniques they used to modify the message. They can specify single-gender target audiences, and craft their messages accordingly. In that case, both girls and boys can develop each message as follows:

	Female Creator	Male Creator
Male Audience		
Female Audience		

DEBATABLE IMAGES

Using a camera or camcorder, pairs of students create an advertisement, one pro and one con, using production "language." Students can specify single-gender target audiences, and craft their messages accordingly. In that case, both girls and boys can develop each message as follows:

	Female Creator	Male Creator
Male Audience		
Female Audience		

Works Cited

Aufderheide, P. (1992). *Proceedings from the National Leadership Conference on Media Literacy.* Washington, DC: Aspen Institute.

Center for Media Literacy. Retrieved February 3, 2005, from http://www.medialit.org.

Collins, R., et al. (2004, Sept.). "Watching sex on television predicts adolescent initiation of sexual behavior." *Pediatrics, 114,* 3, 280–289.

Marlo, Leslie (2004, Fall). "An unscientific survey of teen TV programming." *Young Adult Library Services,* 42–43.

Silverblatt, 2001.

Silverblatt, Art, and Finan, Barbara (1999). *Approaches to media literacy: A handbook.* New York: M. E. Sharpe.

10

Interdependence of Literacies

"There are more things in heaven and earth, Horatio,
Than are dreamt of in your philosophy."
Shakespeare, *Hamlet*

This admonition could well be applied to notions of literacies in the 21st century. No longer does "one size fit all." Literacy has certainly changed in recent decades, morphing from the ability to read and write written/printed text to encompass dozens of competencies in cultural and scientific terms; one may even be fashion literate! Scholars and business, such as UCLA and SBC Global Net, have been reinventing the notions of literacy to address social and economic realities in a digital age. Perhaps it is time to re-define the notion of the "literate" person as, one who exhibits a sophisticated range of abilities and knowledge and has the wherewithal to succeed autonomously within society.

In any case, several literacies have been parsed in this book to determine their unique characteristics. In actuality, they all intersect. This chapter examines how gender and technology fit into this complex picture. As a center of ideas and information, the library offers an optimal learning environment to explore literacies holistically and from many different perspectives. Exercises provide ideas for next steps in gender equity relative to digital literacies.

A Very Short History of Literacies

Literacy has been traditionally linked with reading and writing. Not that illiterate societies couldn't achieve greatness; the Greeks, for instance, created early government and artwork before they created an alphabet. Still, alphabets enabled people to write down their ideas so that these conceptions could be remembered and transferred more easily. In fact, recitation-literates referred to people who could read texts they had memorized, in contrast to scriptorial-literates who could read unfamiliar texts (Blake & Blake, 2002). With the advent of the printing press, a much broader population base could access text so the importance of literacy increased and marked the rise of vernacular language and Protestantism.

In the nineteen century new recording devices emerged that produced photography, sound recording, and film. Not only did these capture the world *in situ*, but they could be readily duplicated and disseminated broadly *with little decoding*. Not that these largely sense-driven media were unfiltered by their recorders. The recorder still had control of *what* to record, and could edit the source in order to communicate a specific message or share a unique perspective. However, that communication was generally one-way; the audience could receive the information but not exchange their views.

The late twentieth century changed that paradigm as digital sources could be manipulated by both the sender and the receiver, given that they had the tools and skills to change the source material. In the process, education changed, from the rather passive task of transmitting the known universe to an interactive exploration that generates new information in an open-ended universe. Moreover, the potential players in this scenario now consist of the entire planet (Rose & Meyer, 1996).

The New Literacies

The New London Group (1996), which is an international think tank, asserts that the languages needed to make meaning are radically changing in three realms of daily existence: working lives, public lives (citizenship), and private lives (lifeworld).

The underlying assumption is that everyone belongs to several communities, and that information gains meaning within the context of its creation and reception — and changes as people design their community futures. The group then discusses design elements in the process of making meaning: linguistic, visual, audio, gestural, spatial, and multimodal. Based on this premise, they then suggest four approaches to teaching: overt instruction, critical framing (i.e., contextualizing meaning), situated practice, and transformed practice (i.e., designing social futures). This approach to information and meaning resonates with today's youth, who are exploring their many roles, both private and public.

Another useful approach to this concept of new literacies builds on librarian philosophy about use of information. Librarians contend that information and ideas exist in myriad formats and representations, and that people can manipulate and communicate ideas and information using a wide variety of strategies. At each point of contact between humans and sources (including other humans), decisions are made as to the tools to use and the way to use them. So rather than thinking strictly about a specific literacy *per se*, focus needs to be on developing a repertoire of tools and processes to use while engaging with ideas and information.

In this model, the following elements of engagement are addressed in terms of the perspective of students, the nature of information, and possible librarian/teacher interventions.

Element	Student	Information	Librarian/ Teacher Intervention
Pre-engagement:	Background, knowledge, capabilities, situation	What are its characteristics? What are the characteristics of the environment in general and at that moment?	Knowledge, role, situation
Origin of Need:	Personal, academic	Producer wants to influence or gain power	Standards, values
Task determinator:	Brainstorming, concept map, strategy choice	Format parameters	Giving directions
First contact:	Attention (may choose to ignore it)	Physical access issues (equipment, availability)	Introduction
Comprehension/ Intellectual Access:	Decoding (e.g., visuals, sound, linguistic language); understanding content (e.g., vocabulary, semiotics, concepts)	Layout, cues to understanding, glossary, dual coding	Phonics instruction; oral reading; simplification; deconstruction; contextualization
Evaluation:	Agreement/ rejection/ incorporation of ideas (based on cognitive, affective, behavioral); Determination of use; Task or need change	Comparative information; peer review	Criteria lists, rubrics; critical thinking skills instruction
Manipulation of Information:	Interpretation; organization; synthesis; re-formatting; changing; relating or combining with other information	Characteristics of information and its representation; malleability desired result; provision of tools	Analytical and manipulation skills instruction; stipulating end product format or
Application/ Use:	Problem-solving; learning; self-change; adding to knowledge base	Generation of new information; change in environment; change in power	Critique; providing venue for implementation

Thus, literacy determining strategies and tools depends on the desired outcome, the nature (and availability) of the information, and the situational context — as well as on the individual's own resources and sense of engagement.

Instead of parsing literacies them according to the social and situational context of the students' needs, both of these models implicity blend them.

Benefits of Literacy Interdependence

By weaving literacies, students can strengthen their performance in each one by shoring up skills in one literacy via the use of another. As an example, the student who has difficulty writing can demonstrate knowledge by drawing a picture that shows deep understanding of a reading selection and choosing passages that inform the details of the image generated. Just as dual coding improves reading, so does dual-literacy deepen learning.

In terms of gender, literacy interdependence helps ameliorate the inequities sometimes associated with a single literacy. For instance, technology literacy (usually favored by boys) motivates and supports their reading abilities (an area usually "cornered" by girls). Likewise, girls' verbal abilities help them solve math problems collaboratively.

Project-based learning offers a rich, student-centered approach to interdependent literacies. For example, as students create a business, they have to use:

1. Information literacy to locate and assess information about starting a business, conduct market research, and evaluate efforts
2. Reading and writing skills to understand legal documents, order supplies, and communicate business plans
3. Technology literacy to locate information, design structures, track the project, keep records, and communicate
4. Numeracy skills to predict, calculate, and maintain budgets
5. Visual literacy to design the environment and produce publications
6. Media literacy to produce advertisements and other public campaigns
7. Aural literacy to listen and communicate, and to consider ambient sounds

Authentic tasks offer a rationale for intellectual and emotional engagement. Essential questions can cross curricular lines and involve skills learned in several classes. Project-based learning usually entails collaboration because the task is complex enough to require several people, thus optimizing the chances that different students' strengths can be put to use — and foster reciprocal teaching. Assessment, too, can be more nuanced as it measures actual performance throughout the project.

Indeed, assessment clearly improves when literacies are combined. Because assessment should be aligned with standards and desired student learning outcomes, incorporating several literacies forces assessment to be more faceted. Thus, students have more ways to demonstrate understanding and skill — and, hopefully, more choices in how they are assessed. Certainly, both process and product can be assessed, and formative assessment along each dimension offers more opportunities for students to get back on track or use more effective learning strategies.

Students should be reflecting on their own efforts, a process called metacognition. This approach to assessment gives students more control of their learning and helps them generalize from their specific situation. When students share their reflections with peers and adults, they get another person's perspective, which further helps them progress— either through confirmation of their current direction or by getting ideas on how to redirect their efforts.

The Librarian's Role

Libraries contain a wide variety of resources in a neutral, interactive environment that models interdependent literacies. The same book or picture might be used by students in different grades for different academic reasons. In order to meet the varied learning styles and needs of boys and girls, librarians need to assess curriculum in light of students, and then acquire and make available highest-quality inclusive collections, and provide access to online and remote resources. Still, it is not enough to have the materials; librarians need to promote those resources proactively, inviting individual members of the school community to engage deeply with them.

As mentioned before, the library's facility itself serves as a model of interdependent literacies. Nooks and crannies of the library appeal to different students to engage in different learning activities. Tables facilitate group work; carrels foster individual concentration. Small study rooms allow collaborative groups to discuss their efforts openly; production areas enable students to generate visual and technological information, adding to the school's knowledge base. Comfy couches invite one to read for pleasure; listening areas allow students to develop their aural literacy. Assistive technology that is easily available enable students with special needs to enjoy the library alongside their peers. All students need to feel comfortable in the facility, and find a spot that "speaks" to them. Hours should be maximized to meet preferences and needs of all students, including accommodations for athletes and night owls. For that reason, as well as others, the library needs to open its virtual doors via a substantial web portal.

Many services that promote literacy interdependency have already been mentioned:

1. Development of webliographies of print, audio-visual, and digital resources
2. Selection of materials in different formats for specific assignments or needs
3. Creation of databases that refer to local sources of information about literacies
4. Circulation of software, hardware, and audio-visual equipment
5. Provision of learning aids in various forms

6. Provision of tutoring and homework assistance
7. Display and archiving of student work in various formats
8. Training of library aides in a variety of duties
9. Sponsoring of programs that encourage a variety of literacies
10. Advising of student clubs that foster different literacies

In some cases, librarians may want to consider targeting one sex for a service. However, the overall sense of service should reflect a sense of inclusivity.

School librarians need to play a pivotal role in instruction as an educational partner. Ideally, curricular units can be designed to meld content, information literacy, and technology literacy standards, with supporting specific-learning activities. The most effective approach, though, is school-wide curriculum development where these literacies are addressed and combined systematically. Because they deal with all students and all classroom teachers, librarians can "translate" literacies across the curriculum so teachers will not feel that they are being further burdened with skills and concepts. Instead, as teachers see how literacies are demonstrated in various academic contexts, they can build on each other's efforts. Not only literacies, but teachers themselves become more interdependent. Content follows, so students can link their learning from classroom to classroom and, thus, transfer their knowledge more easily and apply their skills more effectively.

Coda

In the final analysis, students reflect a broad range of experiences, perspectives, and capabilities. They are exploring their self-identities in a midst of changing environments and expectations. They need to develop their abilities in several literacies so they can find their niche and keep their options open for an uncertain and unknown future. Librarians can help young people in these endeavors, offering a wide range of information and ways to engage in it meaningfully. By being aware of gender issues in this process, students and librarians— and the rest of the community — help ground this exploration and offer ways to help all students fully develop and understand each other within a diverse social construct.

Interdependent Literacies Exercises

VALUING LITERACIES

Ask students to rank-order the following literacies— reading, numeracy, technology, visual, aural, media — in terms of: (1) importance; (2) interest; (3) difficulty. See what gender patterns, if any, emerge. Discuss reasons for the rank orderings and the gender differences, if any.

GRAPHING LITERACIES

Students can keep a time journal describing their use of different literacies (e.g., sample day, one weekday and one weekend day, different days of the week, by course being taken). They can calculate the amount of time they spent on each literacy — and the amount spent on no literacy at all (both sleeping and awake). Remind them that a task may involve several literacies. Ask students to create a bar graph of the relative number of hours spent on each literacy. To what extent does gender impact the distribution of time?

LITERACY STRENGTHS AND CHALLENGES

Ask students to rate their own competencies in different literacies, and to develop a class database of expertise so they can help each other develop literacy competency. See if gender patterns emerge — and change over time.

LINKING LITERACIES

Request that students list the literacy competencies they learn in each class, and then link the competencies to concepts. Next, ask them to link concepts and literacies across classes. The class can then determine to what extent literacies and concepts cross curricular lines. Individual teacher patterns may emerge, which may be linked to gender.

CAREER LITERACIES

Students in mixed pairs can interview or "shadow" an employee, noting the literacies needed to accomplish a job. Students can compare their lists to determine if gender perspectives enter into the findings, and then, with other class members, compare occupations in terms of literacies.

Works Cited

Asselin, M. (2004, June). "New literacies: Towards a renewed role of school libraries." *Teacher Librarian, 31,* 5, 52–53.

Blake, B., and Blake, R. (2002). *Literacy and learning.* Santa Barbara, CA: ABC-CLIO.

New London Group (1996). "A pedagogy of multiliteracies: Designing social futures." *Harvard Educational Review, 61,* 60–92.

Rose, David, and Meyer, Ann. (1996). *Expanding the literacy toolbox.* New York: Scholastic.

Silverblatt, Art, and Finan, Barbara (1999). *Approaches to media literacy: A handbook.* New York: M. E. Sharpe.

Bibliography

Abram, Stephen, and Luther, Judy (2004, May 1). "Born with the chip." *Library Journal, 129,* 8, 34–37.

Agosto, Denise (2004, Jan.). "Gender, educational technologies, and the school library." *School Libraries Worldwide, 10,* 1, 39–51.

Akin, Lynn (1998). "Information Overload and Children: A Survey of Texas Elementary School Students." *School Library Media Research, 1.* Retrieved on February 3, 2005, from http://www.ala.org/ala/aasl/aaslpubsandjournals/slmrb/slmrcontents/volume11998slmqo/akin.htm#research.

Alloway, Nola, et al. (2002). *Boys, literacy, and schooling.* Canberra City, Australia: Department of Education, Science, and Training.

American Association for the Advancement of Science (1999). *Dialogue on early childhood science, mathematics, and technology education.* Washington, DC: American Association for the Advancement of Science.

American Association of School Librarians and Association of Educational Communications and Technology (1988). *Information power: Partners for learning.* Chicago: American Library Association.

American Association of University Women (1992). *Shortchanging girls, shortchanging America.* Washington, DC: American Association of University Women.

_____ (2000). *Tech-savvy: Educating girls in the new computer age.* Washington, DC: American Association of University Women.

American Association of University Women (1999). *Voices of a generation: Teenage girls on sex, school, and self.* Washington, DC: American Association of University Women.

Ames, Pat (2003). "The role of learning style in university students' computer attitudes: Implications relative to the effectiveness of computer-focused and computer-facilitated instruction." Doctoral dissertation, The Claremont Graduate University, 2003. *ProQuest Dissertations and Theses* (AAT 3093249).

Asselin, M. (2004, June). "New literacies: Towards a renewed role of school libraries." *Teacher Librarian, 31,* 5, 52–53.

Aufderheide, P. (1992). *Proceedings from the National Leadership Conference on Media Literacy.* Washington, DC: Aspen Institute.

Bahremand, V. (2003). *24/7 Digital reference services: Does it work for students?* Unpublished master's project. Long Beach, CA: California State University.

Beaulieu, Lionel, et al. (2001). "For whom does the school bell toll? Multi-contextual presence of social capital and student educational achievement." *Journal of Socio-Economics, 30,* 2, 121–127.

Belenky, M. F., McVicker Clinchy, B., Rule Golberger, N., Mattuck Tarule, J. (1986). *Women's ways of knowing: The development of self, voice, and mind.* New York: Basic Books.

Berger, John (1977). *Ways of seeing.* New York: Penguin.

Berman, S. (2003). "Alpha-Numeric System for Classification of Recordings (ANSCR)." Vancover, CA: University of British Columbia. Retrieved February 3, 2005, from http://www.slais.ubc.ca/courses/libr517/03-04-wt2/projects/TP/website/alpha.htm.

Betsky, Aaron (1997). *Building sex: Men, women, architecture, and the construction of sexuality.* Arlington, TX: Quill.

Bhogal, B. (1996). "Discussion about orality and literacy based on Murray Jardine's *Sight, sound, and epistemology: The experiential sources of ethical concepts.*" *JAAR,* 44(1). Retrieved February 3, 2005, from http://cedm.derby.ac.uk/multifaith/images/content/seminarpapers/discussionaboutorallityandliteracy.htm

Binns, Jane, and Branch, Robert (1995). "Gender Stereotyped Computer Clip-Art Images as an Implicit Influence in Instructional Message Design," 315–324. In Beauchamp, Darrell, Braden, Roberts, & Griffin, Robert. (Eds.). *Imagery and visual literacy.* Sugar Grove, IL: International Visual Literacy Association.

Black, Gordon (1995, Fall). *CSMpact for education: Do boys and girls experience education differently?* Rochester, NY: Harris Interactive.

Blake, Brett, and Blake, Robert (2002). *Literacy and learning: A reference handbook.* Santa Barbara, CA: ABC-CLIO.

Block, C., Gambrell, L., and Pressley, M. (Eds.). *Improving comprehension instruction: Rethinking research, theory, and classroom practice.* San Francisco: Jossey-Bass.

Brunner, Cornelia, and Bennett, Dorothy. (1997, Nov.). "Technology perceptions by gender." *NASSP Bulletin, 81,* 46–51.

Boaler, Jo (2002). *Experiencing school mathematics.* Mahwah, NJ: Lawrence Erlbaum.

Brazil, E. (2001). *Cue points: An examination of common sound file formats.* Limerick, University of Limerick.

Brill, J., Kim, D., and Branch, R. (2001). "Visual literacy defined: The results of a Delphi study: Can IVLA (operationally) define visual literacy?" *Selected Readings of the 31st Annual Convention of the International Visual Literacy Association.* Ames, Iowa.

Brozo, W. (2002). *To be a boy, to be a reader: Engaging teen and preteen boys in active literacy.* Newark, DE: International Reading Association.

California Commission on Teacher Credentialing (1997). *California Standards for the Teaching Profession.* Sacramento: California Department of Education.

California Reading and Literature Project. (2004). Los Angeles: University of California, Los Angeles. Retrieved February 3, 2005, from http://www.centerx.gseis.ucla.edu/CRLP/index.php.

California State Department of Education (1997). *Mathematics framework for California public schools kindergarten through grade twelve.* Sacramento: California Department of Education.

Casey, Jean (1997). *Early literacy: The empowerment of technology.* Englewood, CO: Libraries Unlimited.

Cassell, Justine and Henry Jenkins (1998). *From Barbie to Mortal Kombat: Gender and computer games.* Cambridge, MA: MIT Press.

Center for Media Literacy. Retrieved February 3, 2005, from http://www.medialit.org.

Central auditory processing skills (2004). "ThinkQuest for Tomorrow's Teachers." Retrieved February 3, 2005, from http://t3.preservice.org/T0300887/page3.html.

Chartock, R. (2000). *Educational foundations: An anthology.* Upper Saddle River, NJ: Merrill.

Chelton, M., and Cole, Colleen (Eds.). *Youth information-seeking behavior: Theory, models, and issues.* Lanham, MD: Scarecrow.

Chion, Michael (1983). *Guide des objets sonores.* Paris: Buchet/Chastel.

Clarke, J. (1991). *Patterns of thinking.* Needham Heights, MA: Allyn and Bacon.

Clyde, L. A. (2004, Oct.). "M-learning." *Teacher Librarian, 32* (1), 45–46.

Codell, E. (2003). *How to get your child to love reading.* Chapel Hill, NC: Algonquin Books.

Colley, A., North, A., and Hargreaves, D. (2003, April). "Gender bias in the evaluation of new age music." *Scandinavian Journal of Psychology, 44,* 2, 125–31.

Collins, R., et al. (2004, Sept.). "Watching sex on television predicts adolescent initiation of sexual behavior." *Pediatrics, 114,* 3, 280–289.

Colvin, Carolyn, and Schlosser, Linda (1997, Dec.). "Developing academic confidence to build literacy: What teachers can do." *Journal of Adolescent & Adult Literacy, 41,* 4, 272–281.

Conference Board of the Mathematical Sciences (2001). *The mathematical education of teachers, part I.* Washington, DC: Mathematical Association of America.

Costa, Arthur (2001). *Developing minds.* Reston, VA: Association for Supervision and Curriculum Development.

Creany, Anne (1990). "The effect of sex role stereotypes on the gender labels children apply to picture book characters." Indiana, PA: Indiana University of Pennsylvania. *ProQuest Dissertations and Theses.* (AAT 9034352).

Crew, Hilary (1997, Summer). Feminist scholarship and theories of adolescent development: Implications for young adult services in libraries. *Journal of Youth Services in Libraries, 10,* 4, 405–417.

Csikszentmihaly, Mihaly (1998). *Finding flow: The psychology of engagement with everyday life.* New York: Basic Books.

Damarin, S. (1993). "The ascendancy of the visual and issues of gender: Equality versus difference." *Journal of Visual Literacy, 13*(2), 61–71.

Davies, Julia; Marsh, Jackie; and Millard, Elaine (n.d.). "Differently literate: Some ways of working in schools to promote equal access to the language curriculum for boys and girls." Sheffield, UK: University of Sheffield.

Department of Education, Science and Training (2004). *"Your Child's Future — Literacy and Numeracy in Australia's Schools."* Canberra: Australian Government. Retrieved February 3, 2005, from http://www.dest.gov.au/schools/publications/2002/yourchild/english.htm.

Dick, W., and Carey, L. (1996). *The systematic design of instruction* (4th ed.). New York: Harper Collins.

Dishon, Dee, and O'Leary, Pat (1994). *Guidebook of cooperative learning: A technique for creating more effective schools.* Holmes Beach, FL: Learning Publications.

Dobosenski, Laura (2001, Sept.). "Girls and computer technology: Building skills and improving attitudes through a girls' computer club." *Library Talk, 14,* 4, 12–16.

Donalson, M. (1978). *Children's minds.* London: Fontana.

Dresang, Eliza (1998). *Radical change: Books for youth in a digital age.* Bronx, NY: H. W. Wilson.

Eiseman, Leatrice (2000). *Pantone guide to communicating with color.* Cincinnati, OH: North Light Books.

Eisenberg, Michael, and Berkowitz, Robert (1990). *Information problem-solving: The Big Six approach to library and information skills instruction.* Norwood, NJ: Ablex.

Endich, R. (2004). *Media literacy: Activities for understanding the scripted world.* Worthington, OH: Linworth.

English-language arts content standards for California public schools (1997). Sacramento: California State Department of Education.

Everhart, Nancy (2004, Nov.). "Every child ready to read @ your library." *Knowledge Quest, 33,* 2, 77–79.

Fallows, Deborah (2005). "Search engine users." Washington, DC: Pew Internet and American Life Project. Retrieved February 3, 2005, from http://www.pewinternet.org/pdfs/PIP_Searchengine_users.pdf

Farmer, Lesley (1999). *Cooperative learning activities in the library media center.* Westport, CT: Libraries Unlimited.

_____ (2005). *Digital inclusion, teens, and your library.* Westport, CT: Libraries Unlimited.

_____ (1995). *Informing young women: Gender equity through literacy skills.* Jefferson, NC: McFarland.

_____ (2004, Jan.) "Using Internet metasites to foster teenage girls' interest in technology." *School Librarianship Worldwide, 10(1–2),* 92–100.

Ferrington, Gary (1994, Autumn). "Keep your ear-lids open." *Journal of Visual Literacy, 14,* 2, 51–61.

Fessenden, Seth A. (1955). " Levels of Listening — A Theory." *Education, 75* (January 1955), pp. 288–291.

Finders, M. (1997). *Just girls.* New York: Teachers College Press.

Frater, Graham (1997). *Improving boys' literacy: A survey of effective practice in secondary schools.* London: The Basic Skills Agency.

Furger, R. (2004, Sept. 3). "Success stories for learning in the digital age." *Edutopia.*

Furner, Joseph, and Berman, Barbara (2004, Summer). "Building math confidence for a high-tech world." *Academic Exchange Quarterly, 8,* 2, 214–220.

Gilligan, Carol (1982). *In a different voice.* Cambridge, MA: Harvard University Press.

Glenn Commission (1999). *Before it's too late.* Washington, DC: United States Department of Education.

Goldberg, G., and Roswell, B. (2002). *Reading, writing, and gender.* Larchmont, NY: Eye on Education.

Gordon, Carol (2002). "Methods for measuring the influence of concept mapping on student information literacy." *School Library Media Research, 5.* Retrieved February 3, 2005, from http://www.ala.org/ala/aasl/aaslpubsandjournals/slmrb/slmrcontents/volume52002/gordon.htm.

Green, Lucy (1997). *Music, gender, education.* New York: Cambridge University Press.

Gressard, C., and Loyd, B. (1986). "Validation studies of a new computer attitude scale." *Association for Educational Data Systems Journal,* 18(4), 295–301.

Griffin, Robert, et al. (Eds.). (1996). *Eyes on the future: Converging images, ideas and instruction.* Sugar Grove, IL: International Visual Literacy Association.

Gross, Melissa (1997, Spring). "Pilot study on the prevalence of imposed queries in a school library media center." *School Library Media Quarterly, 25,* 3, 157–163.

Gurian, Michael, and Henley, Patricia (2001). "Boys and girls learn differently! A guide for teachers and parents." San Francisco: Jossey-Bass.

Hackbarth, S. (2001, April). "Changes in primary students' computer literacy as a function of classroom use and gender." *TechTrends, 45,* 4, 19–27.

Halle, M., and Stevens, K. (1962). "Speech recognition: A model and a program for research." *IRE Transactions on Information Theory, IT-8,* 155–159.

Hamilton, Anita (2000, Aug. 21). "Meet the new surfer girls." *Time, 156,* 8, 67.

Harding, Sandra (1991). *Whose science? Whose knowledge?* Ithaca, NY: Cornell University Press.

Herb, Steven, and Willoughby-Herb, Sara (1994, Jan.). "The importance of men as role models in literacy." *Catholic Library World, 64,* 3, 46–50.

Higgins, D., and Bryce, J. (1999). "Flow, enjoyment and positive experiences in computer gaming: Preliminary research, theoretical background, results and future research." Unpublished [online], University of Manchester, Manchester, United Kingdom. Retrieved February 3, 2005, from http://www.playingfields.co.uk/content/gamingreport.htm.

Holmes, Bob (1994, Aug. 27). "Fast words speed past dyslexics." *New Scientist,* 1010.

International Society for Technology in Education (2000). *Technology standards for students.* Eugene, OR: International Society for Technology in Education.

International Technology Education Association (2000). *Standards for technological literacy.* Reston, VA: International Technology Education Association.

Jones, S., and Dindia, K. (2004, Winter). "A meta-analytic perspective on sex equity in the classroom." *Review of Educational Research, 74,* 4, 443–471.

Kids and media at the new millennium (1999). Menlo Park, CA: Kaiser Family Foundation. http://www.kff.org/entmedia/1535-index.cfm.

Knight, Heather (1997, May 7). "Study finds few signs of an academic gender gap." *Los Angeles Times,* A1, 33.

Knuth, R., and Jones, B. (1991). *What does research say about reading?* Oak Brook, IL: North Central Regional Educational Laboratory.

Koelsch S. et al. (2003 July 1). "Children processing music: Electric brain responses reveal musical competence and gender differences." *Journal of Cognitive Neuroscience, 15,* 5, 683–93.

Kolb, D. (1984). *Experiential learning.* Englewood Cliffs, NJ: Prentice Hall.

Kuhlthau, Carol (1985). *Teaching the library research process: A step-by-step program for secondary school students.* Englewood Cliffs, NJ: Prentice-Hall.

Kulik, James (2002, Nov.) "School mathematics and science programs benefit from instructional technology." *Infobrief.* Retrieved February 3, 2005, from http://www.nsf.gov/sbe/srs/inf-brief/nsf03301/.

Lacy, L. (1986). *Art and design in children's picture books: An analysis of Caldecott Award-winning illustrations.* Chicago: American Library Association.

Lamb, R., Dolloff, L., and Howe, S. (2002). "Feminism, feminist research, and gender research in music education." In Colwell, R., and Richardson, C. (Eds.). *The new handbook of research on music teaching and learning.* New York: Oxford University Press.

Landy, L., and Atkinson, S. (2004). "EARS: ElectroAcoustic Research Site." Leicester, UK: De Montfort University. Retrieved February 3, 2005, from http://www.mti.dmu.ac.uk/EARS/

Large, Andrew; Beheshti, J.; and Rahman, T. (2002, May). "Gender differences in collaborative web searching behavior: an elementary school study." *Information Processing and Management: an International Journal, 38,* 3, 427- 443.

Laurel, Brenda (1991). *Computers as theater.* Reading, MA: Addison-Wesley.

Lehrman, Sally (1997, May). "Woman." *Stanford Today, 25,* 3, 47–51.

Leu, Donald J., Jr., and Kinzer, Charles (2003). *Effective literacy instruction K-8.* Upper Saddle River, NJ: Merrill.

Ligamari, Joanne, and Goodwin, Katharine (2004, Nov.). "Boys, books and literacy." California School Library Association conference, Sacramento. Nov. 12–15, 2004.

Loertscher, David, and Woolls, Blanche (1999). *Information literacy: A review of the research.* San Jose, CA: Hi Willow.

Loge, Kenneth P. (1993). "Audio: More than meets the eye." AECT conference presentation, New Orleans.

Mann, Charles (2001, August). "Why 14-year-old Japanese girls rule the world." *Yahoo! Internet Life,* 99–103.

Marland, Michael (1981). *Information skills in the secondary curriculum.* New York: Metheun.

Marlo, Leslie (2004, Fall). "An unscientific survey of teen TV programming." *Young Adult Library Services,* 42–43.

Martin, Andrew (2002). *Improving the educational outcomes of boys.* Canberra, Australia: Department of Education. Retrieved February 3, 2005, from www.decs.act.gov.au/publicat/pdf/Ed_Outcomes_Boys.pdf

Martin, Robert (2004, Winter). "A nation of learners." *Threshold,* 32.

Martino, Wayne (1998). "'Dickheads,' 'poofs,' 'try hards' and 'losers': Critical literacy for boys in the English classroom." *English in Aotearoa, 35,* 31–57.

McGrath, Diane (2004, March). "Closing the gender gap." *Learning & Leading with Technology, 31,* 6, 28–31.

McKenzie, Jamie (1996, March). "Making WEB meaning." *Educational Leadership, 54,* 3, 30–32.

Mellon, C. (1988). "Attitudes: The forgotten dimension in library instruction." *Library Journal, 113,* 14, 137–139.

Meltzer, Bonnie (2000, Mar.). "Cheating the kids." *Library Talk, 13,* 2, 31–32.

Miller, Jean Baker (1976). *Toward a new psychology of women.* Boston: Beacon Press.

Moir, Anne, and Jessel, David (1991). *Brain sex.* New York: Dell.

Moller, A.P., and Thornhill, R. (1998, Feb.). "Bilateral symmetry and sexual selection: A meta-analysis." *American Naturalist, 151,* 2, 174–193.

Mullis, I., et al. (1999). *TIMSS 1999 international mathematics report: Findings from IEA's repeat of the third international mathematics and science study at the eighth grade.* Chestnut Hill, MA: Boston College.

Mulvaney, Eileen (1998). "Learning to be audio-literate." 1998 Conference Proceedings. Northridge, CA: Center On Disabilities Technology And Persons With Disabilities Conference. Retrieved February 3, 2005, from http://www.csun.edu/cod/conf/1998/proceedings/csun98_037.htm.

Murdock, Maureen (1990). *Heroine's journey.* Boston: Shambhala.

National Center for Educational Statistics (2004). *The nation's report card.* Washington, DC: Department of Education.

National Council of Teachers of Mathematics (2000). *Principles and standards for school mathematics.* Washington, DC: National Council of Teachers of Mathematics.

National Endowment for the Arts (2004). *Reading at risk.* Washington, DC: National Endowment for the Arts.

National Institute of Child Health and Human Development (2000). *Report of the National Reading Panel: Teaching children to read.* Bethesda, MD: National Institute of Child Health and Human Development.

National Policy Board for Educational Administration (2002). *Instructions to implement standards for advanced programs in educational leadership.* Alexandria, VA: National Policy Board for Educational Administration.

New London Group (1996). "A pedagogy of multiliteracies: Designing social futures." *Harvard Educational Review, 61,* 60–92.

Newkirk, T. (2002). *Misreading masculinity: Boys, literacy, and popular culture.* Portsmouth, NH: Heinemann.

Nichols, Sharon, and Good, Thomas (2004). *America's teenagers — Myths and realities.* Mahwah, NJ: Lawrence Erlbaum.

Noble, C. and Bradford, W. (2000). *Getting it right for boys ... and girls.* London: Routledge.

Nochlin, Linda (1999). *Representing women.* New York: Thames and Hudson.

North, Adrian, Colley, Ann, and Hargreaves, David (2003)." Adolescents' perceptions of the music of male and female composers." *Psychology of Music, 31,* 139–154.

_____, and Hargreaves, David (1999). "Music and adolescent identity." *Music Education Research, 1,* 75–92.

North Central Regional Educational Laboratory (2004). *EnGauge.* Portland, OR: North Central Regional Educational Laboratory.

Ohler, Jason (1998, March). "The promise of MIDI technology." *Learning & Leading with Technology, 25,* 6, 6–10.

Olsson, Bengt (1997). "The social psychology of music education." In Hargreaves, David, and North, Adrian. (Eds.). *The social psychology of music.* New York, Oxford University Press.

Orenstein, Peggy (1994). *School-girls.* New York: Doubleday.

Pappas, Marjorie, and Tepe, Ann (1995). "Preparing the information educator for the future." *School Library Media Annual,* 37–44.

Park, Alice (2004, May 10). "What makes teens tick?" *Time, 163,* 19, 56–65.

Pearson, P., and Taylor, Barbara (2002). *Teaching reading.* Mahwah, NJ: Lawrence Erlbaum.

Pedersen, P., and Hernandez, D. (1997). *Decisional dialogues in a cultural context: Structured exercises.* Thousand Oaks, CA: Sage.

Pellegrini, A. L., Kato, K., Blatchford, P., and Baines, E. (2002, Winter). "A short-term longitudinal study of children's playground games across the first year of school: Implications for social competence and adjustment to school." *America Educational Research Journal, 39,* 4, 991–105.

Philbin, Marge, and Meier, Elizabeth (1995, April). "A survey of gender and learning styles." *Sex Roles: A Journal of Research.*

Pink, Daniel (2005, Feb.). "Revenge of the right brain." *Wired,* 70–72.

Pintrich, P., and Linnenbrink, E. (2002). "Motivation as an enabler for academic success." *School Psychology Review, 31* (3), 313–327.

Pipher, Mary (1994). *Reviving Ophelia: Saving the selves of adolescent girls.* New York: Putnam.

Posner, G. (1992). "Analyzing the curriculum." New York: McGraw-Hill.

Project Slate (2002). "Listening, aural reading, and live reader skills." Lubbock, TX: Texas Tech University. Retrieved February 3, 2005, from http://www.educ.ttu.edu/slate/Braille%20Framework/Listening.htm.

Rainer, Lee, and Horrigan, John (2005). *A decade of adoption: How the internet has woven itself into American life.* Washington, DC: Pew Internet and American Life Project.

Ranjit, S. (n.d.). "How to design attractive and appealing literacy materials for girls and women: Comparisons of successful cases and inadequate cases in terms of visual literacy."

Kathmandu, Nepal: Participatory Rural Appraisal. Retrieved February 3, 2005, from http://www.accu.or.jp/litdbase/pub/dlperson/96SRW/96SRW_03.pdf.

Reach Out and Read National Center. (2005). *Developmental milestones of early literacy.* Somerville, MA: Reach Out and Read National Center.

Resnick, L., and Weaver, P. (1979). *Theory and practice of early reading, volumes I-III.* Hillsdale, NJ: Erlbaum.

Roschelle, Jeremy, et al. (2004, Fall). "Changing how and what children learn in school with computer-based technologies." *The Future of Children.*

Rose, David, and Meyer, Ann (1996). *Expanding the literacy toolbox.* New York: Scholastic.

Sadker, Myra, and Sadker, David (1996). *Failing at fairness: How our schools cheat girls.* New York: Simon & Schuster.

Sadowski, Michael (Ed.) (2003). *Adolescents at school: Perspectives on youth, identity, and education.* Cambridge, MA: Harvard Education Press.

Saettler, Paul (1998, Jan.). "Antecedents, origins, and theoretical evolution of AECT." *TechTrends, 43,* 1, 51–57.

Savolainen, Reijo, and Kari, Jarkko (2004). "Placing the Internet in information source horizons." *Library and Information Science Research, 26,* 415–433.

Scherer, Marge (2002, Sept.). "Do students care about learning?" *Educational Leadership, 60,* 1, 12–17.

Sheehy, Gail (1995). *New passages.* New York: Random House.

Shenton, Andrew, and Dixon, Pat (2004). "Issues arising form youngsters' information-seeking behavior." *Library & Information Science Research, 26,* 177–200.

Silverblatt, Art (2001). *Media Literacy: Keys to interpreting media messages.* Westport, CT: Praeger.

_____, and Finan, Barbara (1999). *Approaches to media literacy: A handbook.* New York: M. E. Sharpe.

Sloboda J. (1993). "Musical ability." *Ciba Foundation Symposium Proceedings, 178,* 106–13.

Smith, M., and Wilhelm, J. (2002). *Reading don't fix no Chevys: Literacy in the lives of young men.* Portsmouth, NH: Heinemann.

Sousa, David (2001). *How the brain learns.* 2d ed. Thousand Oaks, CA: Corwin Press.

_____ (2005). *How the brain learns to read.* Thousand Oaks, CA: Corwin Press.

Spain, D. (1985). *Gendered space.* Chapel Hill: University of North Carolina Press.

Steen, Lynn (1999, Oct.). "Numeracy: The new literacy for a data-drenched society." *Educational Leadership, 57,* 2, 8–13.

_____ (2001). *Mathematics and democracy.* Princeton, NJ: National Council on Education and the Discipline.

Stein, N. (1999, Dec.). "Listening to— and learning—from girls." *Educational Leadership,* 18–20.

Stonehill, Brian (1998). "The on-line visual literacy project." Claremont, CA: Pomona College. Retrieved February 3, 2005, from http://www.pomona.edu/Academics/courserelated/classprojects/Visual-lit/intro/intro.html.

Study art (2005). Rockford, IL: Sanford. Retrieved February 3, 2005, from http://www.sanford-artedventures.com/study/study.html.

Sullivan, Michael (2003). *Connecting boys with books: What libraries can do.* Chicago: American Library Association.

Sullivan, Michael (2004, Aug.). "Why Johnny won't read." *School Library Journal,* 36–39.

Tarrant, M., North, A., and Hargreaves, D. (2000). "English and American adolescents' reasons for listening to music." *Psychology of Music, 28,* 166–173.

Teele, Sue (2004). *Overcoming barricades to reading.* Thousand Oaks, CA: Corwin Press.

U.S. Department of Education (2003). *The facts about good teachers.* Washington, DC: U. S. Department of Education.

_____ (2005). *National Educational Technology Plan.* Washington, DC: U. S. Department of Education. Retrieved February 3, 2005, from http://www.nationaledtechplan.org.

U.S. Department of Labor (2001). *Secretary's Commission on Achieving Necessary Skills.* Washington, DC: Government Printing Office.

Van Scoter, Judy, and Ellis, Debbie (2001). *Technology in early childhood: Finding the balance.* Portland, OR: Northwest Regional Education Laboratory.

Vandergrift, K. (2003). "Color preference and gender research." Princeton, NJ: Rutgers University. Retrieved February 3, 2005, from http://www.scils.rutgers.edu/~kvander/gender_project/bibliography/bibliography1.htm.

Venezky, Richard (Ed.) (1990). *Toward defining literacy.* Newark, DE: International Reading Association.

Wiggins, Grant, and McTighe, Jay (2001). *Understanding by design.* Englewood Cliffs, NJ: Prentice Hall.

Willinsky, J. (1990). *The New Literacy: Redefining Reading and Writing in the Schools.* New York: Routledge.

Wilson, M. (Summer, 2000). "Evolution or entropy? Changing reference/user culture and the future of reference librarians." *Reference & User Services Quarterly.* 39: 387–390.

Wolfe, Patricia, and Nevills, Pamela (2004). *Building the reading brain, pre K-3.* Thousand Oaks, CA: Corwin Press.

Wollman-Bonilla, Julie (2003, Nov.). "E-mail as genre: A beginning writer learns the conventions." *Language Arts, 81,* 2, 126–130.

Wright, H. (2000). "Nailing jell-o to the wall." *Educational Researcher, 29,* 5, 4–13.

Zull, James (2004, Sep.). "The art of changing the brain." *Educational Leadership, 62,* 1, 68–72.

Zillman, Dolf, and Gan, Su-lin (1997). "Musical taste in adolescence." In Hargreaves, David, and North, Adrian (Eds.). *The social psychology of music.* New York: Oxford University Press. Vancouver: University of British Columbia. Retrieved February 3, 2005, from http://www.slais.ubc.ca/courses/libr517/03–04-wt2/projects/TP/website/alpha.htm.

Index